Suburban D

A cop's guide to protecting your home and neighborhood during riots, civil war, or SHTF.

by Don Shift

"If you are not prepared to use force to defend civilization, then be prepared to accept barbarism." -Thomas Sowell

The first two rules of Matt Graham's Killhouse Rules:
1. Nobody is coming to save you.
2. Everything is your responsibility.
Originally published June 13, 2016.
http://grahamcombat.com/the-killhouse-rules/

Introduction

One night I was taking a walk through my suburban neighborhood and wondered what combat would look like on the streets. This grew into an idea of how I could defend my street against some sort of attack by marauding bandits. Then the riots of 2020 came and suddenly neighborhoods being invaded by hostile mobs became a reality. Thus a lot of the focus is on dealing with a large group of angry people.

I've presented my thoughts and observations here aimed at answering the question "How does a suburbanite with a little bit of tactical interest or experience organize a defense?" That's what this book is about. Using mainly military and police manuals, I've adapted their tactics to a suburban neighborhood in a way that amateurs could use.

Many prepper and survivalist experts give up suburbia as lost, focusing on rural communities where the idea of "dense" housing is two-acre lots. The little I've seen that deal with neighborhood defense seem to over-estimate the ability of the residents and have a one-size fits all strategy of "shoot everyone." Rather, this guide is aimed towards those of us trapped in suburbia and provides many less-lethal methods of defense.

The astute reader will notice a lack of basics on topics of tactical gunfights, advanced driving techniques, undercover work, surviving in a third world country, or general survival advice, etc. This is not a survival manual. It is not a tactical shooting, room clearing, SWAT team and military tactics for the civilian book.

This also isn't a book that will be telling you how or that you should become a prepper. Survival and stockpiling tips along with the reasons why and horror stories of those who didn't elsewhere in the world aren't in my wheelhouse. There are no "red" or "black" pills in this book to try and wake you up to the danger that our civilization is in. If you haven't been paying attention to the fragility of modern American society, this book isn't to convince you we are at that point or to tell you how we got there.

My book can't cover everything in detail, nor should it. Better books exist that cover gunfighting, carrying a gun, first aid, small unit tactics, the intricacies of radio communication, intelligence, and preparedness. It would do everyone a disservice to try and create a comprehensive work on suburban survival. This is just a patrol cop's[1] thoughts on how to stop major league trouble when law and order breaks down. This is for:

- Folks who suddenly woke up one morning and realized they have to be their own security force;
- People who bought guns and ammo for self-defense but have no clue about tactical stuff;
- People with tactical training and experience but haven't thought about how to secure a neighborhood during civil unrest; or,
- Cops, soldiers, and "sheepdog" civilians who need help figuring out how to protect their neighborhood in a situation that isn't guerilla warfare.

This is not:

- How to be a guerilla or operate with military-type tactics;
- How to use a gun or a guide to gunfighting skills;
- A primer on tactical first aid;
- Prepping for dummies;
- How to use a radio for dummies; or,
- A bug out guide.

---

[1] I wasn't on SWAT or anything fancy. I'm not an expert.

Critical Event Categories

Definitions

SHTF: Shit Hits the Fan.[2] Any emergency event that deviates from our normal condition of civil order beyond a limited disaster and implies a partial or total collapse of law and order.

WROL: Without the Rule of Law. This is a situation where police and courts are non-existent; a total collapse of law and order. Criminals will not be arrested and prosecuted. It is the law of the jungle; kill or be killed; only the fittest survive. This situation is essentially lawless and resembles war more than a disaster.

Grid down: A disaster or situation where nationally or across your region the utility and communications systems collapse totally, along with the supply chain. There is no electricity, city water, Internet, phones, nor distribution of groceries, fuel, or other essentials. You must be self-sufficient to survive.

Introduction

What I intend to look at here are situations where policing is ineffective or totally absent. To keep it simple, here are three broad categories:

---

[2] I'm not bowdlerizing this initialism explanation, but from here on it will just be SHTF.

- **Ineffective policing**; where police do exist but are unable to do much more than apprehend criminals after-the-fact. The criminal justice system functions in this scenario and may be politically biased towards those that resist the locally dominant ideology. All laws apply, but enforcement and protection are unavailable and uneven in application.
- **Temporary chaos**; police may or may not be present but law enforcement and the criminal justice system are temporarily suspended. Police and prosecutorial activity are rare and operates almost at random. Excesses related to personal defense are likely to be prosecuted in the future when the situation stabilizes. An example of this would be what occurred during Hurricane Katrina in New Orleans.
- **Without the rule of law (WROL)**; law enforcement and the criminal justice system have completely failed and are totally absent. Individual citizens are responsible for their defense and the law serves as no deterrent. Crimes go unpunished by the traditional governmental systems and those acting in self-defense may utilize means generally illegal during normal times.

Ineffective policing is the risk of our time. Many criminals report they have lost their respect for cops as they know the courts and politicians will not support the officers. The "Ferguson Effect" is the fruit of de-policing, where officers deliberately reduce their enforcement activity in order to avoid excessive scrutiny or reduce the possibility they will be prosecuted under political pressure. Outside the contemporary United States, ineffective policing would include police strikes.

In 2020, this has been seen in communities like Minneapolis where officers have been prevented from tackling criminal activity in certain areas or restricted from more aggressively curbing rioting. Seattle's CHAZ autonomous zone was abandoned by police under orders from city leadership, quickly causing the Capitol Hill neighborhood to become home to violence like shootings and beatings. "Security" in CHAZ was maintained by an armed thug militia that targeted journalists and anyone they thought were police spies.

With rioting in particular, in 2015 Baltimore mayor Stephanie Rawlings-Blake said, "we also gave those who wished to destroy space to do that," during the riots there, where we first saw police being actively held back. Portland is the most notable example in 2020 of police being politically restrained as the mayor prohibited use of things like tear gas and refused to protect the federal courthouse.

Here I examine not what caused the event, but how humans react and how that reaction may be a threat to you. These crises could be short term or they could be long term. Numbers 3 and 4 trend to long-term. I have framed these events in terms of civil unrest.

---

1. "Mostly peaceful protest."

Small scale acts of vandalism and violence often done in revenge or to further antagonize, that is not stopped by police usually because of politics.

In cities too numerous to mention, protests marched down residential streets with the intention of making a lot of noise to annoy, harass, and intimidate the residents. The reasoning behind this is the supposed culpability of your average suburbanite for being part of a system the protesters don't like. These events were characterized by yelling/chanting, trespassing across lawns and driveways, and banging on doors and windows. Sporadic vandalism occurred. Police mainly observed the events. Protesters typically moved through the area once they felt they made their point.

What was not seen in these incidents were burglary or personal violence. Practically never did the protesters attack anyone or force their way into homes. Vandalism was limited to mostly childish destruction, such as trashing mailboxes, damaging cars, and spray painting things. Someone's flowers probably got trampled on too.

The criminal violations are minor: obstructing traffic, jaywalking, perhaps trespassing (although it is not illegal to walk up to someone's door or across their lawn), and usually misdemeanor vandalism. Incidents of explosives, arson, or major vandalism have so-far been mostly isolated incidents by someone with a bone to pick against a certain house or resident. Police generally do not make arrests.

These neighborhood invasions are like an outdoor version of burglary for the feelings they cause in reaction. A burglary is an invasion of your space and often leaves victims with a feeling of vulnerability and that an unquantifiable thing, the sanctity of their private home, was stolen. Burglaries are initially frightening, then often an angering experience to see your home rifled through and things missing.

Persons who have experienced such aggressive residential protests and marches report feeling emotions afterwards similar to burglary victims. While infuriating to see a bunch of petulant troublemakers violate the sanctity of one's neighborhood by those who wish you harm, you cannot allow the feelings of helplessness and anger dictate your actions.

For those of us watching hooligans terrify, destroy, and loot with impunity on television as police do nothing, it is even worse for those who had to experience it first hand. In that moment, one has to consider what will happen next. Will the mob pass on by or will they escalate to arson and forcing entry? In these moments, police have failed the citizens they are sworn to protect by allowing this to go on, often for political reasons. "Give them room to riot," politicians say.

Fortunately, in the residential areas the protesters did remain "mostly peaceful." Little physical harm was done. All that one had to do to stay safe was remain in a locked home, away from the windows with the curtains drawn, and arm themselves in the event things escalated. While in a sane world, police would have cracked down to send a message that this behavior wouldn't be tolerated.

Characteristics

- These incidents occur in residential neighborhoods, either targeted or as a spontaneous spillover from another location. This may be a reaction to police dispersal from another area.
- Mob participants are mostly protesters there to demonstrate verbally and with signs.
- Front and unfenced yards are trespassed on, but no entry is made to homes.
- Homes are targeted for repeated doorbell ringing, banging on doors and windows, or surrounded for verbal intimidation.
- Destruction is limited generally to minor vandalism and trampling of landscaping. Broken windows may

happen in some incidents, but not as an attempt to enter the home.

- Police are monitoring or following the crowd, but not intervening to disperse the crowd or make arrests.
- The incident usually ends when the mob finishes moving through the area or it self-disperses within a few hours at most.
- Traffic is usually blocked from leaving the area by the size of the crowd or by active intervention from participants.

Defense preparation

- Firearms should be carried at all times (concealed carry preferred), along with discreet wearing/staging of tactical gear.
- If there is sufficient advance warning (such as social media posts before the event) or word that a crowd is moving towards the neighborhood, pre-deployed rapid window covers can be installed. This shouldn't take more than a few minutes to cover large front windows.
- Vehicles should be moved off the street and into a garage where possible, to the side/behind the house, or the driveway at a minimum.
- All doors, windows, and gates should be locked and barred. Deploy "no trespassing" signs to your yard and gates.
- All windows should have their blinds, drapes, or curtains closed.
- No interior lights should be visible from outside the house, but exterior lighting should be turned on.
- Fire extinguishers and other response equipment should be taken from storage and pre-deployed in case things escalate.
- Bug out bags should be ready to go.
- Move non-combatants to a safe part of the house. Turn on TV, video, or music to distract children or scared household members.

- If you have gas masks, get those out in the event police deploy tear gas.

Defense tactics

- Do not engage the crowd unless absolutely necessary; no political back-and-forth, no taunting.
- With all windows closed and lights off, avoid even being seen by the crowd. Do not give them an audience. Remain inside.
- Turn on sprinklers on the lawn to take advantage of people not wanting to get wet to force them away from that part of the house.
- This is not a situation to use force unless the mob escalates it into one. Do not try to make arrests, etc. Lie low, let them pass by.
- Carefully observe the crowd via video cameras or from viewing places where you cannot be seen (window slit in a dark room, peephole, knot in the fence, etc.).
- If your home is specifically targeted, the mob want a response, so don't give them one. Call the police so at a minimum your fears are on record. As frustrating and humiliating as it is, suck it up and let the crowd burn themselves out yelling at an unreactive house.
- If a window is broken, monitor the room for anyone attempting entry or throwing an incendiary device. Handle such an escalation appropriately. If you are able, barricade the broken window and secure the room from the rest of the house.

Pre-emptive measures

- Landscape your yard with a fence or other features to keep the crowd from just walking across your lawn. Perhaps install a driveway gate or barricade chain.
- Make your perimeter walls and fences non-conducive to jumping,
- Install security film on your front windows in case you are unable to board them up.

- Remove all flags, political signs, or other indicators of identity or belief, including bumper stickers on cars.

"Why didn't you tell us to get our neighbors together and stand around with guns to frighten them off?"

First, you are likely to be outnumbered. Should the crowd see your weapons as a bluff, which they probably are, they will challenge you. At that point, you will need to escalate to using force, possibly lethal force, without legal justification, or have to back down. Backing down will embolden the crowd and should you actually need to mount an armed defense in the future, the crowd may misinterpret your earlier retreat as weakness.

I understand that it feels like you're doing something and standing up to these bullies by going outside with your guns. An argument can be made for discreetly carrying (perhaps openly carried pistols vs. tactical gear and AR-15s) and standing in a large group to show resolve. The videos I've seen of these incidents varied in the details, but armed neighbors showing resolve and remaining impassive (versus engaging with the crowd or yelling political stuff back) worked successfully.

We are approaching a time when such an approach may result in the intruders escalating their actions to force a violent response, to which they can respond with more force. The decision on forming your own picket line will have to be a local one made on the merits of the situation and a read of the incident. I offer the most conservative approach that serves the best chance to not get any defenders in legal trouble. Often de-escalation and refusing the fight wins the battle, as un-sexy as it might be.

Remember that your actions can have adverse

consequences, even if you start within the law or have the best of intentions. Your actions might influence a stupid mob to do stupid things. Slowly we are seeing these groups becoming bolder and more confrontational. All it takes is the perception of weakness or one agitator looking to intensify the conflict to call your bluff.

Intermediate event: specific targeting of your home

Your home may be singled out for particular attention during a riot or protest. This could be because someone saw multiple political signs and flags in front of your house or because you supported an unpopular cause. It is easy to "dox," or use public records and information to reveal personal information including an address, for harassment purposes. This is often done by unhinged and unscrupulous enemies on the other side of an issue.

Fox News anchor Tucker Carlson had his Washington DC home surrounded in 2018 by protesters who vandalized the house and terrorized his wife (Carlson was live on TV at the time so the instigators knew she would be alone). In December of 2020, a Michigan man had his home targeted by a bomber over political signs on his front lawn. One "victim" didn't even live at the home that was vandalized. The *former* home of Barry Brodd, a use of force witness for Minneapolis Police officer Derek Chauvin, was splattered with pig's blood and the animal's head left behind.

No real harm was done, yet the events were disturbing and an indication that there is a low-intensity civil conflict going on in our country. These events were low-grade terrorism. The perpetrators got away without any consequences and there was nothing the victims could do to stop it from happening. This could happen to you.

Many people have been "cancelled" for saying things that the social media mobs didn't want to hear, so jobs were lost and homes picketed. The protests may then turn from bad to worse. A one-sided incident can be spun up by people who hate you to result in harassment at your home. No matter how hard the protesters banged on the Carlson's door, no matter how many people stood on random suburban lawns condemning the residents for being white, rich, or middle-class, there is nothing you can do but endure it.

Mrs. Carlson couldn't shoot the people for harassing her, even though in the frontier days if an Indian tried the same thing a settler would have shot the Indian. Police can't and won't arrest people for occupying your lawn, rattling your door knob, and heckling you. There is little investigatorial will to identify the vandals graffitiing the garage door. In the case of the bombing incident, police will put out a little more effort because of the obvious danger of explosives.

Restraint is the key to getting through these situations. If you can move to an area that is not politically divided, do so. Harden your home and the perimeter so it is difficult for anyone unbidden to easily approach the house. Remain armed in a secure home and hope that the police can do something.

Example of blowback on the defender

St. Louis, Missouri, 2020: An angry mob breaks down a gate and enters the lawn of a wealthy couple's mansion. The couple was charged with felonies and ultimately pled guilty to misdemeanors. The husband of former Los Angeles District Attorney Jackie Lacey was charged with brandishing for pointing a gun at an angry mob outside his home months prior to the 2020 unrest. See the section on brandishing in the "Self-Defense" chapter for more details.

2. Violent unrest

A temporary and localized loss of civil order that is beyond the ability of police to stop but are able to contain.

An example of this situation would be the 1965 Watts riot in Los Angeles, the 1967 Detroit riot, the 1992 Rodney King riots, and the WTO protest in Seattle. In current context, this would also include the events of Ferguson, Missouri, in 2014 and the 2020 George Floyd riots in Minneapolis, Philadelphia, Los Angeles, and many other cities. These events are where violent assaults, widespread looting, arson, and vandalism occur in specific areas of a metropolitan area, although it could happen in smaller towns too.

For your defensive considerations, riots that fit the pattern of historical ones are simply a variation of "normal" times. By that I mean that morally and legally, every consideration that applies in your day-to-day life, including self-defense laws, still applies. That means you can't beat someone up or shoot them for walking down your street. Challenging them and encouraging them to go somewhere else is legal but there is nothing to do if they refuse.

In everything you do, be sure it remains within the law, except minor things you *must* do to stay safe, like blocking the street. Blocking the street is probably going to earn you a parking citation or traffic violation at worst, should anyone care. Many acts that would be customarily frowned upon will be ignored by police. Members of the public will likely understand and empathize with average people taking reasonable and responsible steps to protect themselves. Whatever you do, ask yourself: what would a jury think of this?

In these events, police are unable to maintain order and stop felony acts from happening. All police can really do is rescue innocents, try to keep a lid on things, and try to keep the riots from spreading across the city. Mostly police standby and let it happen; look at the videos from 2020 showing not a cop in sight as police cars are looted and burned. Looting and vandalism is like an out-of-control fire that the fire fighters are letting burn itself out.

In Minneapolis, the 3rd Precinct station was abandoned by police and overrun by rioters who burned the building. This transpired even though the building was barricaded and had been protected for a time by police. Politicians and police brass simply did not have the political will to protect the building. At a smaller scale, we saw this with the widespread abandonment of police cars to be looted and burned.

Failing to defend a police station sends an extremely

bad signal that police will not even defend "their" property, so why would they defend the public? On a symbolic level, letting a police station be taken and burned is like reducing "law and order" to a physical concept that is torn apart, burned, and then pissed on all while the cops do nothing.

The station being destroyed through an unwillingness to appear oppressive is a first-order effect. A second-order effect is the encouragement to continue rioting or become more aggressive because no opposition is encountered. A third order effect is that respect for law and order, or at least the fear of enforcement and punishment, is diminished. A fourth order effect is a lost of trust in the police by the public, leading the public to take matters into their own hands. Should civil unrest continue to occur with little police intervention, soon civilians will begin to respond on their own and they will *not* be as self-controlled as police.

Generally in historic riots, businesses were the target for arson, theft, vandalism, and looting. Physical violence was contained in the areas of unrest and usually between participants in the riots or those unlucky enough to be caught in them. Gang violence is common. Residential areas were left relatively unaffected, although current trends indicate *politically* motivated riots will likely affect residential neighborhoods in the future.

What is characteristic about these events are two-fold; the "message" of the movement is subordinated by the second-order effects of troublemakers looking to behave badly under the cover of the event. The looters know they can empty out Target because the police can't/won't protect it and the looters know this. Whatever brought people out to the streets is almost irrelevant once "the cause" becomes a catalyst and excuse for civil disorder.

For most people, if you don't live in a big city, you have nothing to worry about. In my county, there were protests in several cities. Ventura County[3] is pretty white and Hispanic, mostly middle class, so these events were nothing more than marching in traffic so teenagers, college students, and leftists could virtue signal. The largest impact was the blocking of traffic for a bit. A woman got pepper sprayed and an idiot walking in traffic got hit by a car. The sheriff's department did take an alert posture and sent deputies to the outlet mall.

Symbols or highly visible areas are popular. Las Vegas saw protests on the Strip and downtown in 2020 and Washington DC's monuments were gathering points and targets of vandalism. In fact, in most of the major riots in recent American history, riots tend to be rather confined to downtown or "big city" urban areas that lean heavily towards minority racial demographics. Using 1992 as an example (I'm from California) if you didn't live in the ghetto, the riot threat was pretty limited.

Intermediate event: flash mobs and flash riots.

Flash mobs became a phenomenon as text messaging proliferated. Now flash looting mobs can show up at a store and empty the place in minutes out of nowhere. Sometimes people get hurt. As the social and economic situation deteriorates, these forms of theft/robbery will become more common. A flash looting mob at a liquor store was a catalyst for the 1992 LA riots. Using force to defend a home or business

---

[3] An hour west of Los Angeles. It is a mix of rural and suburban communities and mostly middle class.

may amplify the anger of the crowd or those that sympathize with the perpetrators turned victims.

A likely event might be the future crash of the EBT system, a cyber attack on the financial system, or foot shortages. Angry, hungry people begin looting a grocery store and wrecking the place. This has actually happened when localized EBT system failures happened at the beginning of a month. It lasted a few hours and service was restored, but if memory serves me right, shoplifting and some violence happened at a Walmart.

Just imagine if a major disaster or war that interrupted the supply chains happens *and* people can't pay for their food. Imagine Texas during the cold snap of 2021 when millions realize that food isn't going to quickly fill the shelves back up and the lights won't go back on. Almost anywhere could see food riots and if the conditions are right, they may explode into widespread unrest. These flash mobs can grow out of control. One never knows when a small spark will turn into a forest fire.

Sidebar: What if urban civil unrest turns into an uprising?

We saw this across the Middle East in the last decade where protests against tyranny became riotous and resulted in true insurrections. During the Arab spring, most Arab countries had protests of one kind or another, resulting in five countries undergoing regime change, and several others making important governmental reforms. Libya's dictator was killed and Syria is still working through a civil war.

Not every riot or incident of unrest will result in a civil war. When riots stay in lock-step with politics and transform into uprisings, seeking political change through violence, beware. We do need to take heed that in today's fractious political environment, riots can be come something far more dangerous. In the next category, we look at when localized lawlessness spreads.

Characteristics

- The unrest during these incidents is geographically isolated, even though the troublesome areas may be widespread or occurring sympathetically in cities across the state/nation.
- Areas in the closest proximity to riots are at highest risk, usually economically disadvantaged areas with high minority populations (the ghetto).
- Suburban areas and adjoining communities far from the unrest are usually unaffected.
- These events usually start in response to a specific event, but the catalyst that starts the riots is incidental to the follow-on effects of lawlessness.
- Violence can be specifically targeted against political opponents, other races, upper classes, etc.
- As violence spirals out of control, the atmosphere is used as a license to burn, loot, rob, beat, destroy, and so on, with little relation to the initiating event.
- Police are often powerless to control the riots or protect the public; sometimes this is because of political decisions at the city/state level.
- The riots continue for several days until law enforcement and the National Guard are able to get a handle on the situation (weather changes have also been a cause for riots to fizzle out).
- The rule of law is still in effect, even if it isn't being enforced to stop the riots. If *you* break the law, especially if it is an egregious overreaction or politically unpopular, expect to be prosecuted. Conduct yourself

to the legal standards as you would every single day of normal life.

Defensive preparations

- Much of Category 1 is applicable, depending on the proximity one's residence has to the riot itself. If close to the riots, or rioting is expected locally, make preparations as in Category 1. Otherwise:
  - Monitor the extent and spread of the riots in case the situation intensifies or expands. In 2020, we saw intent to spread looting from metropolitan areas to suburbs under the observation that suburbs were unprepared and wealthier. Use this opportunity to practice your skills monitoring police radio traffic and open source news to develop intelligence on the situation.
  - Maintain a heightened level of awareness and if you do not regularly carry a weapon, do so. Consider a "trunk gun" long-arm if you are comfortable with such a weapon and can carry it legally (and securely) in your vehicle.
  - If you work in affected areas, modify your work routine or work from home if possible. Don't go to work in areas with active riots.
- If the riots are in your part of the city or in your neighborhood, take more extensive measures to control access to the neighborhood.
  - Start talking to your neighbors (if you haven't already done so) about creating a mutual assistance group to watch the neighborhood. If there is interest, see that plan into action.
  - Harden the front of your home at this time and other weak areas. This is the time to accept inconveniences like boarding up the front windows.
  - Monitor the street (go out front and look around) and take short walks/drives around your immediate area to get an idea of what is going on.

- Have someone at home always awake and monitoring news, scanners, and outside. Ideally this is a family member but a trusted neighbor who can alert everyone is ideal.
- Move street barricades into place, but do not close the street until danger is imminent. You may inadvertently block a neighbor who is trying to get home to safety.
- If you are not carrying your long-guns or wearing tactical gear, keep it at hand at all times.

Defense tactics

- If you are outside, wear a helmet and eye protection if possible and use weapon retention devices (like a sling for a rifle).
- Barricade the street as the rioters approach and mount your guard. Depending on the exact nature of the mob, you may not erect barricades and may choose to simply maintain a visible presence while armed to serve as a soft deterrent if more disruptive/aggressive measures are not called for.
- Do not engage the crowd unless absolutely necessary; no political back-and-forth, no taunting. Stand well back from the barricade and crowd if possible to avoid the appearance you are trying to go toe-to-toe with them, which may encourage them to stop and heckle.
- Challenge rioters or strangers who are attempting to enter your neighborhood/street.
- Refrain from using force except in a direct attack on you or someone else (this includes aiming weapons at anyone).
- Perhaps have someone with a camcorder record the mob as it passes so they know they are being filmed and seen.
- Should your barricade be forced, tactically withdraw to a second perimeter, if possible, or back to your home.

    - The crowd may have forced its way down the street, but as the street is technically public property, with law and order still intact, do not try and actively stop them from coming down.
    - Do not use force against a crowd that is not a threat to life.
    - Depending on local laws, you may use non-lethal force against persons trying to enter your yard (trespassing).
    - If you should be threatened with violence or objects are being thrown, go inside and lock down.
    - Be alert for persons trying to infiltrate your property at unobserved locations.
- If the rioters attempt to kill or seriously wound someone, respond appropriately to the persons presenting the threat. Handle attempted arson attacks on occupied structures as outlined in that section.
- If you are violently overrun, use non-lethal tactics to disperse the crowd and/or create some space for you and your team to retreat into a home, otherwise only ever use force against specific persons when justified under self-defense laws, not generally against the crowd.
- Retreat inside if police arrive on scene.

Example of blowback on the defender

In August 2020, 17-year old Kyle Rittenhouse came to Kenosha, Wisconsin, to help defend a friend's business during the protests/riots after the police shooting of Jacob Blake. Rittenhouse spent the day helping to clean up and repair damage from the previous night's unrest. During a confused situation, Kyle was set upon by three members of the mob and violently attacked. Kyle opened fire with an AR-15 he was carrying, killing two protesters and injuring another.

All of the protesters had criminal records and were captured on video attempting to assault Rittenhouse. The survivor was shot as he attempted to draw a pistol. Despite the video being obvious evidence of self-defense, Rittenhouse was charged with murder, among other crimes. He and his friends were characterized as "vigilantes" by the sheriff, who did little to protect businesses.

3. Short-term near-WROL

A widespread loss of civil order where evildoers are often not stopped by authorities, but prosecution may come after-the fact.

The closest situation to a true SHTF scenario modern America has seen is what happened after Hurricane Katrina in New Orleans. Law and order totally collapsed as police deserted the city and government was rendered impotent. For days, even weeks, citizens were essentially on their own in a city filled with desperate predators. We have all heard the stories of murders, robberies, home invasions, violent looters, and gang warfare in the flooded streets (real or imagined).

As bad as the situation was, it was temporary and all

knew it. Police were still extant (if practically worthless), the court system still functioned, and both Louisiana and the nation were still in business. The National Guard and mutual aid police officers from across the country came in to reestablish order. For law-abiding citizens, every law and consideration when using force or protecting one's home/neighborhood was still in effect during and after the crisis as it was before the storm.

Extreme measures that may be morally acceptable, or excessive but understandable, were prosecuted. These situations are almost always temporary in nature and the situation reverts back to law and order. This is not a free-for-all situation where one can go weapons-free and do whatever they feel is necessary for survival. Expect disproportionate behavior to be investigated and punished afterwards.

An example of how this works out can be taken from war crime trials; the defendants never thought they would lose the war and be prosecuted. I understand that the situation may be so dark and perilous that there is a great temptation to throw away restraint and behave how a soldier might, but what you do during a temporary dark age may come back to haunt you. Never lose your morality or humanity, even if you must harden your heart. Your morality is your compass to staying out of legal trouble (as far as possible) and not committing atrocities.

My two nuclear war novels, *Limited Exchange* and *Late for Doomsday*, deals with a world where certain harsh measures have to be taken, yet the characters are not absolved of legal or moral responsibilities. One such instance is how to handle a defensive shooting after an attempted carjacking before radioactive fallout arrives.

For the average person responding to the crisis, police may not be doing anything, but they will again someday. This means you don't get to preemptively shoot threatening people, use force against an angry mob just for coming down your street, or killing looters. Criminals might be encouraged to pillage the town with the police gone, yet you still need to respond to them according to established law. Whenever and wherever you exceed the law, it must be something that you can live with, if caught and punished, and/or something so necessary, reasonable, and restrained that a jury would be sympathetic to you.

Characteristics

- These events are usually in combination with a natural disaster. They could be the beginning stages of a total collapse type situation depending on what is happening nationally.
- The area of the event is widespread across a major metropolitan area, a region, multiple states, or even the entire nation.
- There is usually a failure of the supply chain (stores are closed/empty) and utilities may be interrupted.
- Duration of the event is from several weeks to months. Law-and-order, utilities, and municipal governance are eventually restored. Life returns to normal.
- For all practical purposes, law enforcement is totally absent. Police cannot be relied upon for proactive protection (deterrence) or emergency response.
    - Citizens must protect themselves from attack and theft as well as serve as their own deterrent to crime.
    - Police will not be able to accept citizen's arrests.

    - Any law enforcement activity is likely to be a sporadic, unhelpful appearance where the officers are unable to do anything.
    - Law enforcement may be actively hostile against armed/proactive citizens.
    - Criminals will take advantage of absent policing to engage in overt criminal activity. Expect greater threats, more aggressive criminals, and persons who wouldn't ordinarily break the law to commit crimes.
- The personal safety threat shifts from large, rioting mobs or hyper-specific incidents against individuals or their homes/businesses to pervasive and random attacks, usually of opportunity or on soft targets.
- Burglaries, home invasions, robberies, carjacking, looting, theft, and assaults occur at a higher rate than before and outside of traditionally "bad" neighborhoods.
- Your defensive posture will shift from manning a barricade and fronting off a mob (short duration) to patrolling and being alert for surreptitious or aggressive burglaries, home invasions, etc.
- Persons from all walks of life and responsibilities behave abnormally; from failure of those in positions of responsibility to take charge to your fellow citizens behaving irrationally.
- You may feel tempted yourself to behave in extreme ways, such as shooting a non-violent looter, but such action is not appropriate nor justified.
- It seems like civilization has stepped out of the room for a moment.

Defensive preparations

- Typical disaster and long-term emergency supplies and preparations are needed. This is where being a prepper is a huge advantage. Look to those resources for guidance.

  - Have a sufficient store of food, water, and necessities for at least three months *prior* to any trouble on the horizon. If you are unable to do so, buy as much supplies as you can.
  - Have redundant means of communications (radios) and a way to generate your own electricity, like a generator or solar panel system.
  - Be mentally prepared to survive on your own without government help for a long time.
  - Evacuate to a safer location if possible.
- Activate your neighborhood mutual defense group if you have created one already or at least coordinate defenses/security with anyone who is not evacuating.
- Make sure all neighbors have a way to call for help to each other; 911 may not work.
- Someone, preferably two people, need to be on security watch at all times, including patrolling the immediate area to keep and eye out for people who may be sneaking in to do bad things.
- Barricade your street but be mindful that neighbors may still need to come and go. Consider a night-only total closure of the street to vehicle traffic.
- Remember when boarding up windows that you may need daylight or ventilation if utilities are absent or marginal.
- Keep armed at all times and a long-gun at hand, even if tactical gear isn't always worn.
- As far as possible, keep your home secured. Burglaries are common when windows are left open in warm weather, for example.
- Make your home look like an unappealing target, rather than a high-tech hard target like you have something to protect. Think crappy salvaged boards over the windows versus some sort of purchased high-tech defense. Let your landscape go unkempt.
- Take serious precautions to conceal any supplies that you have; do not let anyone, even a neighbor, know you are riding out the storm comfortably. Criminals may target you for robbery and even a friend, when

desperate, could turn against you. An example of this is generator thefts in the South after a hurricane.

Defensive tactics

- A slightly relaxed rules of engagement would be appropriate in order to affect your safety as ordinary means of dealing with suspicious persons and criminals through the police is absent.
- Your defensive posture will be vigilance: watching for intruders into your neighborhood and your home. This is accomplished by observational duty in static posts watching and by patrolling the area. If you are alone, do not leave your home unattended unless absolutely necessary.
- Challenge intruders; if they claim to live in the neighborhood, make them identify themselves to your satisfaction. If they cannot prove they belong there, send them on their way. Consider having someone snap a photo of them for later identification if necessary.
- Spraying someone with water to make them uncomfortable and annoy them may be one way to get them to leave, but this could be construed as assault.
- If you must go physical with someone to encourage them to leave, physically restrain them and walk them out of the area.
- For persons engaging in criminal activity who refuse to leave or return, if you are able to apprehend them (use handcuffs or zip ties), but you can't find police to turn over your arrestee to, drive them far away and drop them off. Note that this may be extra-legal and construed as kidnapping.
- It is tempting to smack a bad guy around, but if you use unnecessary roughness, or decide to beat someone up, to disincentivize them from returning, understand you may be prosecuted or sued later.

- Most persons looking to assault or steal will be deterred by a neighbor's presence and the additional challenges and resistance from an armed person will only accentuate their desire to leave. However, be prepared for a desperate or deranged person who escalates the situation to violence. This is where pepper spray, a Taser, impact weapons, or firearms are handy.

Example of blowback on the defender

Hospital workers euthanized stranded patients who could not be evacuated from deteriorating hospitals.[4] In the Danziger bridge incident, several New Orleans police officers shot unarmed civilians. It appears officers grossly overreacted in a tense situation where they operated as if the world had ended. In other words, they panicked, shot first and asked questions later, then tried to cover it up. The officers were prosecuted and convicted.[5]

If there was no rule of law in a true SHTF situation, we probably would have heard nothing of these incidents. Both of those incidents were inexcusable from a moral standpoint, yet the fear and desperation that lead to those bad decisions being made can be understood.

4. Long-term WROL

[4] No one was convicted for the deaths of the patients caused by morphine or Versed overdoses.

[5] All officers had their sentences reduced after it was revealed the prosecution engaged in misconduct.

(a n a r c h y)

The absence of government authority and a reversion to an uncivilized world (i.e. survival of the fittest).

My fictional works, the VCSO EMP series, *Hard Favored Rage* and *Blood Dimmed Tide*, deal with a WROL scenario. Electromagnetic Pulse (EMP) and nuclear war are high-impact, low probability events. Decades ago, we would have said the same thing about a second civil war, but here we are. For a WROL scenario to occur, America would have to change drastically. Most likely scenarios are a civil war or a full-scale economic collapse.

For an example, we have to look outside the United States at Sarajevo 1992-1996. During much of the siege, the city was entirely lawless. The rule of law collapsed and survival by any means necessary was justified. Crimes were perpetrated freely, without any police-type force to intervene. Predators were free to prey on the populace and average citizens did use extreme measures to stay safe.

Retaliation and the odd war-crime trial for high profile individuals aside, no one faced repercussions for what they did in these events. While that is bad for the evil people, this allows you to use a broader spectrum of defense and offense typically reserved for wartime. Survival is not a given thing and you must be prepared to survive at all costs and do things that would normally be off-limits for civilian self-defense.

Without going into graphic detail, one should be

prepared for extreme circumstances that would lead individuals to do things they ordinarily wouldn't. The horrors that happen overseas in war and famine will happen here.

The 1990s siege of Sarajevo, old enough for most people in their thirties to remember, was a real horror show. The writings by a survivor known as "Selco"[6] detail how awful it was. Genocide was commonplace. Snipers shot people for fun. Neighbors stole from and betrayed one another. Women were abducted by gangs and rival factions to be gang raped as sex slaves. Civilization and decency totally broke down during the siege.

During something as horrific as the siege of Sarajevo, one must do whatever they can to survive. It truly is kill or be killed, where decisions to feed your children while the kids next door starve to death have to be made, even after you shot their father for stealing vegetables from your garden.

How best to survive this? The joke answer is a time machine or a plane ticket to a sensible country. If you can move now, move to a rural community in a conservative state and buy your own self-sufficient, defensible property.

Characteristics

- The situation is marked by total disorganization and disintegration of the normal social order caused by disaster or war.
- For all intents and purposes, civilized society is non-existent.

---

[6] Selco Begovic: *The Dark Secrets of SHTF Survival: The Brutal Truth About Violence, Death, & Mayhem You Must Know to Survive* and *SHTF Survival Stories: Memories from the Balkan War*

- Ordinary commercial, private, and government services are out of business. Often utilities, transportation, and communications have been interrupted.
- Day-to-day life is a survival situation where the final outcome has a high probability of death.
- The situation is regional, with very limited chances of escape, or even statewide or national.
- Local intervention is not possible; i.e. the National Guard isn't coming to save you. In fact, no one is coming to save you. If you are very lucky, in the late stages aid organizations like the Red Cross may come in, but then it will be too late for many people.
- Morality will go out the window for many people and horrific things will be done, such as cannibalism. Killing will be among the first answers to interpersonal difficulties and criminality. Predators will exploit the situation for their gain or to satisfy their perversions.
- Obtaining food, water, and medical care will be impossible, very expensive, or extremely difficult.
- Power will be exercised by force and not necessarily by police, the military, or good guys. Citizens pledge support to whoever can take over and provide safety, supplies, or just won't hurt them.

Defensive preparations

- Implement the foregoing suggestions.
- If at all possible, move outside large cities and metropolitan areas. Even moving to relatively isolated small cities or towns within half a tank of gas of a large city is preferable to staying very near large population centers.
- Stockpile *years* worth of food and supplies. Identify alternative sources of water and have various means of collecting and purifying water.
- Invest in serious firearms and defensive tactical training.
- Make permanent modifications to your home or be able to make them when the situation deteriorates,

such as barring or boarding up windows and adding bulletproof materials.

- Consolidate all relatives into a single home or adjacent homes. The more eyes and ears looking out, the better.
- Create a defensive team from *reliable* and *well-prepared* neighbors. If you have a mutual assistance group in other parts of the town, consider moving into the same neighborhood, even if this means taking over abandoned homes.
- Barricade the street and restrict all entry to those who live there and only their verified guests. Use force to keep anyone else out. No one else has business on your street and could be a spy, thief, or saboteur.
- Never leave children, the sick, disabled, or elderly persons alone. If women are unable or unprepared to defend themselves, do not leave them alone. In times of mass rape, women and children may need to remain in doors or in fenced backyards at all times.
- Make your neighborhood look unappealing with poor landscaping, poor superficial maintenance, and garbage strewn about. Don't look like you have anything worth stealing. Look like ragtag survivors, not people who planned for this.
- Institute communication protocols for a WROL scenario, including using equipment, frequencies, or techniques that are ordinarily prohibied (i.e. encryption).

Defensive tactics

- Understand that you may need to do things that violate our innate Western sense of charity and fair play. Only do things that you are morally prepared to accept having done when the situation normalizes.
- Don't be evil; if in war it would be a war crime, don't do it. History does not look well upon atrocities, even if it seems necessary or proper at the time.
- Loosen the rules of engagement to handle threats preemptively.

- Deploy your armed neighborhood watch around the clock. Make sure that anyone watching *you* sees that you are on the lookout for *them*.
- If someone is threatening you and demanding goods or services, do not give in, no matter what.
- Politely refuse demands from interlopers or refugees who want goods or services. The same goes for persons in authority if authority is meaningless; do not give in or admit strangers. Have the men and arms to back up your refusal.

Postures

Defense posture 1: low threat

Description: This would be in the event of rioting or a disaster where police are spread thin, but "the system" is still functioning.

Threat: There is a low to medium chance of property damage, theft, or vandalism and escalation to personal violence is low. Violence may be in your city but not in your neighborhood.

Criminal status: Mainly opportunistic criminals are taking advantage of the "strength in numbers" factor and that police are busy elsewhere.

Watch status: All defending neighbors should discuss the situation and be on personal alert. Persons should be monitoring social media, news, and scanner traffic. If action is expected in your area, periodic reconnaissance patrols by vehicle should be made.

Guard status: A guard doesn't have to be mounted unless a threat is imminent. At least one person should be awake and visually monitoring the neighborhood at all times.

Barricade status: Do not close the street, but be prepared to should the situation warrant it. Any closure would likely be temporary and mostly a visual deterrent.

Weapons: Don't go full tactical; open carry may be appropriate where you live depending on the culture.

Rules of engagement: Presence and verbal commands are generally all the force that is necessary.

Offensive: Expect to be a visual deterrent force vs. taking kinetic action. Keep your distance and don't engage if you don't have to.

Shelter in place: Fall back to inside the houses or front yard perimeters should things get rough.

Defense posture 2: medium threat

Description: Widespread looting/rioting in residential areas with no police response or a major disaster elevating theft risk. No neighborhood is safe.

Threat: There is a medium to high chance of property damage, theft, or vandalism and escalation to personal violence is elevated.

Criminal status: Criminals are emboldened due to the inability of police to respond and are actively taking advantage of the situation to further their own ends.

Watch status: All defending neighbors are on alert and

intelligence sources are monitored. At least two people are on watch on the street at all times.

Guard status: The two people watching the street are in a position to respond to any immediate threat. If a specific threat, like a mob approaches, the combatants volunteer for guard duty.

Barricade status: Vehicle barricades can be staged and deployed as necessary; a manned checkpoint at night may be desirable for people who need to come and go.

Weapons: Long-guns may not need to be carried, but pistols would be indicated with long-guns stashed nearby.

Rules of engagement: Commands may need to be more forceful and backed by subtle intimidation or the visual deterrent effect of the guard increased.

Offensive: Suspicious persons can be challenged and non-residents with no business turned away.

Shelter in place: During times of immediate threats, non-combatants should shelter in place. If overrun, combatants should shelter in place rather than using lethal force.

Defensive posture 3: high threat, near-WROL

Description: A violent insurrection in your area, widespread looting/riots that are targeting the suburbs without police intervention, or a major disaster like Hurricane Katrina. Restoration of order is short term (weeks to months).

Threat: High risk of property damage, theft, vandalism, and personal violence in your neighborhood. Certain areas may be experiencing a higher threat but random incidents can be expected anywhere.

Criminal status: Criminals know that police interference is practically non-existent and behave aggressively and often openly in ways and to degrees they may not have before.
Watch status: Common radio frequencies that coordinated groups may be using are monitored.
Guard status: A guard is constantly mounted at each entrance point. Regular rotations are made.
Barricade status: Barricades are fully erected and manned. Checkpoint entry/exit restricted to only necessary trips.
Weapons: Full tactical gear and long-guns are carried, along with any other tactical response items.
Rules of engagement: Standard justifiable homicide with looser restrictions on less-lethal force to preempt any attack. Less-lethal items may be used judiciously to stop non-violent crimes or warn off persistent intruders. Consideration should be given to less-lethal force and other deterrent tactics to keep crowds off your street.
Offensive: Aggressive commands, aiming of less-lethal (or lethal weapons when justified), and audio/visual warnings are used to deter suspicious persons or potential intruders. Less-lethal weapons can be employed to drive off people who are or seem reasonably intent on criminal activity. Extreme measures that may be legally questionable generally are not appropriate.
Shelter in place: Non-combatants should shelter in place. If overrun, combatants should fall back and attempt to defend homes from the outside, going inside if conditions are too unsafe.

Defensive posture 4: high threat, WROL

Description: Police and government have collapsed and a restoration of order will not occur in the near future. Prosecution for crimes is unlikely and criminality is rampant. The situation is "survival of the fittest."
Threat: High risk of property damage, theft, vandalism, and personal violence universally. Genocide and warfare may be a risk.
Criminal status: Professional criminals, gangs, cartels, and organized predatory groups are attacking even hard targets. Regular persons who are otherwise law-abiding are preying on others to survive. Psychopaths and especially violent people may be living out their fantasies.
Watch status: Common radio frequencies that coordinated groups may be using are monitored. Someone is always watching the street, often outside. Patrols monitor the neighborhood and surrounding areas. Homeowners should ensure that no one enters their yard to steal food or enter homes.
Guard status: A guard is always mounted, even if in a general watching capacity, but armed men are always ready to immediately respond. Imminent threats see full manning of the barricade.
Barricade status: The street is entirely closed to all entry/exit except when absolutely necessary. Guards are either present at the barricade or actually observing it. Checkpoints have anti-vehicle barricades in place.
Weapons carry: All adults carry weapons. Tactical gear and long-guns are carried on patrol, guard duty, or watch.

Outside the "wire," everyone moves in a heavily armed group or as "gray" men with discreet backup and long guns.

Rules of engagement: Suspicious persons are warned off and less-lethal munitions may be used to encourage them to leave or stop their advance. Actual or highly suspected threats are engaged with lethal force immediately. Crowds or mobs may be turned away with extreme prejudice.

Offensive: A hard target is presented as a deterrent. Very little leeway is given to actual or suspected threats. Preemptive engagement of future threats may be reasonable. Doing what is necessary to survive is done.

Shelter in place: All non-combatants shelter in place. Everyone but armed patrols stay within the secure zone unless it is absolutely necessary to leave (food, medical care, etc.). Children should play within fenced yards under adult supervision. During heightened threats, consolidation to one or a few specially hardened homes may be warranted.

Checklist

Early warning

Know what's going on.

- Follow the news/local social media enough to know when unrest is likely.
- Identify what the local issue is, what they "want" and when and where they plan on protesting (or what they are saying they will target).
- Ensure your loved ones know what is going on, that they know to stay in contact, and where everyone is going to be during potentially dangerous times. Stay in contact with each other.

- Make your decision as to whether you are going to stay home or evacuate.

Go tactical.

- Dress as a "gray man."
- Carry your weapon (if you don't usually/can't legally).
- Carry spare magazines or replace your pocket gun with a larger one.
- Cancel all extracurricular activities; no sports league, no walking/jogging, no going to the playground, no whatever practice, no dinner out, no playdates. Stay home.

Prepper up.

- Fuel all vehicles to "Full."
- Stock up on any food or supplies you need.
- Make sure all electronics have charged batteries.
- Make sure your weapons are cleaned and loaded.
- Have your fighting gear prepped and ready to go.
- Place your barricade/boarding-up supplies out and ready to go.
- Either you or a trusted neighbor needs to monitor the area, social media, the mainstream news, and any radio scanners for advance warning of trouble.
- Don't patrol the neighborhood or shut down the street yet. Discreetly walk around with concealed weapons.

Immediately before

Secure the perimeter.

- Close and lock all gates. String up your driveway chain.
- Keep all doors and windows closed and locked at all times, even when just going outside "for a second."
- Check the function of all lights, cameras, and detectors.
- Secure any outbuildings, outdoor furniture or objects, and anything that could be stolen, damaged, or thrown/used against you.

- Park in the garage if possible.

Ready for trouble.

- Stage fire extinguishers and have a garden hose ready for fire fighting.
- Take down any flags or signage (including stickers on your car).
- Put barricades in place, or, be prepared to do so with little warning and in minutes.
- Have weapons out of the safe and all tactical gear staged.

Take action.

- Monitor social media and radio/scanner traffic constantly.
- Talk to your neighbors/self-defense group to make sure everyone is alert and aware.
- Evacuate now if this is part of your plan and it is safe for you to do so (your home can be secured, your destination is not being threatened, and the route you are taking is safe from trouble).

Threat imminent

- Weapons and tactical gear are worn/carried at all times.
- Barricade home.
- Establish street guards, patrols, and checkpoints.
- Put blockade material in place and ready to go when the threat level rises to needing to block off the street.
- A handgun needs to be on the body at all times and any long-guns within arm's reach.
- Someone in the house needs to be awake at all times, whether actively guarding or not.
- Stay home, period. If you don't have it, and it's not life threatening, go without.

Threat has arrived

- Street barricades and guard force is fully established to ward off the bad guys (in other words, you are in contact with the enemy).
- All non-combatants need to stay in the house, away from the street, in the interior rooms least likely to be affected by gunfire.
- Non-combatants are briefed on evacuation criteria and routes.
- Don't show any white light from inside the house; close all windows and keep the lights off in rooms that could be seen by the public. Only use exterior lights to deny the advantage of darkness to bad guys.
- All defenses are deployed in full and defensive plans are implemented (actually in-action).
- All non-essential activities and communication cease.

Neighbors and Defenders

Disclaimer: This book was written on the assumption on pretty much everyone but the reader being unprepared for a crisis and having no interest being part of a defense group *until* the wolf blows the house down. Everything in this chapter is predicated on that, not some unicorn neighborhood filled with preppers.

This book, particularly this chapter, is intended for persons and groups who *are not* able to or going to form a prepper or mutual assistance group. If you are that type, please seek advice on how to form such a group elsewhere, but odds are you already know how or have. Most existing groups of this type (or the more patriot militia styled ones) come from people who meet in other settings—like gun clubs—and coalesce.

Lone-wolfing it won't work

Your neighborhood will have to act as a team to survive. Lone wolves die alone. You alone, by yourself, or even with your typical four-person American family won't last. Using war as an example, even our super soldiers don't travel alone, but in small squads of at least four men. Strength in numbers is a saying for a reason.

You can't be alert all the time. Having a team allows everyone to get some rest, relax, and attend to chores. If you are alone, there will be no one to help you if you are sick or injured. Can your wife handle foraging for food, the chores, tending to your wounds, all while keeping watch and running off bad guys? Is your teenage son physically able to drag you to medical care? A family alone will have a bad time.

Your wife isn't intended to be your battle buddy. In real SHTF scenarios, women reverted to gender roles from days past. They stayed home, took care of the children and the house, did the cooking, cleaning, etc. Women who had no men were forced to go out and forage for food in addition to their home duties. These women were also taken advantage of without anyone to protect them.

A group, like a family, gives you a mutual drive to protect and survive. Each member of a group draws strength from one another and helps share the physical and mental burden of survival. Neighbors are united by their homes. Each has their family and their property to protect, which can create a sense of teamwork and purpose where there may not have been one before.

Group creation

For those who intentionally want to create a mutual defense group, finding persons with the desire, requisite skills, and discretion to participate within your own neighborhood will be difficult. Let's be honest; few of us know our neighbors in the suburbs. Knocking on doors, introducing yourself to random strangers, and bringing up the topics in this book, even in the most vague, diplomatic way possible, is a non-starter. It will get you marked down as a weirdo or potentially some sort of domestic terrorist if you talk to the wrong person.

Very few people in most communities, let alone urban areas, will have any interest in, or concept of, teaming up to survive SHTF. Anyone who is involved in prepping or survivalism knows just how clueless and unprepared most Americans are. For this reason I'm entirely skeptical of the idea that random suburbanites are going to form any sort of coherent defensive group before any crisis.

The most likely scenario is that no one will participate or team up until SHTF. Normalcy bias will be in control up to then. Then when people are scared and looking to defend they will start asking each other what to do. This is your moment to act and organize. Forming a defensive group will not seem strange when danger is at the door and everyone is looking for a solution.

One way to explore the human capital in advance is to "poll" neighbors who express concerns in person or online. Get them thinking defensively like "What would we do if rioters came down our street?" when someone posts a video of rioting in a neighborhood on Facebook or whatever. Keep track of who responds in a way that signals they may be useful when things reach an organization stage.

Defensive team

When I say, "defensive team," I mean people who are ready to go outside and fight if necessary. These are people who will stand watch with a gun and help contain an angry crowd or looting mob. These are your fighters—your warriors.

I can almost guarantee your group won't be a civilian facsimile of a military unit. If you have an experienced ham radio operator and a nurse, that's fantastic. On the other hand, you may have a bunch of white-collar guys who can't change a tire. Realistically appraising the strengths and weaknesses of your group is important.

Consider the fitness level of your group. Most Americans are technically obese and out of shape. Even if you have a corps of ex-military guys, or if some guy shows up with all the right gear, don't assume he is capable of military standards. The best you should expect is that these people can stand for hours on end keeping watch and then run the length of the street once or twice to take shelter or respond to stuff without passing out.

Are your neighbors proficient with firearms? You may not have the chance to do a "group shoot" with them, but are they careless with firearms? Do they point the muzzle at people or are fingering their trigger? Do they get edgy when you make safety suggestions to them? You may have to take what you can get. Don't expect that anyone will show any interest in training or practicing.

Leaders

Don't try to be a leader. Don't claim "I read this book by this veteran law enforcement guy and I have some ideas..." Be the organizer and the person who is looking for a natural leader who will step up and can organize and motivate people in a way you can't. Be wary of the people who *want* to be in charge. Start out as the guy with ideas and suggestions. Be the first to volunteer for anything and set a good example. Start by doing and people will follow.

An example I'll use is the person who means well but interjects their past authority or experience into a situation in lieu of actual leadership. I'm talking about the guy who announces he's a reserve deputy and a retired USMC sergeant major who starts giving orders and criticizes people. We've all met the "know it all" type who, with no authority, tries to order people around. Compare this with the quiet guy who makes a good suggestion that the group follows.

Group harmony

What is the makeup of your neighborhood? Is it mostly elderly people, unable to engage in physical activity or self-defense? Perhaps it is a neighborhood with gang, drug, or crime problems. Are your neighbors in and out of jail or prison? Some communities may be diverse enough that there is no natural cohesion between races or cultures. Consider politics. Are you a Trump supporter in a deep blue state in a deep blue suburb? Maybe your neighbors support what's going on and will have a case of Stockholm syndrome if you suggest resistance.

Can you trust these people? Not that you are going to have all that many secrets, but will they be ones to run away or cave when the pressure is on? If you have to use force, will they suddenly be horrified and turn you into the police or try to interfere?

Avoid persons who sympathize with the troublemakers.

You or they might be on the same part of the political spectrum as the protesters/rioters, but what the people in the streets *really* want is not the same as you. Don't unintentionally invite a wolf into your fold. Be wary.

I suggest that religion and politics stay out of neighborhood defense. Don't bring it up at all. I know a lot of people can't help themselves but learn to police your tongue. Don't alienate someone because you want to let slip some snide political remark or are looking for a sympathetic ear who shares your politics. Your number one priority and unifying factor is the safety of your neighborhood.

Personality and people problems

Ever here of the 80/20 rule? 20% of the people do 80% of the work. Expect to have neighbors who only do the bare minimum and rely on others to do the heavy, the boring, the tiring, or the dangerous stuff. Be prepared for when most of your neighbors decide to cower in their homes instead of reacting. Lots of people want to do badass stuff until it comes time to actually do the badass stuff.

Don't be surprised to have traitors in your neighborhood. People may seem to be on board while they are scared, but when the barbarians are no longer at the gates, they may succumb to social pressure. Karen the Cowardly Neighbor doesn't want to feel like the "monster" all her friends are calling her on Facebook, so she thinks she can redeem herself by ratting you out for openly carrying a gun, blocking the street, or something.

Trust within your group will be a premium. Very few people can be trusted under stress, especially when facing an existential threat. Add guns and potentially a hostile political dynamic that might reward betrayal and you have a dangerous combination. Operational security and keeping mum about what preparations or supplies you have at home is also crucial. People are selfish and many are not moral enough to keep themselves from taking advantage of you out of desperation.

Many people are not outright cowards but are weak in the face of confrontation or danger. Let's be honest; most suburban people avoid confrontation. Dealing with the situations you may face will be beyond what suburbanites can handle. That's why they pay police. Expect and prepare for desertion, retreats, and people simply bugging out. Those who remain steadfast in the face of danger and don't cut and run after the first hairy night are the ones you will be able to count on.

Biased collective thinking is another obstacle that might occur. A domineering leader may actively or subconsciously steer the opinions of the group. Some members may be afraid to voice dissent or alternatives for fear of upsetting others or being ostracized. Or the entire group could simply adopt the same idea and no one could question it (groupthink).

The worst scenario, and the most realistic one, is that the group doesn't want to confront negative things or outcomes and thus are unrealistically optimistic. This can be most problematic and both leaders and members have to challenge their own thinking to ensure fantasy thinking isn't happening.

Appearance

Appearance is key. Consider what you look like; do you look like you're part of the mob or an unruly group of amateurs? Dress smart. Not that you are going to a funeral or job interview, but look presentable, as if you wanted to make a good impression on someone. Your neighbors, strangers, and police will react differently if you are in a clean work shirt and khaki work pants than dressed in all black with a Punisher T-shirt on.

Instead of maybe looking like you are wannabes, throw that battle rattle over your work clothes. Remember you want to look like what you are, normal folks trying to protect themselves. Use your dress to send that subliminal message. Officials and juries will likely react better to a mix of street clothes and plate carriers than looking like GI Joe.

Militias have gotten a bad rap because of the idiots in decades past who wanted to overthrow the government. What will your neighbors and the police think if you pull out all your battle rattle and show up looking like a discount version of the National Guard? Police may also get offended that you are usurping official authority. Save your camo for when you actually need to hide. That's probably not going to be in any situation where the police exist.

Uniforms probably aren't going to happen. A loose group of civilians of varying interests and abilities aren't going to be able to purchase uniforms once they've organized (loosely) after a crisis begins. Everyone should wear clothes they can get dirty. Colors should be primarily of dark or earth tones. Bright clothing should be avoided unless there is no time to change. Pants and long-sleeved shirts are recommended to protect the skin against irritants, bullet fragments, and abrasions when taking cover.

Identify yourselves to each other. Not everyone is going to know everyone. You can make neighborhood armbands that everyone can wear. Perhaps some sort of uniform hat, or scarf, etc. Ideas are endless. The simplest idea is that everyone wears the same color on a given day; this could be a shirt, a hat, or some other prominent piece of clothing. Many law enforcement agencies have a so-called "color of the day" that undercover and plainclothes officers wear to subtly identify themselves to each other.

"Uniform"

I recommend staying away from camouflage. Your neighbors aren't going to have it and you will definitely stand out. Pick dark clothing that is durable and protects your skin. Try and coordinate basic colors or patterns, like a dark green shirt and blue jeans for your defensive team. At a glance, you can see who each other is and verify by looking for an armband or at the face.

- Dark clothing (earth tones preferably).
- Avoid all black or similar clothes to what the mob is wearing.
- Heavy, closed toe shoes or boots.
- A helmet or a hat.
- Pants and long-sleeved shirts.

- Colored armband or piece of fabric changed every day, to identify friend from foe.

Gray man appearance

Uniforms and tactical gear can create an impression of strength and preparedness. This has its pros and cons. To a weak enemy, this is a deterrent. For a strong enemy this can be an indication that you have something valuable that may be worth the risk in taking. A danger is *appearing* strong when you are not. An observant enemy can tell when a show of force is a bluff.

In the context of handgun carry, one issue many concealed carriers and instructors have with open carry is that they feel a visible handgun makes a person a target. Statistically this is an unjustifiable fear, yet the hesitation these people have are reasonable. Carrying a gun does not make you safe and yes, criminals do exploit people who are carrying (in both manners) who fail to use a proper holster and maintain situational awareness. These criminals know that the person they are snatching the gun from is unaware of the subtle cues that precede an attack, are unable to retain their weapon, and probably unwilling to use it.

To avoid this problem, many instructors suggest a "gray man" approach. This is a person who blends in with their human environment and doesn't stand out from the crowd. Practically, that means concealed weapons, no visible tactical gear, and no outward evidence of preparation. If the people you are with are wearing dirty, dingy clothes, so are you.

Going gray man would be for a situation where it is better *not* to stand out than it is to look tough. Predators unafraid of hard targets may target you as a challenge. Using an example from (mainly) fiction, noted gunfighters had problems with being tested by other gunslingers who wanted the bragging rights of killing some other badass.

In SHTF, the most likely scenario is that you will be giving away that you are prepared and/or have something worth guarding. You may not be attacked right then and there, but you could be followed from a market back home. A weaker enemy may identify you, observe you, then attack when you are unprepared. Or an enemy may learn that your fancy weapons and clothes are just a bluff.

You will need to discern whether a "hard" or "soft" appearance is the best tactic for your situation. I would suggest that tactical gear be worn overtly in situations where force is highly probable, such as during a neighborhood defense. Appearing prepared and competent (as reflected by proper gear) may be a decisive factor in having your enemy *not* take the field.

If you are out and about, being discreet is a better idea. Sure, everyone may have a pistol carried openly or concealed, and maybe a rifle, but their clothing will probably be regular clothes and very little, if any, tactical gear will be carried. Going shopping in a plate carrier with your night vision mounted to a helmet will be very conspicuous. You are better off looking poor and hungry like everyone else. Let your demeanor and your eyes do the silent "tough talk" for you.

Social camouflage, versus traditional camouflage where you are trying to blend into the environment, is about blending in with the people around you. Most people in a

SHTF world will be in jeans, not BDU pants. Mimic this and have clothes specifically for looking like less well-off survivors.

Hiking clothes and boots fulfill many of the same needs as tactical clothing and they can be purchased in earth tones. Consider dying clothes with Rit dye to mute light colors and add a worn or dirty look. A plaid pattern with the light colors dyed out will still look like ordinary clothing but adds some camouflaging properties. Utilize hiking or backpacking packs instead of military ones in camouflage or with MOLLE webbing on the outside.

Shifts

Shift work sucks and shifts will cause you problems. Practically no one is going to want to work an overnight shift unless the danger is close and pressing. I would expect no volunteers for after midnight on a quiet night and if there are, expect them to desert their post or fall asleep. This is the prime time for attack but also when the human consciousness is at its lowest ebb. Plan for that fact.

Working nights can be difficult. The more you try and force yourself to stay awake when exhausted, the more you want to sleep. As the night drags on, your mind will play tricks on you. Lots of times at night I've seen black shapes run across the road. One time I thought the overcast sky was a bridge as I was coming up a hill and panicked, thinking the big object I was hauling on a trailer would hit the low-bridge. Just imagine what could happen if you are armed, jittery, and having "soft" hallucinations because you want to sleep.

Active threat

The easiest time to get people to stay out and "man the walls" will be when the threat is active and immediate. Nearly every defender will want to be up and ready during those times. However, there will be ebbs and flows in the "battle rhythm" where exhaustion and personal weakness can set in.

My suggestion is to make a "party" of things. Sentry detail seems a lot less like some boring duty when a bunch of guys are sitting or standing around shooting the breeze. It builds camaraderie, helps with confidence in tense times, and everyone is better off with more bodies guarding the gate. Multiple people will keep each other awake.

General threat

War has been described as "boredom punctuated by moments of extreme terror." Having an enemy at your gates or trouble brewing a few streets over will be a fraction of the time. A constant manning of guard posts is not going to happen "just in case." I deride advice that assumes you can maintain a guard force of suburbanites like that. Realistically, at night it will be a single observer on patrol, if that, who can wake everyone up.

If things are quiet, assume the entire neighborhood is asleep and oblivious. Your team needs to react like minutemen. The first warning of an attack could be vehicles pulling up and gunfire starting. You will already be behind the curve. Maybe you have to be the one who wakes up at 3 AM or stays up all night.

Tips

Maximum guard shifts should be four hours, two if possible. I would recommend two hour rotations if things are really tense or during darkness. Switch up night duty as much as possible so no one gets burnt out on it. The wee hours of the morning, 2 AM to dawn, are when things typically quiet down because rioters want to go to sleep, but that is also when people are most tired/sound asleep, so bad guys like to attack then. So depending on the threat, things could quiet down then, or they could be most dangerous.

It would be better to discuss night shifts, have the natural leader volunteer for the worst shift (usually 2 AM to dawn) and let everyone else fall in line. Let the natural night owls stay up late. The early riser might pick 4 AM to dawn because he's just waking up an hour early anyway.

Mix things up. Don't let anyone get complacent. That goes for you too! Get to know the different rhythms of the day. As far as selecting shifts, poll everyone's strengths and weaknesses. The weak people will choose early shifts; don't stop them. You won't want to force them to stay awake when you don't want them to. Forcing people to cover shifts they don't want or aren't capable of staying alert on doesn't do anyone any good.

Work out some sort of rotation so that within everyone's best time range, the shifts change a bit. Maybe have one

"dog watch" in the wee hours that rotates and maybe one slot is selected by drawing for the short straw. This way no one gets stuck working that shift forever.
During daylight hours shifts and guards can be relaxed. More people will be awake and outside to keep tabs on the neighborhood. One person who can observe both ends of the street could serve as the watchman and alert everyone else. Shifts can be longer too with the danger of falling asleep being less during daytime and with more stimulation. Other neighbors can spell the watchman during the day as well.

Command

Your group should work as a democracy (except in a fight). Why? Because a loose group of individuals who are united only by their addresses and the desire to protect their homes will act like individuals. When it gets too hard or too scary, people will leave. There will be differences in opinions and ideas. Not everyone will be able to participate like the fit, motivated, ex-military or law enforcement neighbors can.

I know some of you are thinking you should operate under military protocols and that's not going to happen. Average civilians who may struggle with basic firearms competency and bladder control may flat-out refuse orders. Military-style top-down leadership will be viewed as a dictatorship and it will be resisted leading to a collapse in discipline.

Reaching a consensus by mutual accord is better than a "raise your hands vote." Do you really want to something critical defeated by a narrow vote? Discussion comes first. When the debate has naturally ended, then proceed to the decision. Someone should suggest an idea and if it is accepted, the leader should look around and ask for confirmation. Not a vote, but an agreement of accord, like everyone nodding their heads. No more debate, but "yay" or "nay." If most of the group nods, grunts, or at least doesn't object, the motion passes by acclamation.

Why not use a system that uses ambiguity to your favor? A hard "no" may be pressured to go along to get along because he has no allies. Why give the soft "noes" solidarity? This isn't picking where to eat lunch, this is survival. The beauty of this method of "tricking" everyone to go along with the decision is that it avoids creating an obvious split. Once the group has made its decision, move on without a chance for someone to change their mind. Stalling and debating after the discussion has been had is like introducing cancer.

Leaders should issue hard orders in tactical situations only. The tactical leader should be capable of making snap decisions and trusted by the group to do so. Democracy has no place in a firefight. Everyone in your group who is willing to be a combatant needs to agree to abide by moral orders that the leader gives in an emergency.

Group activation

When to activate the group:

- When police are not able or willing to control the situation;
- When police have effectively disbanded or no longer responding to calls for service;
- When there is an attack by burglars, bandits, or raiders; or,

- When a riot or looting mob enters your neighborhood.

Uninvolved neighbors

Uninvolved persons will act in two ways: neutral or against you. Neutral can still be bad if, when a crisis occurs, the person makes the situation worse. An example of this is the horror movie trope of the person who flees in a panic but leaves the door open for the killer. Though everyone is seemingly invested in the safety of the neighborhood, for various reasons cooperation will not be uniform.

Uninvolved neighbors can either passively oppose you or they can be actively hostile. Passive opposition can be harmfully benign; not that they want to hurt you or see something bad happen on the street, but they only care about themselves. This would be a person who wants to get through a barricade to go to work or go out and return whenever they want. Or this person doesn't think the measures you are taking are right and calls the police to complain.

An actively hostile neighbor is one that supports whatever cause or group is trying to attack you. Perhaps they identify with them in some way or another and are willing to sabotage you. Odds are, you know who these people are already or they will make themselves obvious once festivities begin. In a WROL situation, you must be wary of them and plan to deal with them.

Non-participating individuals can be placed in two categories: *can't* and *won't*. Neither group has to be considered an enemy. Most will be neutral and some will be slightly useful. The *can't* group is composed mostly of people who actually cannot assist in the defense.

The *won't* groups are problematic. The lone wolf who doesn't want to get involved, but is otherwise interested in self-preservation, is not as much of a problem as the others. The *won't* group is composed of the obstinate, the cowards, and those ideologically opposed to you. At best, they are simply unhelpful dead weight who get in the way. At worst, they are enemies.

The "cant's"

The *can't* group is composed mostly of people who do not have the physical ability or skills to engage in survival or defense efforts. This would be children, the elderly, the chronically ill, or the disabled. Those who *can't* may still be useful in other contexts, such as babysitting, watching cameras or out a window, monitoring radios, scanners, or social media, or helping with general survival or daily living tasks.

Those who can't probably know their weakness. They may be eager to help in whatever way they can or at least stay out of the way not to be a burden. You will need to plan for those who can't and are not able to contribute. When things go topsy-turvey, in a civilized society the strong protect the weak.

Consider moving all the children (or elderly) into one house for babysitting. This will free up adults to protect the neighborhood. A small team can then protect that house. Outlying or other vulnerable homes can be temporarily evacuated, as well as any homes in the "line of fire" so to speak. Consolidating everyone in a few homes means a smaller inner defensive perimeter.

Wont's

The emotional "wont's"

People deal negatively with disasters and emergencies in several ways. The first is denial. Either they have not mentally prepared themselves to accept and handle the challenge or they are so psychologically fragile that they cannot bear to accept the danger of the situation.

Some people are just so stupid that they can't comprehend peril and act like "it" isn't happening. If this were a movie, this is the guy driving home through a crowd of zombies and complaining about all the "damn jaywalkers." This subset often does dumb things out of ignorance.

Thankfully, the clueless are often easy enough to redirect and do get some sense back. You just never know who will break and run, making your problems that much more complicated. The worst thing the ignorant do is come into a situation totally unprepared expecting everything to work as it always has. If they survive, the learning curve is steep, but they get through it.

More broadly, the main reactionary styles are personified as *deniers, avoiders,* and *the futile.* All three are related and often appear together in various stages as part of a maladaptive emotional response. In short, it's all a form of denial and a poor handling of grief.

Others lack the overall awareness of an approaching emergency. The calamity hits them suddenly and it becomes a race to adjust and respond. The first two responses—a form of denial—are ways to pace one's emotional reaction to gradually come to acceptance. This mental brake all operates to some degree within everyone and keeps us from being overwhelmed. Some need much more time than others to accept. The question is will they do so quickly enough to survive a crisis?

Many of us have gotten devastating news. Our first reaction is often a sense of emotional numbness. The horror of the moment drops us into a sudden emotional overload and we blank out. Instead of working things out, some just give up entirely. This *futility* can turn a person who gives up into dead weight that has to be protected, worked around, or even abandoned.

Many in this group don't have the will or ability to survive. The situation may not even be life or death; they could just be too psychologically fragile to ever come to acceptance. The outlook may be too bleak for them to comprehend so they never do. They feel hopeless and give into that emotion becoming helpless.

The toll is largely upon them, potentially becoming basket cases when things turn stressful. Manifestations may be a delusional deliberate avoidance of the changed circumstances or imposing threat to emotional withdrawal. This group will be dead weight to you. Their negative emotions may become a source of negativity which could affect morale. At worst they will probably just be in the way or another mouth to feed. In a survival situation, this group is the one that "just lays down and dies."

Deniers often:

- Refuse to acknowledge the threat;
- Become angry when their denial and inaction is challenged;
- Attempt to rationalize why the threat is not a danger to them and justify why they don't need to act; or,
- Become anxious, depressed, or hopeless when they begin to accept the danger, but are not ready to "deal with it."

In the Kübler-Ross Grief Cycle, this would look something like denial, anger, bargaining, and depression. Someone who gives up runs through the entire denial, fear, and futility reactions.

In a crisis, this presents actively as:

- A failure to heed warnings or take precautions ("It won't happen, so I don't have to prepare.");
- Acting, or attempting, to act normally without regard for changing circumstances ("This isn't happening.");
- Hostility or interference with those who are taking precautions or dealing with the situation ("Why are you blocking the street? I need to get to work!");
- Using avoidance and false rationalization to avoid dealing with the emotions of being caught unprepared;
- Acting totally unreasonably or in a counter-productive manner when the threat confronts them (getting in the way); or,
- Becoming totally hopeless and helpless (giving up).

Failure to prepare puts the denier at personal risk mostly but can turn them into a potential threat if they, for instance, try to steal supplies from the prepared. Deniers who refuse to acknowledge the security situation may insist on trying to live normally when it is not safe to go out at night, in another example.

Avoiders

Fear, denial, and avoidance go hand-in-hand. Denial is improper control of fear by refusing to acknowledge the threat. Avoidance is acknowledging of the threat but minimizing or ignoring it. The avoider is dealing with their fear by engaging in often counterproductive behavior. They do this by deferring any proper response or behaving in a totally contradictory manner.

An example is someone who insists on going about their daily routine even as the world falls apart. This group will present the largest challenge among the three fear-based uninvolved types. Disputes are likely to occur when preparations close the street or defenses take away the atmosphere of normality.

Avoidance will manifest this way:

- Minimalization of the threat;
- Deliberate avoidance of anything that reminds them of the threat;
- Using specious rationalization to dismiss the threat; or,
- Acting in an irrational, counterproductive manner.

While mostly annoying, manifested avoidance isn't necessarily dangerous unless you are counting on these people in some way. Avoiders' behavior may affect you in these ways:

- Anger and belittling towards those who are preparing;
- Interference or harassment towards your preparations or defenses for inconveniencing them or (in their mind) increasing the likelihood of attack;

- Entering/exiting the security perimeter or barricade at inconvenient times or doing things that frustrate security measures;
- Not sharing the burden of security or defense;
- Calling the police or local authorities to complain about preparations or defenders;
- Removing physical defenses; and,
- Failure to make any or adequate preparations and turning to others for support after the fact (or preying on others).

Oppositional neighbors

Ideological opponents are those who are totally opposed to your way of thinking. This may range from soft opposition, such as a neighbor who agrees with the ideals of the protesters, to hard opposition, where the neighbor is willing to kill you over their beliefs.

Politics aren't necessarily the problem. It could be racial or ethnic. Lord knows in myriad conflicts all over the world we've seen otherwise indistinguishable citizens of a country turn on their slightly different ethnic neighbors.

The real threat of a hardcore ideological opponent is the one that supports the violent extremes. In today's terms, this is Antifa and the boogaloo accelerationists. I'd say that most Americans are equally wary of both. If you have a person who will, or really does, want to harm you for what your politics are, in your neighborhood, then that person is the ideological opponent I'm talking about.

If an opponent wants to harm neighborhood defense, this could be done in several ways:

- Calling the police for blocking the road or engaging in anti-riot tactics;
- Providing false or exaggerated testimony to prosecutors;
- Reporting or informing on defenders if a society takes a tyrannical turn;
- Bullying or harassing defenders;
- Destroying or sabotaging defenses;
- Actively letting in bandits, thieves, rioters, etc. to target homes;
- Assassinations or arson;
- Localized theft;
- Beating or intimidation; and,
- Passing on intelligence to rioters, looters, bandits, etc.

All of this is done to weaken you, destroy you, or submit you to the will of the oppressing force. I see this at the highest probability in a civil war situation where the country fractures like the Balkans did. In a disaster/economic collapse scenario, I believe that it is much more likely that people will come together than factionalize.

I can't make suggestions on what to do with these people. Ignore them the best you can. Don't let them antagonize you and don't hate someone because of some superficial difference. If they are not a threat to you or your neighborhood, live and let live. Just be wary of the ones that hate for hate's sake and are willing to destroy from within.

How to deal with people getting in the way

First of all, be polite to your annoying or adversarial neighbors. Do not argue with them, yell back at them, or insult them. Ignore what they say and try to accommodate them the best you can. For instance, if they want to yell at you as they drive through the barricade a zillion times, let them, opening and closing it as long as it won't harm anyone's safety. In time, the neighbor may finish going through their crisis adaptation phase and come around to your point of view. Why make an enemy?

One situation you may encounter is someone who wants to keep coming in and out of a roadblock. They may do this just to annoy you. Rather than pull them from the car, beat them, and then disable the vehicle, offer to let them park just outside the barricade. Your group can observe it and keep it safe, calling the owner to move it should it be at risk of theft or vandalism.

Do not engage in political discussions. Frankly, the time for that is past. Only deal with the situation at hand and the steps to resolve it. Be united by the people who are breaking the bonds of civilization to try and hurt you, not divided by politics.

Do not take petty revenge. You may find yourself in a situation where no police means no fear of the law and an antagonist could easily escalate a long-standing feud or any argument to violence. More serious forms of revenge or coercion should be avoided as well. Taking the road of violence may create an attitude in your neighborhood that taking things to the extreme is a way of solving problems when it is not.

Someone who actively supports or sides with outsiders that wish to destroy your neighborhood will be tricky. They need to be considered a security risk and no "secret" information should be shared with them. Information will leak, but at least try to keep them out of the loop. If you can, keep their house outside your defenses. Monitor all visitors and if you can do so discreetly, photograph their faces and record their license plates.

Intelligence

Your purpose of intelligence

Your purpose of intelligence gathering is:

- To be aware of developing trends before they evolve into a threat,
- Warn of an imminent threat, and
- Gain a tactical advantage to respond to a crisis.

You will not be gathering data on various gangs or factions and assembling profiles of their members in order to facilitate some sort of offensive action. Remember, this book is aimed at *defense* for average citizens.

Know where you live

Knowing where you live and all about the area is important. This is basic situational awareness. We all want to know which side of the tracks is the "wrong" side, what parts of town are dangerous, and what natural hazards could harm us. All of this is basic background intelligence on your geographic area.

Many of us who have lived in a place for a long time know these things naturally. We know that the west side of town is inhabited by lower economic class minorities who tend to fall into gangs, thus it is dangerous. We know that the river floods every ten years and the cheap houses there are not a good bargain.

If you don't know your area well, are new to an area, or are looking to move, you will want to research your region. Realistically ask yourself how well you know where you live. Make a mental map of the hospitals, the fire stations, and the police stations. Are there any dangerous factories or power plants nearby? Is there a neighborhood or district of the city that is plagued with gang or drug problems?

As a cop, this came naturally to me. I quickly learned who lived where, what kind of things happened around town, and where infrastructure was. There were only a handful of streets I could not immediately place without a map. If a fleeing suspect took to a storm drain, I knew what neighborhoods it went through and where he might pop out if he followed it all the way.

You might only understand your town as it relates to your daily life. How to get to work, how to get to the store, a vague idea of where the "other" Walmart is, and some idea that the shortcut past the school is a bad idea on weekdays. If a violent mob attacks your neighborhood, this isn't the time to wonder what is on the other side of the row of houses behind yours.

The first task of knowing where you live is to learn the geography of your area. Learn how to get around. How are the neighborhoods laid out? Are they grid patterns that can be easily traversed to get across town or are they split into clusters with limited entrances and exits? Do terrain features like ridges, hills, or rivers divide the city? Create a mental map so that you don't have to look up general areas of town to know what someone is talking about. Make sure you can navigate generally about town without any kind of map or directions.

If you haven't found and studied a topographical map of your area study one. Look at aerial and satellite photos and study them well. If you can't read a map, you need to learn how ASAP. Know what your neighborhood looks like from above (satellite view) and internalize that view. Be able to have a 2D representation (map) of your area in your head, not just the understanding you have from your daily life. An inability to think geographically results in locations having no real meaning to you unless you look them up.

Do you live behind a target that is tempting for looters, like a strip mall? Is a police station or courthouse, a potential magnet for protests, close by? Perhaps the factory a half-mile away makes rocket fuel and has multiple safety violations for "small" fires. You might learn the abandoned high school down the road was closed because it lay below an airport flight path and authorities were concerned airplanes might crash into it.

Look up demographic data. Use census data, things like the Racial Dot Map, and household income data to build a general demographic profile of your area. Population density, income, and crime rates often correlate. How? Low population density, high income, and low crime rates correlate—the inversion is also usually correct as well. Past behavior is the best predictor of future outcomes. If residents of an area have rioted in the past, they may do so again.

An unfortunate reality is that non-white communities in the United States tend to have much more poverty, which drives up gang, drug, and general crime. Parts of a city with high proportions of certain minorities can be a predictor of what neighborhoods may be troubled in a period of civil unrest.

Crime maps are great tools to not just see where crimes are happening, but what kind of crime? The data won't be too specific; an assault could be a man beating up his wife or it could be a gang crime. A double homicide could have happened one street over, but was it a home invasion gone wrong or was it a sick husband who killed his wife and then committed suicide? The neighborhood where I grew up had more police shootings than any other reporting district in my hometown (two in a year), but the neighborhood is practically "leave your door unlocked" safe. Read the news stories about these incidents and decide if it is just the stuff that happens that no one can really predict or if the neighborhood is unsafe.

Using my hometown as an example, I know my parents live in a very safe neighborhood. The town is virtually all middle to upper class, and though the demographics are varied, there is no racial strife in town. There is no flood or fire danger to my parents' home.

What does concern me is a freeway runs directly through the city (thank you city fathers), something which many California towns share. Los Angeles has three main routes north into our county, and although in 1992 and 2020 no rioters came north, in a super-bad situation, it is possible. In a major disaster affecting LA, our county would be ground zero for refugees. Not to brag or anything, but I do know our law enforcement locally is highly competent.

Knowing my local area, I can immediately point at a map and show you where out-of-towners might enter the area from and where the danger/chokepoints might be. I know my parents' neighborhood will be hard to secure with at a half-dozen entrances, but I have more than just one way out if necessary.

- Study road and topographical maps, satellite photos, and city/county utility maps (keep hard copies!)
- Research the demographics of your area.
- Learn where government and significant commercial buildings or centers are located.
- Monitor crime reports and crime maps to understand the nature of crime in your area.
- Walk your area both day and night, exploring natural areas, storm drains, and other places off the beaten path.

Observation and situational awareness

Observational intelligence

Physical, on the ground intelligence is the hardest to get, but often tells you things you can't learn any other way. For instance, during the George Floyd riots, many areas in big urban cities were supposedly "safe" because they were not near downtown where people gathered. Yet the big box stores (Target and Walmart) in the outlying areas were closing early and barricading their entrances.

Would the stores have done that if things were truly "safe?" In hindsight, I learned it was out of an abundance of caution (in my area), but that day, no one knew what nightfall would bring. Had I not gone out to check for myself, I might have assumed everything in my area was going to be hunky-dory.

Sporting goods retailers, if they had guns and ammo left to sell, pulled those items off the shelves. In the case of all these stores, they did this because they *expected* something to happen. Gauging other people's reactions, especially when those reactions, if wrong, could have an economic impact, is a good way of judging the seriousness of the situation. Stores don't hide products, close early, hire armed guards, and barricade the entrance because of simple anxiety.

Analysis requires discernment. If you wanted to see what items were facing a shortage, you would go to the grocery store and see what people filled their carts with. In Winter 2020, this was toilet paper and bottled water. That would be a clue of what shortages to expect, beyond the masks and cleansers. Poor intelligence analysis would have told you that there was some threat that required massive amounts of toilet paper and would cause a water shortage.

Maybe on a drive around town you notice that the officers, who are usually solo, have doubled up on patrol. The citizen patrol is off the street. Officers might be donning helmets when they exit their vehicle.[7] Are officers conducting extra patrols or stationary observation at certain buildings, like big box stores, government buildings, or infrastructure?

Perhaps the threat is greater than what they told you. Seeing official behavior that contradicts what the authorities are saying is a clue that something isn't right.

Situational awareness

Situational awareness distilled is nothing more than mindful observation. You see and hear what's going on, process that information, and make decisions based on it. You are constantly observing and assessing, rather than reacting. Continuous observation of present information allows you to make projections about what will happen in the short-term future. This allows you to be *proactive* rather than *reactive*.

An example from driving is that traffic slows down. You begin looking far down the road and at the shoulder for signs of road construction while you increase your following distance. An unaware driver merely reacts, slamming on the brakes and wondering why traffic just stopped, totally unaware a lane ahead is blocked off. I've seen drivers so unaware they stopped right behind a police car that was parked with all the lights flashing.

A common example of poor situational awareness is walking in a busy public area staring down at your phone (or the ground) and not paying attention. People like this are

---

[7] Wearing helmets outside a vehicle was a regular practice for police in the 1960s-1970s in part because of the unrest of the times.

targets for muggers. Awareness is more than seeing the guy in the ski mask coming. It's noticing that a certain car drove by slowly while staring at you several times. The proactive part is deciding this is suspicious, could be dangerous, and planning what to do to get out of the situation or react to it should a threat emerge.

We have all have had moments where things seem out of place or suspicious. Can you articulate why? If not, start observing people and things, make a guess about what's going on based on what you can see and hear, and watch to see if you're right. We all have an understanding of what is normal in our neighborhood, or do we?

Understand the baseline activity of your city, your neighborhood, or your commuting route.

- What is the usual level of traffic?
- What is the usual amount of police activity: response, enforcement, and proactive patrol?
- What are the typical patterns of crime in your area (infrequent property crimes or rampant violence)?
- How does inclement weather affect things?
- What is the racial, socio-economic, and political make up of your community?
- Has unrest occurred in that area before?
- How do the residents of that area behave towards each other and how safe do they feel?

Identifying people

Threat identification in your neighborhood or on your street can be as simple as seeing a stranger who is out of place. Familiarity is one factor in telling sheep from wolves among strangers, but little behavioral clues tip us off. We may not recognize a strange face, but from the person's clothing, their quick pace, and that they are looking straight ahead, we can conclude that they are probably on an evening walk.

Persons who are legitimately passing through tend to do so quickly or directly to their destination. They aren't constantly looking around. The types of people who go slow, or stop, while eyeballing the area are probably bad guys reconnoitering the area. The same goes for someone with no evident purpose being in the area and loitering.

Anything that hides someone's identity is also suspicious, like a hood and hat at night or wearing a mask now that the mask mandates have expired. It would behoove you to pay attention to someone lurking in the shadows or moving through areas that are hard to see.

Human threat identification becomes more difficult in dense cities or neighborhoods. A cul-de-sac can barricade easily, but a large high-density urban development doesn't have that same option. Your daily living situation might be one that precludes you from excluding all but those who belong, leaving your street open to reconnaissance. Learn who belongs and to identify suspicious behavior by actively watching.

Intelligence basics

Intelligence is a broad term that means both the process of being properly informed so that you can prepare or act appropriately and it also refers to information that has been distilled to be useful. *Information* is raw data or knowledge. Information is of little value if you cannot contextualize it or apply it practically. *Intelligence* is information that has been analyzed and refined into a useable product. Multiple sources and applying critical thinking turn information and observations into intelligence.

Intelligence analysis takes raw information and does several things to it. Collection and collation puts the data into a format where it can be studied. That data and the sources behind it are evaluated as to their veracity and reliability. Finally, that product, *intelligence*, is used to prepare for a specific event or understand larger, general trends for local strategic planning.

An example of information is knowing that one section of your city has a gang problem. That information is highly unspecific and not directly helpful. However, if you learn that the major gang problem is from MS-13, most of the police arrests occur within a two-block radius of a certain intersection, the gang members typically focus their crime on Hispanic neighborhoods, and the police estimate the size of the gang is 200 people, you're getting somewhere. Analysis requires that more specific information, things that can assist you in planning or reacting, be gathered.

So perhaps you start talking to Hispanics in your area. They tell you that while their businesses haven't been harassed, their cousin that lives closer to the ghetto has heard that the gang is starting to rob houses, rather than extort business for protection. Next you gather police data on burglaries, corollate that with the victims being Hispanic, and all have something in common, like they make obvious displays of wealth in this one club everyone who has been victimized meets at regularly. Now you have the beginnings of intelligence.

Analysis is not just a presentation of the facts. It verifies the quality of the source of the information and its usefulness. By identifying things beyond the facts you can see patterns or problems you didn't see before or gain a new understanding of a situation. You can begin to anticipate the future or understand where else to look. Analysis is making information turn into decisions.

To analyze intelligence, a set of goals must be met. Libraries are great but just a curiosity unless you have something you're looking for. Intelligence gathering and analysis allows you to identify specific targets, problems, or weaknesses that need to be addressed.

What is the problem that you are trying to solve?

- What threats to the neighborhood should we be expecting and planning for?
- Who has been perpetrating these crimes and how can we stop or mitigate them?

What information do we already have and how can we get more information?

- You have reports that daytime burglaries are on the rise and suspect vehicle information.
- You begin knocking on doors, asking people if they have seen the suspect vehicle, any suspicious activity, and if anyone has camera footage of the vehicle.

What implications does this information have for us?

- The vehicle description fits the pattern of a vicious burglary crew that has been seen in other parts of the city; meaning that your neighborhood is likely being targeted by these creeps.

Is this information reliable and are their other explanations?

- Can you trust what the gossiping, half-blind neighbor who rarely looks outside says?
- Are *your* burglars actually the same burglars that have been beating and tying up people they found at home, or is it a copycat trying to throw the police off?
- Do you need to obtain more information?

How can you or your group take action with this information?

- Increase patrols and general awareness in the neighborhood to raise the alarm if these guys are seen again.
- Maybe setup daytime checkpoints to screen cars coming in.

What do you seek to gain by incident analysis?

- How is the crime or attack usually carried out?
- Who (or what) do the suspects seem to target?
- What vulnerabilities are exploited?
- What techniques do the bad guys use and what equipment do they have?
- Are there any tactics that work against them?
- What are the costs to the public due to crimes so far?

Determining the modus operandi (MO) of suspects allows you to examine your own weaknesses to the enemy's operation. Do they work from within to exploit a neighbor who is sympathetic to them? Perhaps they have a large vehicle that will bash through barricades or are experts at stealth attacks.

Who are they? Do they have criminal associations, such as are they part of a gang, are they alone, a revolutionary militia, or is this a bandit group? This allows you to understand the scope of your threat. Roving bandits or gangs might pass through like locust, but generally aren't going to return repeatedly. An ideological militia may return to extort or cause harm to achieve their political end. A lone thief might not warrant any change other than increased alertness.

Where do they live and where do they commit their crimes or activities? Do they have weapons and if so, how well do they employ them? Do they have any special skills or unusual equipment?

Strategic vs. tactical

For this chapter, I'm breaking this down into *strategic intelligence*—big picture—and *tactical intelligence*—happening in the moment. For you intelligence analysts out there, please remember this is grossly oversimplified.

Strategic intelligence focuses on the larger picture and the long term. Nationally, understanding that the country is divided politically, race and political protests are occurring everywhere, and the economy is failing is helpful to understand where things may begin to destabilize locally. Yet much of the national picture is like the science behind an earthquake; it's interesting to hear the scientists from CalTech talk about the epicenter, strength, and depth of the quake, but you need to know when the water will come back on and if the freeway to your in-laws' house is still standing.

Local *strategic intelligence* is information that relates to the broad and long term pictures. This is identification of trends and patterns. For instance, knowing that X city has a Hispanic gang problem, predominately MS-13 (a violent gang), that is expanding its crimes from drugs to robberies and burglaries of the suburbs, permits you to make overall decisions to harden your home and neighborhood security.

Strategic intelligence gathering can be summed up poorly as understanding the signs of the times. If foreclosures are going up and jobs are being lost, crime may increase in the short term. You may need to be more alert in public and keep your home secure. Another example is that police officers are retiring or quitting in large numbers. As far as taking action, think of this as hurricane season. If the forecasters are saying that this year will be extremely bad, wouldn't it befit you to make sure your generator and preps are all good to go?

Ignoring the strategic picture by burying your head in the sand will lead to major problems down the road. Hopefully, you are not reading this book when police are deserting the force and cities are descending into chaos. Knowing that the United States is on a path of decline towards violence and hardship will allow you to begin preparations. Strategic planning is preparation for a general threat; it becomes tactical when the threat becomes specific and immediate.

Tactical intelligence will be comparatively short-term in nature and restricted to that which *requires* action on your part or helps guide your *reaction* in a defensive situation. This would be like in the middle of a citywide riot and hearing that the looting mob finished with the mall and is moving into the adjacent neighborhoods. Again, tactical intelligence is *specific* and *immediate* (all relative, of course).

Tactical intelligence is usually gathered in the moment of crisis and used to direct your response. Strategic intelligence has told you to expect massive riots this weekend when the banking system shuts down, but tactical intelligence is hearing the police announce the rioters are entering your part of town. Another example of tactical intelligence is hearing on your scanner a crew of bandits plotting to imminently assault your barricade in force.

Strategic assessments identify the wide-scale, long term problems and their first, second, and third order, etc. effects. This allows you to prioritize the threats, determine what resources or preparations you will need, and begin making those outlays and planning tactical response strategies. The goal here is preparation.

A *tactical assessment* identifies the current threat(s) and the immediate actions needed to neutralize or mitigate that threat. You tailor your actions directly against the threat in the best way the intelligence dictates to immediately end the situation and preserve what you are protecting. Overall tactical goals are to end the threat and prevent the situation from further deterioration.

Validation

Information must be verified and validated. That is, a rumor might be true, but general information about what is going on without specifics it does little good. On the other hand, highly specific information could be given to you that is just plain wrong (a car pulling up at night is not a burglar, but the boyfriend sneaking in) or misinformation.

Any evaluation has to assess the reliability of the source and the veracity of the information itself. Rumors don't come with the whole story, even though they might be correct in a larger sense. Someone who does provide specifics might be entirely mistaken or flat-out lying to you for malicious reasons. Even your own interpolation of the data/evidence could be incorrect or biased.

Profiles

You will want to establish beforehand *problem profiles* and *target profiles*. Profiles are pre-incident identifiers of risk and guide your planning and preparation. Understanding what the most likely perils you will face are will allow you to allocate resources, train, plan, and prepare defenses. These are preparatory analyses and actions, not reactionary ones.

A *target* is a particular person, group, or place that will in the future present a risk. A *problem* is a scenario or situation that may occur, although the troublemakers are unknown. Target: what is the likelihood that Crazy Neighbor becomes an active shooter on the street and how will we deal with it? Problem: how likely is it that [rioting, looting, bandits] come to our street and what are our plans for each situation?

These are also known as threat assessments; what you believe the dangers facing you are and what you know about them. You can also examine what you *don't* know and what you need to find out. This is the time and place to discuss how these actions will affect you, what your response would be, what the effectiveness of that response might be, and what reaction *your* response might generate.

Background intelligence: a basic understanding of problems and players involved. This includes an understanding of the area you live in, both from a physical perspective and a demographic one.

Estimative intelligence: what might happen and what to expect if it does (strategic).

Warning intelligence: that something is happening or is about to happen and more specific information on how it might go down rather than just speculation.

Tactical intelligence: information processed on current events to immediately respond to the situation.

Analytic considerations

Data collection and assessment

Analysis of crime does the following:

- Identify crime patterns and trends using crime reports and crime maps.
    - Strategic assessment can put you on alert to monitor for indicators of specific problems or target behavior.
    - This includes not just crimes, but all negative incidents that pose a threat.
- Pattern analysis allows you to monitor when crime-conducive conditions occur. Pattern analysis includes:
    - Incident analysis (what and how it happened).
    - Match this crime with overall trends.

- This allows you to:
    - Predict future threats or connect the dots.
    - Recognize patterns in seemingly random data/events.
    - Make assumptions and predictions based on historical activities/patterns of activities.

Operating environment

At a narrow level, this is your street and your neighborhood. Then it enlarges to your section of a city, if large, or town, if small. Moving outward, you look at your county and region. Where will *you* be and where do you expect trouble will be coming from/ or affecting?

High risk areas

- History of riots and unrest.
- Areas with large minority and immigrant populations.
- Low income neighborhoods.
- Near colleges/universities.
- Near prisons or work camps.
- Close proximity to a military base.
- Malls and large retail centers.
- Near major government buildings.
- Symbolic places or large gathering spaces.
- An "autonomous" zone.

Demographics

- What are the demographics in your area?
- Is there demographic change occurring and what are the likely strategic implications of this?
- What are the types and impacts of criminality in your area?
- Has a change in attitude or behavior occurred among the population in your area?

- Are there racial, religious, or class tensions in your area?

Operational

- How are victims selected?
- What tools, techniques, or ruses do the bad guys use?
- How have police or other entities dealt with this problem in the past or in other places?
- Are there established and proven techniques already out there?
- Do the bad guys exploit any physical, geographic, political, social, or government weaknesses?

Intent and capabilities

- Intent is "what do the bad guys want?"
- Genocide?
- Material or financial enrichment?
- Just to cause trouble?
- Political revolution?
- Has the intent or priorities of the person or group changed, for instance from protests to targeted violence?

What are they capable of:

What criminal or harmful activities are your potential adversaries engaged in?

- What are they likely to engage in if overall circumstances change?
- How has this person or group behaved in the past and how are they likely to behave if there is less of a chance of police interdiction?
- What are their technical (skills and equipment) capabilities?
- Do they have the weapons, training, and numbers to target you?
- Can they feasibly leave their enclave 20 miles across town and attack you?

If you know what they want and what they can do, this allows you to make educated guesses about their courses of action.

From among these, you will need to decide on the Most Likely Course of Action (MLCA). Objectivity is important here. What does the *data* say they are most likely to do? Not what you optimistically want them to do.

SWOT

SWOT stands for "Strengths, Weaknesses, Opportunities, and Threats." This is a planning tool in business to evaluate new goals or development. This can be used in SHTF to evaluate yourself, your group, an enemy or a situation you may face.

To SWOT yourself, evaluate your position, what you need to improve, and what threats you will need to plan to face. For an enemy, what do they have that can be successful against you? For a situation, how will a given scenario be handled by you or your group with what you have?

Strengths evaluate positive attributes. This includes skills, assets, or successful tactics or procedures. **Weaknesses** are detractors, like a lack of supplies or skills on your end or vulnerabilities of an enemy. **Opportunities** are places for improvement or exploitation of a situation or enemy. **Threats** are what could harm you or where you could fail; this will dovetail in with your analysis and planning elsewhere.

All of this is meant to be expanded outward. Such as, how can you exploit your strengths to improve your survivability or overcome weaknesses? How can your weakness be exploited or how can you exploit an enemy's weaknesses? Opportunities might be a window of gain for you or a way to examine how an enemy may take advantage of the situation. Threat analysis is covered in this chapter as part of the intelligence process, but it can be looked at as a way of examining the consequences of failure.

Intelligence gathering

The main goal of your intelligence gathering and investigation efforts is to identify indicators that can be used to prevent a threat from reoccurring (or happening to you) or mitigating the consequences should prevention fail. How did this happen and what do we need to look for, and do, to stop it from happening again? This is why we study signs of impending threats and incidents that have already transpired.

Incident analysis looks at problems and targets to determine how future incidents (or crimes) can be prevented or mitigated. Investigative analysis is about identifying and apprehending (or neutralizing) a particular suspect. In the civilian's case, this would be about turning information on the suspect over to police for arrest or if you are on your own, to specifically prevent the suspect from returning to re-offend.

Passive collection is done through observation and open sources. You monitor radios, cameras, look out the window, or research things online. This could also include things you learn through general conversation without specifically looking for anything.

Active collection is done by talking to specific sources

to gather information (such as victims) and going out to observe your enemy, collecting information about/from him (surveillance). This is much more about going outside and *doing* rather than staying inside and researching. Think of passive as collecting things you come across and active as searching things out.

Types of information

In order of least credible to most credible:

- Rumors and gossip.
- Media and social media reports with specifics.
- Eyewitness observation of the events (including radio interception of enemy operations).
- Verified reports of criminal activity (confirmed by police or by you).

Open source intelligence

Your primary method of grid-up SHTF intelligence will probably be from social media, news reports, and Internet searches. These are known as "open sources" meaning that you don't have to compromise anyone or hack into anything. The information is publicly available for anyone to access.

Newspaper articles and TV news reports are *not* real time intelligence unless the field reporter is live tweeting or broadcasting breaking news from the scene. What hours or days old reports are good for is establishing a reference point and background. What kind of incidents occur in your area, why, and how do they affect the community?

Social media

Social media in the right context is like having second sight. Take the NextDoor app; did you ever know there were so many suspicious things happening or petty crimes in your neighborhood? On one hand, it can be unsettling, while on the other, it is good to really know what's going on.

While everyone seems to loathe Twitter, if the right accounts are followed it can be a great source of open source intelligence. Other social media platforms can be as well, but Twitter seems to excel at real time news. Social media intelligence comes in two forms: aggregate or scouring.

Scouring is searching accounts, topics, phases, and #hashtags to locate information. In other words, you are manually filtering through the platform to find information relevant to your area. While this can be rather effective in times of crisis when lots of people are posting in near-real time, it can be more difficult to find relevant information and accounts that may give advance warning. Not all of us can dedicate huge chunks of our time to analyze who the troublemakers are locally and monitor their postings regularly.

Accounts that find and share the information for you are much easier sources of intelligence gathering, but they don't exist in all areas. The aggregators are people who search out relevant information and post it online. This can be sharing posts, sharing links to livestream feeds of an event, to monitoring radio traffic and posting that. Many large cities have one or more police scanner Twitter feeds that often share more than what police are saying on the radio including information about protests, emergencies, or disasters.

Social media posts can be your forewarning that a protest is scheduled. Vigilant posters can share updates of unrest or emergencies as they begin. Livestreams, videos, and photos taken at or near where critical incidents are unfolding can be the eyes and ears on the ground you don't have.

Local area social media apps like NextDoor are a good source for firsthand accounts from your neighbors. Those who use that app now know it is a way to keep tabs on what's going on in the neighborhood. You can use these reports to establish a baseline of local activity (criminal or otherwise) and track how it changes. As crisis situations develop, real time reports can be shared allowing you another source of remote intelligence.

The way these apps and other local social media pages work is also excellent as a sort of meeting ground to share individual observations, what's known as Human Intelligence (HUMINT). In the past, you'd have to talk to all these neighbors individually to get all the information you can just easily scan.

I know these apps become a toxic wasteland for petty squabbles and gossip, but you don't need to comment. Just create an account, read, and track. Monitoring alone is a great way to poll the attitude of the neighborhood. The Internet is used as a semi-anonymous dumping ground for people to vent and express things that they wouldn't in person. Are people's comments reflecting fear, hostility, or tension that you wouldn't be able to learn otherwise? Perhaps you can identify friction points before they explode into real-world incidents

Electronic intelligence

Communications intelligence, or COMINT, is about gathering information from communications. This means radio traffic for the most part, as you won't have the ability to intercept cellular signals. SIGINT[8], or signals intelligence, is about the analyzing of raw radio signals. This could be direction finding and ranging transmissions from the bad guys, but this is beyond the ability of most average people and best left to an experienced ham radio operator.

Note that most communications in a grid-up world will be done over cellphones. Radio traffic will be secondary. If the grid goes down, expect radio communication between bad guys to increase. However, a lot of bad things happen without electronic communication, so there may be no COMINT to gather.

Radio scanners

Radio scanners are excellent tools for information and intelligence beyond the general morbid curiosity of what the police are doing. Scanners are simply a radio receiver and memory bank that rapidly tunes to potentially thousands of channels in a matter of seconds. Most decent models can get everything from public safety, aviation, marine,

---

[8] COMINT is often erroneously referred to as SIGINT.

unencrypted military, business, amateur (ham), and personal use radio traffic. You are suddenly able to gather your own information based on what people are saying between themselves. This could save your life.

In 2018, the Thomas Fire struck Ventura County, California, in what was then the state's largest brush fire in history. This fire was consuming one acre every second at its height as gale force winds drove it. I was listening to the fire department on the radio when one of the fire fighters announced that the city of Ventura had two hours to prepare for impact in a certain neighborhood. Since the point of origin of the fire and Ventura are about 10-15 miles apart, this seemed odd to me.

Using a map, I was able to listen to the various updates on where the fire was. It was indeed moving that fast. A neighborhood that burned to the ground had two hours to prepare. Unfortunately, local broadcast news wasn't covering the story, but had gone to regular evening programs. Being "just another brushfire" in a remote part of a rural county 50 miles west of LA wasn't in the interest of the local news folks.

Even the county webpage that *is* updated during times like these was not being updated with this critical information. Only those of us listening to the real time radio calls of the fire fighters knew that this situation was serious and that the city of Ventura was in real trouble. Thankfully, a scanner enthusiast and a ham radio operator were pushing updates out in real time on Twitter, which was the only reliable source of immediate information.

Sadly, the two-hour warning never seemed to make it to the people on the northeastern end of Ventura, which runs up into the coastal foothills in neighborhoods separated by wide gullies, or barrancas. The area hadn't burned in decades and was filled with rich fuels. The official warning came when police and deputies began making evacuation announcements, which was far too late.

Being your own source of information and intelligence is absolutely vital. Never assume that the police or the media will tell you if you are in danger. It's up to you. Get a scanner, learn the lingo of what you're listening to, and monitor it to know what is going on.

Never rely on online streaming services; I don't care how easy or comprehensive the Broadcastify app on your phone is. A generous citizen has his own scanner wired to a computer which uploads the audio to the website; it isn't a government service. Streaming requires an Internet connection on both your end and the broadcaster's end.

The feed is often delayed, seldom covers anything other than main dispatch channels, and is totally under the control of the service and the streamer. In a major catastrophe, the electricity, Internet, and cell service may be down at your end and the streamer's end. Be able to listen using only your own resources.

To anyone not in the emergency services, the learning curve to hear what's going on will be steep. Find your local "ten codes" or whatever and learn those. In much of America, ten codes are somewhat standard with local variations or different meanings. Police codes are very much like different languages and dialects. For instance, 10-19 to me means "return to ____ (or station if unspecified)" whereas in Alaska, it essentially means "en route." NYPD's "officer needs help" code is 10-13, whereas that's a weather check for me.

Learning the lingo isn't hard but understanding who is who is much more complicated. Some agencies have lists of their call signs. These vary widely between agencies. You will also want to learn not just what units are calling, but what geographic area they are operating in. A murder 1-A-12 got assigned to might be sensational, but it matters little to you if it is ten miles across the city and your local car is 16-X-81. Try putting in a public record request for call signs and beat maps from your police agency. Fire departments often have the station and battalion information online.

Should all this fail, keep a log with the call sign, the frequency, the time, the action of the unit, and the geographic area of the call. If you track and plot this, you will see patterns emerge. "C" units might be in the city "Central" beat, for example. "Tom" and "Mary" units that make a lot of traffic stops and get sent to car accidents might be traffic enforcement units.

Tactical COMINT gathering

Radio traffic won't give you the big picture. Government users aren't out there to give you a play-by-play of an emergency. Remember that when listening to police radio you aren't going to learn what the officers are doing. You will hear dispatch put out the call and then the officers advising of their status. It's not uncommon to feel like you're missing out on something. Fire fighters often do a lot of coordination and updates via the radio, much more than police.

I don't care for the "Close Call" features that give priority to geographically close transmissions. The receiver scans a huge swath of the spectrum and I often get false positives, a lot of which is unreadable. Various scanners may have advanced programming that will allow you to narrowly tailor this feature to specific frequencies or bands. This will allow you to hear transmissions close by, such as in your neighborhood, by scanning short-range radio frequencies.

Whether you use "Close Call" or low-power bands bad guys are likely to use, this is an advantage in that you can hear what is being said in your immediate area and thus have insight on the super-local picture. You could learn about the situation that others are in by what they say. Or you may hear the transmission of a group of raiders who are coordinating a hit.

Identifying your enemies' radios will give you insight into what frequencies to monitor. Antifa uses Baofengs often illegally on frequencies they have no business being on and without licenses. Accordingly, you would monitor the VHF and UHF bands that Baofengs transmit on until you hear radio traffic describing events you are seeing. An ad hoc group of looters or raiders may be using cheap blister pack GMRS radios. A more organized group could be using stolen police/fire radios or business radios.

Monitor your local radio traffic across the most likely bands that bad guys would be using. It helps if this is done while criminal activity is ongoing to match activity to transmission. Radio discipline within many of these groups will be poor. Gang members and stupid people like to brag. Couple this tendency with the notion that radios aren't "fun" unless you are talking into it and someone is talking back. These poor habits can give you great intelligence.

Be your own detective

Police typically handle the questioning of crime victims and witnesses. One way to get suspect and crime information is to request a copy of the reports for the incident, but these may be difficult to get in a timely manner due to bureaucracy and if the information is in progress. Your state public record laws may limit what information can be released. Even if police are still responding, you may need to know who the suspects were and what they wanted in order to plan your defense accordingly.

Consider being your own detectives and interviewing crime victims. If the police aren't doing it, who else is going to? You can gather valuable information that may possibly lead to the identification of the perpetrator, clues as to why they are doing what they are doing (organized gang vs. opportunistic), and if this was random or if there is a chance they might return. Perhaps the criminal was another neighbor.[9]

If you have to conduct your own investigation, you will need to seek out victims and witnesses, establish a rapport, and conduct an interview. It may be uncomfortable to approach a crime victim, or a witness may be too intimidated to talk, but how else are you supposed to get the information you are looking for? They may post about the incident on social media, if it is functional, but that does not replace an in-depth conversation.

- Interview victims of crimes or intimidation to gain information on the perpetrators.

---

[9] This book is not about what to do with the perpetrators should you find them or if you should look for them.

- Use intelligence gained from these interviews to make a risk assessment for future attacks and to plan a response/defense.
- If you detain a suspicious person, try to get any identifying information on them and photograph them as well.

Interview styles

Casual interview

A casual interview is talking to people you encounter in daily life specifically to gain information of intelligence value. An example is being a tourist and asking people on the street what the good restaurants are and the cool spots only locals know about. In an SHTF world, you may be standing in line at a food distribution center and asking people in line how crime and violence is in their area.

These conversations can start out with friendly small talk and chit-chat, but you will need to steer them towards the information you want to learn about. If you don't know how to move a conversation in a direction you want, or how to "share" thoughts, feelings, or experiences to elicit the same from someone else, you need to get out of the basement.

As information of interest is presented, you can start asking more detailed and pointed questions. To not seem weird, you can say things like "Wow, we had something a lot like that happen just last week. What car were they driving? Maybe it was the same people."

Victim/witness interview

In military parlance, this is called a *debrief*. For law

enforcement, an interview is an integral part of an investigation. How the crime happened and what exactly happened are vital to successful prosecution. As for the details of the crime, you only really need to know the bare minimum of what they did (i.e. robbed the house, beat up and intimidated someone, raped women, etc.). You don't need to establish the elements of the crime, so awkward questions or pointed questioning isn't necessary.

The purpose of your interview is to gather indicators of a potential recurrence. That is, you want to know who did it and how they did it to identify and counter them later. I have found it best to ask a person to tell you what happened in their own words first so you understand what happened before proceeding to direct questioning. Letting them talk freely also may give you additional nuggets that you wouldn't have thought to ask about.

Direct questioning serves both to clarify what they said and to get the specific answers you want. This answers the "5W1H[10]" questions. Before you go in, have a mental list of any specific questions you want answered; such as, did the suspect have a particular tattoo that might indicate this is a certain guy who made threats earlier? Keep in mind new questions may arise as the interview goes on. Save any hard questions or pressing people for direct or specific answers to the end so as not to turn them off.

You probably will not be arresting suspects, but if you do, interview them in a similar manner to above.

Canvassing

Canvassing is basically knocking on doors or going

---

[10] Who, What, When, Where, Why, and How?

around and asking people if they have information of interest. This can be done to identify victims or witnesses or see if anyone has any specific information regarding subject or an incident. One way of doing this is after an incident to get additional information from witnesses or victims.

The other purpose of canvassing is to gain information about threats, occurrences, or trends you may not be aware of. Think of this as conducting a poll. Social media has done away with the need to hang around the water cooler and listen to rumors and gossip, but if SHTF, it might be your only way of learning of things that aren't immediately apparent.

Field interview

Field interview is a term I borrowed from law enforcement; usually in a field interview (or interrogation), a suspicious person is quizzed for information. There may not be enough evidence of a crime to arrest them, but at least we can identify them and see what they will tell us. In military intelligence this is known as *tactical questioning* and can often be done as part of a *snatch and grab* operation to take an enemy captive for interrogation of tactical intelligence.

You won't be grabbing people, but in dynamic situations you will encounter people. Talk to them and see if they can offer any information of value. Get answers to the 5W1H questions.

Who: Identify them and if they are part of a larger organization.

What: Get their version of events, especially if you didn't observe everything they did.

Where: Origin, destination, route, point of entry/egress.

Why: What was the purpose of their act and what were

they trying to achieve?

How: Details on what tools, methods, or techniques they used to commit the act.

When talking to a suspect, act like you already know most, if not all, of the answers, and are just filling in gaps. If you can throw something at them to blindside them (such as if you saw them do something they thought no one saw), it enhances the effect.

You can also question people you encounter during patrols or defensive activity. Such as talking to a semi-cooperative intruder or people you find walking the area. This won't be like in the military where you rush from your defensive line into the enemy and snatch one of them for questioning. Although if you can capture an intruder and talk to them away from any of their friends, this can provide valuable intelligence.

A sympathetic intruder might come up to you and say something like: "I hate your president, but you're not bad people. Some really bad dudes with guns are gonna come here and shoot you up." You need to quickly extract specific information fast; the guy isn't going to stick around long.

"When?"

"I heard this like 15 minutes ago. They have to walk down from the park [20 minutes away]."

"How many of them?"

"Six guys."

"What kind of guns?

"AR-15s and pistols."

"Do they have anything else? Any bombs or Molotov cocktails?"

"Yeah, they're planning to burn you guys."

Brief interviews can also be done while engaged in security duties, like a modified form of canvassing above. Though you are not likely to be on patrol, you can always ask people you encounter highly specific questions to aid you in your mission. This would, for example, be asking for a suspect description and direction of travel as you chased a dark clad burglar down. Keep your questions brief and simple. Remember any neutral person you talk with may not want to talk with you for fear of being targeted.

A field interview as part of a screening process at a checkpoint is another excellent way of getting information. Before letting people into your neighborhood, you will want to identify them and why they are visiting, right? If they are cooperative, ask them for information. What are things like in their area? Did they notice anything strange or suspicious on their way over? For a non-cooperative individual, you will obviously screen them further to see if they are a jerk on legitimate business or up to no good. Someone who is up to no good should be treated like a suspect and interrogated and identified before sending them on their way.

Reporting

Write stuff down! Keep a record of what you have learned. You will never know when it may become useful. Any written form is good, but if you have an old laptop that is not connected to the Internet, it can be a stand-alone intelligence collection device. It should be password protected and encrypted. The advantage to digital collection and storage of intelligence is that it is easier to search (Ctrl + F). Photos and maps can be linked as well.

Terms

Spot report

A spot report is intended to quickly convey intelligence of an immediate nature, such as in a tactical situation. You would usually be transmitting this via radio or mouth to inform others.

Event: who, what, when, where, why, and how. (5W1H)
Assessment: how the event will or may affect you and what actions should be taken?
Evaluation: how credible and actionable is the source/information?

SALT, SALUTE

SALT and SALUTE are initialisms for remembering what information to report in a *very* short format, such as observers to the intelligence analyst team member. SALUTE is the long-format main reporting form and SALT is the short or supplementary form. Both cover the basics leaders need to know to make decisions.

SALUTE: Size, Activity, Location, Uniform/Unit, Time, Equipment

"Approximately 100 person mob, chanting and vandalizing their way down Madison Ave from Main Street, all dressed in black, approaching now, carrying torches and pitchforks."

SALT: Size, Activity, Location, Time

"Five men just broke off and are making Molotov cocktails in front of Joe's house, just now."

The exact format doesn't have to be repeated as in the initialism or examples, but that information needs to be conveyed. Further details or observations can follow or be requested.

5 W 1 H

Who, What, When, Where, Why, and How?

Who: Name, identity, and biographical information of your subject and/or any identifying information, including physical descriptions of persons or vehicles.
What: A narrative of the event; the nature of the incident (what was done) and how it happened.
When: The time frame of the incident or how long ago it occurred. Is the timing of the incident significant?
Where: The location of the incident, where someone or property was taken, from where access was made, etc. Are there weak points somewhere or do the locations in question have some significance?
Why: What was the goal or motive of the incident? If one was not obvious, can you piece the clues together to ascertain one?
How: Details regarding techniques, methods, tools, etc. on how the incident was accomplished; not a narrative of *what* happened, but *how* it was done.

Communications

Have you thought about how you will communicate if the cell network goes down? The modern telecommunication system can be taken down through cyberwarfare, hackers, or a natural disaster. Cell towers only have a limited amount of fuel in their generators to keep running after a power outage. The regular telephone system is resilient but is now more than ever dependent on the Internet to facilitate calls. Robust forms of communications are necessary for your family, information gathering, and tactical self-defense use.

Apps and the Internet

Absent SHTF, the Internet and the various websites, programs, and apps it provides for us is a fantastic tool. You should already be taking advantage of things like NextDoor to network, gather intelligence, and communicate with your neighbors. As things deteriorate, information sharing, and coordination will become vital. However, such established "Big Tech" platforms will likely eventually crackdown on citizens using their platform for self-defense coordination.

In these times of discord and suspicion, secure communications on your cell phone are important. You don't want Google, Facebook, or the government spying on you. Of course, the NSA can probably read or hear everything, but why make it easy? Get critical communication off the open networks.

The alternative, while still using the Internet and modern

communications, is to move to private communication apps, like Telegram or Signal. Download a secure group messaging app like these. They are best for non-emergency communications and the privacy makes it that much harder for your communications to be intercepted.

A tech-savvy individual could also create a website with a forum for locals. Worst case, create an email list. Everyone can email each other like the old newsgroups.

Radios

Radios are good when you need immediate communication at the push of a button. You aren't texting in a gunfight and dialing a call is too long. Also everyone on your team can hear a radio transmission. Radios will be the primary form of communication in a major grid-down type of disaster. The downside to radio is that in the forms that you will likely have access to, there is zero privacy, all frequencies are shared, and are short range.

Remember to replace that cheap, short "rubber ducky" antenna on your radios and scanners with taller, high gain ones. For tactical use, folding flexible antennas exist.

Privacy and discretion

The majority of your radio usage, especially in an emergency, should be monitoring the radio. Just like you listen to talk or news radio and eavesdrop on conversations to get information, you will do the same with your radios and scanners. Many people who do not understand there is no privacy on the radio will be broadcasting all sorts of information. Listen and learn. This is known as COMINT, for Communications Intelligence.

Unless you have a business that is licensed to have encrypted radios, any radio traffic you send will be able to be intercepted. This goes for ham radio, GMRS/FRS, and CB radio. Privacy codes? Forget it. All those do is tune your radio to ignore other traffic on the same frequency. Anyone with a decent scanner or those privacy codes turned off can hear you.

Using encryption is a sticky subject and some feel that means that private codes are a no-no. To some, that means everything must be easily understood by a listener. I think that's a little pedantic. I would say that anything that is encoded specifically to deceive would be illegal encryption. However, I think the FCC would have a hard time arguing in court why nicknames for places, things, and behavior would be illegal encryption. Read up on the ham forums and decide for yourself.

For legal purposes, obey all FCC regulations. That means if you need a license, get a license. Use your legal call signs. Do not use the radios for illegal purposes. After the January 6, 2021, US Capitol storming, the FCC reminded everyone that the public airwaves are not to be used for nefarious purposes. Just go ahead and assume legally protecting your neighborhood will eventually be deemed "nefarious" and the FCC might prosecute you.

Call signs are publicly available information; you can look up anyone in the FCC database and see who they are and where they live. Be sure to register your call sign to a PO box so no one can easily tell that WANK247 lives at 742 Evergreen Terrace.

Radios should be kept at the lowest volume to still hear them without being so loud others can hear. Ideally, you should be using a headset or earpiece so nothing is broadcast out. Most likely, your devices will be handheld radios with no advanced features. Again, keep the volume low and clip them someplace on your vest or jacket close to your ear if you can.

To limit interception, keep the radio turned to the lowest power (transmitter wattage) possible to accomplish what you need. You need but half a watt to reach the end of the street instead of blasting 5-8 watts all over the town. Keep transmissions as short as possible using brevity codes, nicknames, etc. The longer you transmit, the easier it is for someone to home in on your signal and locate you (if they have that kind of equipment). And the more you talk, the more info they get to fill in the blanks in their intelligence about you.

Remember that you can legally transmit on any frequency to summon help (or provide assistance) even without a license.[11]

Radio band types

UHF: Usually in the 400 MHz range and often found in the non-ham radios commonly available in stores (GMRS and FRS). For hams, this includes the 70cm AKA 440 MHz band (Technician-level amateur operator license required at minimum). This is

[11] 47 CFR Subpart E, §97.403 & §97.405

for short range (<5 miles) communication.

VHF: Usually in the 30-200 MHz range for civilian radios. This is most common for 2m band (144-148 MHz) ham radios, like the ever popular Baofeng radio. The 2m band requires at least a Technician-level amateur operator license at minimum. This is for short range (<5 miles) communication.

VHF and UHF are line of sight radios, meaning they cannot be used to talk over obstacles like mountains. UHF radio is better for indoor usage and in urban areas. Both will suffer if you have terrain or large buildings in between users. If you are on top of a high hill, you may be able to talk out to the often advertised range of 25+ miles if someone is equally as high as you are.

Range is never what is advertised. The long ranges for these radios are predicated on ideal conditions, such as from one mountain peak to another. Higher wattage radios and larger antennas help, but for these radios how high you are and the fewer the obstacles you have, the better. In the city expect 1-2 miles on the ground between walkie-talkies up to five miles if the antenna is high.

HF/shortwave: Usually 26.965-27.405 MHz for CB (unlicensed) and 28.000-29.700 for the 10m amateur band. You will need at least a General-level amateur license for this, except for a very small portion of the spectrum (28.3-28.5 MHz for voice at the Technician level). This is for medium range (10-30 mile) communication. Shortwave receivers also pickup your standard commercial-type radio broadcasts and some models can pickup ham bands. The latter feature will give you listen-only capabilities for long range, amateur communications.

Unlicensed options

Our discussion will be limited to bands that do not require an amateur operator's license.[12] If you plan on using anything other than simple, pre-programmed radios in the neighborhood, do some serious research. You don't need to necessarily get a license for all of these options but do learn how the various bands work in the application you want to use. Learn what equipment works best and how to install and program it. Use your Google Fu!

Note: Dual-band radios that operate on both UHF and VHF (usually 70cm/GMRS/FRS and 2m) are available for the use of hams. These radios, which include the ever popular Baofeng series, can transmit on GMRS, but not legally. Dual-band radios are best for monitoring only, WROL use, or for licensed hams.

GMRS: General Mobile Radio Service. Used for family communications, popular with off-roaders, often used without a license (illegally) by anyone needing a short-range radio. The license is $70 as of this writing, supposedly to be lowered to $35 later in 2021. The license is good for 10 years and practically any close relative can use your license. I have not heard of the FCC prosecuting unlicensed use.

---

[12] Yes, I know GMRS requires a license but the test that puts so many people off their ham license is not required.

You can install repeaters and use radios up to 50 watts. This is a poor-man's UHF ham analogue, but lots of people are using few channels, so you have less options. Portable radios are usually 5 watts, which will give you 1-3 miles in town without connecting to a rooftop antenna. 50 watt radios and a rooftop antenna could cover up to 15 miles depending on the terrain.

For usage if the cell network is down, my suggestion is to put a mobile GMRS 50 watt mobile radio in each vehicle, plus a 50 watt radio stationary version at home. You can purchase multiples of the same radio and simply connect the home unit to a dedicated power supply or even disconnect the car radio when at home and use it as a base station.

If each car in the family has a radio with a suitable antenna mounted on the roof of the car, talking to a 50 watt station at home with a rooftop antenna (they sell 6ft tall poles that are unobtrusive) would be a breeze across a relatively flat suburban city. Each family member could also have a portable radio (walkie-talkie) with them.

My recommendation is GMRS walkie-talkies for each adult in your family. You may want spares for friends/relatives who drop in or to give to a trusted neighbor. Install a 50 watt base station at your house with a 6ft antenna on the roof. Install a 50 watt mobile unit in your car. For a convoy, handheld radios with replacement antennas should be sufficient.

FRS: Family Radio Service. Basically your cheap blister pack radio. Only good for talking within a few blocks, like one end of the street to the other mostly. Though the frequencies and possibly the radio would have greater capabilities, you can't replace the crappy antenna.

Remember that so-called "privacy" modes are anything but. What they do is essentially transmit a code so that only you and the other radios in that same mode can hear each other. Everyone else listening to that frequency can still hear you. This is sort of like yelling across a room at a party in French on the assumption no one else speaks French. In fact, on any radio frequency, whatever you say in any mode can be intercepted.

CB radio: Citizen's Band radio falls at the high end of the HF spectrum. Yes, it is the uncool radio that truckers use and is filled with trash transmitting garbage. You too can have an ugly antenna sticking off the side of your station wagon!

CBs are right on the border between "long range" HF/High Frequency and "short range" VHF/Very High Frequency. Maximum legal wattage is 4 watts, which won't reach far, but if you buy illegal amplifiers, you can increase power dramatically to reach across whole counties, depending on the terrain. Under the right conditions and with the right equipment, a CB radio base station could reach out around 30 miles or so, giving you medium range communications without a repeater.

CB can be used while driving during an emergency or not. After all, most use is on the highway. A few sources recommend it for convoy travel, although I would say a convoy should be tight enough that a few miles from a GMRS radio with a rooftop antenna would be fine. A CB radio base station with a good antenna mounted up high and a very powerful amplifier would be better as a home base radio.

Recommendations

I recommend a home GMRS watt base station and at least one car with a 50 watt mobile radio. This would replace a cell phone when driving around town when the grid is down. Each family member would have a GMRS walkie-talkie; the older folks would get the more expensive models with longer antennas and the kids would get the bubble pack ones when they go play down the street. To talk to friends or relatives across the county, this would be done with a CB radio mounted on the house.

What is ham radio?

"Ham" radio is properly known as the Amateur Radio Service and is licensed by the FCC. An amateur operator license requires that one pass a test and pay a fee ($15-35 depending on the time of reading). Morse code is *not* required any longer. The tests are put on by many ham radio organizations around the country on a regular basis. There is one near you, wherever you live.

If you would like greater flexibility and the benefits of better radios and frequency choices, pursue your amateur license. The material for a Technician license isn't overly complicated and study guides provide a good introduction to the test material. Studying for the test can be done by simply memorizing the question pool. Knowledge of Morse code is no longer required. Don't let the study material and test throw you off; once you pass, for most entry-level radio usage the knowledge is practical versus technical.

Ham radio is divided into three license grades: Technician, General, and Amateur Extra. Technician is the easiest level to achieve and gives you access to VHF and UHF bands. The main advantage over just using GMRS/FRS radios with their no-test license is that ham radios allow you more power, more features in the radio, and better ability to attach peripherals like microphones, antennas, and accessories.

Passing the amateur operations license test is a matter of studying the test questions. Very little actual technical knowledge is required when using the radios or to pass the test. The general knowledge about how radio waves and antennas work is easy enough to learn from simple introductory books ("Dummies Guide") and YouTube videos. If you just want the license, studying to the test is enough to pass. I recommend studying for a general license to obtain an additional range of frequencies/bands you can use.

Why get a ham license?

"In SHTF, I will just transmit without a license," many say. I partially agree, and I have a license. No one will stop anyone and we each will have bigger problems than worrying about the FCC. I personally don't want to be broadcasting my callsign for the bad guys to hear and find out who I am and where I live. That's great for me because I have a license now and can practice legally *and* I have years of experience using a mobile VHF radio.

Obtaining a ham license is a positive because:

- It allows you to practice legally now.
- It allows you to legally use your radio in situations that are less than WROL/SHTF.
- If the FCC does engage in targeted prosecution of unlicensed operators, you won't get in trouble.
- With the right equipment and learned experience, it will be your only form of non-phone or Internet communication for long distances (greater than 30 miles).
- Restricting yourself to CB/GMRS may cause you to limit yourself to those bands and equipment, hindering any switch to other bands later due to lack of experience/complacency.

If you don't get a license, there are some radios (GMRS/FRS/CB) you can use but be aware that the frequencies will probably be clogged with traffic from other unlicensed users.

Scanners

Radio scanners are excellent tools for information and intelligence. Scanners are simply a radio receiver and memory bank that rapidly tunes to potentially thousands of channels in a matter of seconds. Most decent models can get everything from public safety, aviation, marine, unencrypted military, business, amateur (ham), and personal use radio traffic. Get a scanner, learn the lingo of what you're listening to, and monitor it to know what is going on.

Never rely on online streaming services; I don't care how easy or comprehensive the Broadcastify app on your phone is. The feed is often delayed, seldom covers anything other than main dispatch channels, and is totally under the control of the service and the streamer. In a major catastrophe, the electricity, Internet, and cell service may be down at your end and the streamer's end. Be able to listen using your own resources.

When buying a scanner, options can be overwhelming. One easy option is pre-programmed scanners like the Uniden Home Patrol series. These scanners are preloaded with frequencies and can also be edited to create custom lists on your computer. They are expensive but are easy to use without compromising on features. Simple scanners that take direct entry are available cheaply, but these come with very limited features, a narrow range of channels you can save, and can't capture all radio transmissions.

Know what kind of radios are used by the emergency services in your area or you might have a dead scanner. Simplex (or conventional analog) radio is what most people are familiar with; you hear what is transmitted on the frequency you've dialed in. On a scanner, the frequency can be directly entered and signals received. These systems are common in smaller and rural communities.

Trunked radio systems are much more complicated and requires a trunking scanner. These systems share a set of frequencies, but instead of transmitting on a dedicated frequency, a controller only sends the traffic to radios tuned to receive specific traffic (called "talk groups"). Skipping the detailed explanation, one has to program in the control frequencies for a trunked network and the individual talk groups. Programming is more complicated because the control frequencies and the talk groups must be input.

Trunking is why older scanners don't work with modern

systems, but this doesn't mean that the radio traffic is encrypted. LAPD uses a trunked system that is unencrypted. Nevada state agencies, for example, are on trunked systems, but among those, only Las Vegas Metro Police have encrypted radio. In another example, St. Louis Police is part of the Missouri Statewide Wireless Interoperable Network, also unencrypted. Check what your local agencies use.

One thing to keep in mind when monitoring trunked systems is that the voice traffic sounds unnatural. It sounds "digital" and "choppy." If you've listened to online streams, you probably know what I'm talking about. This has to do with the fact that consumer scanners aren't often included with the same technology and antennas to properly receive the signals in the same quality very expensive public safety radios can. Unfortunately for the civilian listener, traffic can be garbled, part of the transmission can be missed, and the lack of detail tends to drop out important contextual cues like background noises or tone of voice.

Have a hardcopy of all the frequencies you want to monitor along with the hardcopy instruction manual of your scanner. You can't get online to RadioReference.com if the world has ended or the power is out. In fact, program your scanner now and listen.

I prefer to have pre-set groups of frequencies I want to check. For instance, for SHTF intelligence I have a list of frequencies that average people (or bad guys) might be using. The typical radios someone will use in an SHTF situation will be those that are readily available, meaning GMRS/FRS, CB, business/MURS, and dual-band Baofeng type radios. Most criminals are lazy and unsophisticated; they will use what they have access to and aren't going to be running some sort of high-tech digital or encrypted radio but whatever they bought cheaply or more likely stole.

I don't put much stock in the "Close Call" features that pickup nearby radio transmissions. In practice, these pickup far too much traffic and are often inundated on each "sweep" of the frequencies by digital data when scanning ham bands. I don't want to check thousands of frequencies and get a lot of false positives. By scanning the frequencies bad guys are most likely to be using, I can hear if the neighborhood group in the development across the arroyo is getting attacked or if a gang is coordinating a raid.

With an off-the-shelf scanner, I'm using a dinky little rubber ducky antenna and most likely so is whoever I'm trying to listen to. Transmissions far away aren't going to be received if they have a weak signal, so by the nature of the equipment, I'm going to pick up close transmissions anyway.

Sound discipline

Walkie-talkies should have earpieces to minimize the spillover of radio traffic when outside. If your team's radios do not have earpieces, as they probably won't, sound discipline must be tightly maintained. This avoids the sound unintentionally alerting someone to your position or anyone up close enough to hear the transmission from eavesdropping without their own radio.

One method would be to have a radio set to the lowest volume that can still be heard from your belt, etc. Everyone transmits just a call sign and waits for a response to continue. When the first call is heard, everyone with a radio turns down the volume and puts the speaker to their ear like a phone so the transmission isn't loudly broadcast everywhere.

It should go without saying that music needs to be prohibited when on guard or watch duty. That means no stereos and no earbuds. All attention needs to be on the situation at hand. Rebroadcasting even police scanner traffic could cause an issue with interference in acoustic observations. One person should be dedicated to monitoring scanner traffic or radio traffic. A dedicated radio operator may be desirable if there is a lot of radio traffic in your group and action on the street.

ComSec; Communication Security

Everything you say on a radio can be intercepted. What you say and where you transmit from can be easily identified. Should you have access to encrypted business radios, those can be decrypted by the government, if they are so inclined. Dedicated amateurs practice locating transmitters (especially unlicensed or foul mouthed operators) and breaking digital mode transmissions (which are not encrypted).

Until the federal government is unable to enforce the law, all FCC regulations apply. This means that licenses are needed on licensed frequencies, call signs must be used, and no encrypted traffic can be sent. The FCC can't monitor everything, but keep in mind that "white night" ham radio operators may turn you in or interfere with you for violating regulations. Keep in mind that using radios improperly when defending yourself could be used as a weapon to prosecute you federally if you are politically unfavorable.

The so-called "privacy modes" on your family radios only silence people outside your group; everyone else can hear you in those modes. It's also important to understand that even if you don't hear anyone else on the radio, someone could still be listening.

Efficiency of communications helps avoid giving away intelligence and cuts down the amount of time that traffic can be intercepted. Think of it as whispering in a dark room; the shorter and quieter you whisper, the less chance anything you say will be understood and the harder it will be to home in on your voice. Understand that radio traffic can be detected as soon as you key the mic without even saying a word.

Keep anything you say to a minimum. Communicate only information that is vital to your mission. Do not make conversation. If you have a talkative or joking individual in your group, consider taking away their radio and ignoring any idle chatter from them. If you are making a long report, say "break" and stop transmitting every so often so that someone with emergency traffic can break in. Radios aren't like cell phones; you cannot talk over another radio signal at the same time.

Keep any specific information discreet. If you can avoid transmitting real names, addresses, and your actions, the better. True codes tend to be frowned upon in normal times, but in a WROL radio procedure should use special call signs and codes. By "codes" I mean concealing names and locations, not trying to mimic police or military radio codes.

Use plain speech as much as possible to give orders or request things, while only obfuscating that which your enemy may intercept. Don't use 10-codes or things like that. Average people aren't going to be able to memorize and correctly use a whole host of code phrases. Your job isn't to sound cool.

As much as possible, generic descriptions and first names should be used (aside from call signs). Example: "John, this is Dick. Go to southeast corner and report," versus the poor "John, Dick Wilson here. Can you go down Maple Street to the corner of Ash Drive by the Jones' house? Tell me what's going on down there." The first strikes a good balance between vagueness to frustrate electronic eavesdropping and quickly transmitting information. In the second version, John just gave away Dick's last name and unwittingly broadcasted his cross-streets.

As far as code phrases, restrict those to only orders that would be compromised if intercepted by radio, such as ordering a retreat. An example would be instead of radioing "Retreat, retreat," you would say "Doghouse, doghouse." The bad guys won't know what "doghouse" means. A bad use would be "Buick, move with Ford to Dallas. Use the Big Stick to Jet Ski." That's five things to remember and all the code words could be confusing. Only encode what you absolutely must.

Good practice all the time

- Replace the rubber ducky antenna with a better one.
- Keep transmissions brief and specific.
- Speak loudly, slowly, and clearly.
- Do not use the radio for conversations.
- Vary the channels and frequencies you use regularly.
- Keep the volume low.

- Never attempt to jam or harass your enemy; listen and use them as a source of intelligence.

"Normal" times protocol

- Use call signs as required by the FCC.
- Use only frequencies you are licensed to use.
- Do not use codes, although nicknames for places and persons within a group is likely permissible.
- Do not use the radio to coordinate activities of questionable legality.

WROL only protocol

- Use first names as they are easy to remember and still somewhat vague.
- Change channels regularly to complicate interception.
- Operate outside of approved bands for given licenses.
- Never use exact locations except in an emergency; assign code names to your streets and local landmarks. Your radios won't be transmitting that far so you won't have to rename the whole state.
- Perhaps have code phrases for certain common or very important actions (keep it simple).
- Have a duress code if you think someone is listening to the radio so everyone can be extra discreet. One code word could indicate to switch to a pre-decided secondary channel.

Self-Defense Legalities

Self-defense and justifiable homicide laws govern when you can use force and what kind. The key is proportionality; was the force you used reasonable to stop the offense? That is what a judge and jury will look at. What might seem like the end of the world to you might not actually be, so any extreme circumstances you find yourself in may not be "weapons free" for kinetic solutions.

This chapter is merely a general introduction to broad concepts. I am not an attorney nor qualified to speak expertly on any state's laws. I caution everyone to have a thorough understanding of their local self-defense laws and take a class on them from an attorney or licensed concealed carry instructor.

Self-defense in general (non-violent crimes)

You may resist the commission of a crime if you or another person will be harmed. This includes using reasonable force to prevent damage to, or theft of, your property. Resistance sufficient to prevent the offense is allowed. In other words, the force you use must be proportionate to the force the suspect is using, i.e. grabbing a thief or restraining someone from punching you, but not shooting them.

Deadly force is *not* permitted to stop a property crime, such as shooting a burglar or a shoplifter running away with loot. This would also apply to driving through an angry mob simply because they are in the road but not actively trying to kill you.

Note that robbery and burglary of an occupied home, both crimes that usually involve theft, are considered violent crimes and not just property crimes. Robberies involve force and/or fear of death or serious injury (often with weapons). Burglaries of occupied homes have been traditionally recognized as having a potential for more than just theft and deadly force is generally permitted against a burglar.

In the event of physical violence that is not inherently deadly, such as a fistfight or an assault, you cannot use deadly force. You may however fight the suspect off using whatever means are *not* likely to cause death until the assault ceases. A slap cannot be answered with a gunshot.

Use of retaliatory force is not permitted. You may not beat someone up for stealing from you or committing some other property crime "to teach them a lesson." The only force you may use is that necessary to stop the crime from happening, to legally effect an arrest, or to prevent them from hurting you. Even in a WROL scenario, a vindictive beating may only result in your opponent coming back to exact revenge on you.

Generally, you may come to the aid of another. Some states condition their self-defense guidelines to only protecting yourself or a close relative. For deadly force, almost universally you are permitted to come to the aid of the victim regardless of any relationship to them.

In most states, private persons are allowed to make arrests (citizen's arrest) for a felony or a crime (misdemeanor) that was committed in their presence.[13] Force sufficient to

---

[13] Note that a felony usually *does not* have to be committed in the presence of the arrestor.

make the arrest (usually physical strength to restrain the person) is permitted. Private citizens then need to immediately turn their arrestee over to the police or a judge (details may vary).

- Self-defense is usually allowed on behalf of others.
- Non-deadly force must be reasonable and be proportionate to stop the offense.
- Deadly force can't be used in response to property crimes.
- You cannot use force on someone for mere words, in retaliation or revenge.
- You may arrest someone committing a crime in your presence and restrain them until you can turn them over to the authorities.

See also: "Use of Force Continuum" in the "Riot and Crowd Control" chapter.

Justifiable homicide

Justifiable (or excusable) homicide is killing when it is necessary to do so for a greater good; i.e. in self-defense, rather than maliciously (murder) or negligently (manslaughter). Most states define it as: "the killing of a human being in necessary self-defense." This includes use of deadly force, even if the person does not die.

The killing must be necessary to prevent an immediate danger of death or serious injury against you, a family member, or a third person in your presence. Some states include in defense of an occupied home or motor vehicle. A serious injury usually includes being crippled, losing a part of your body, rape or sodomy, or an injury that could be potentially life threatening if not immediately treated (such as being shot or stabbed).

Many states excuse the killing of burglars breaking into a home, "in a violent, riotous, or tumultuous manner," if the defender can ascertain or believes that the burglar is trying to break in to offer violence to the inhabitants. This would include home invasion robberies or an angry mob trying to force its way in to harm someone. Some states add "surreptitious" manner, as in someone trying to sneak in through a window undetected.

You should be cautioned to never shoot someone who is in your home unlawfully unless they are actually a danger to you or could reasonably be perceived to be a danger. Sometimes the mentally ill, elderly people with dementia, or drunk people enter the wrong home with no intention to do harm. Killing them absent any indication of danger would be illegal. If the person is not actually a threat, do not automatically just shoot them. It may turn out that the dark figure in your home is actually a relative who is home early or up late.

Shooting someone who has committed a felony is generally only reserved for law enforcement and is governed by the case *Tennessee v. Garner*. Fleeing felons must be a danger to the public if they escape, such as a serial killer or violent robber. You cannot shoot someone for a property crime, even if it is a felony.

Usually inflicting non-deadly injuries, mainly serious injuries, (or using less-than-lethal force, including physical strength) is permitted if the use of force otherwise conforms with justifiable homicide.

Fear and threats

Merely claiming a bare fear is not enough to justify killing. You must have actually been afraid and the circumstances and evidence must support this. For brave souls, feeling the emotion of fear isn't necessary, but having the intellectual fear of death or harm is enough. You cannot just state you were "afraid for your life;" another reasonable person in the same situation must also have ben afraid of being killed or seriously injured.

Credible threats with immediate danger of them being carried out are also generally justifiable ("I'm going to kill you," said the axe wielding maniac). Future harm is generally not considered justifiable no matter how great the threat of harm is (i.e. "I shot him because he said, 'one day, I'll get you when your back is turned.'"). In a WROL situation, it may be reasonable and prudent to preemptively address threats that you can honestly and reasonably say will turn deadly, such as a gang coming back at night or an opponent who will ambush you. In a civilized world, this preemption is *not* legal.

Provocation

You cannot create a situation where it becomes necessary to exercise self-defense, such as picking a fight and then claiming you shot the other guy because he pulled a knife. Provoking someone to cause violence so you can hurt or kill is never permitted. If you do start a fight and it escalates to deadly force, you must have taken every good faith measure to quit the fight. In this case you have a duty to retreat and stop fighting before you can legally defend yourself.

Please note that the danger of being labeled the aggressor and prosecuted for self-defense is great when you are facing off with a politically advantaged person or group. What you and I might deem reasonable measures to protect your neighborhood, such as openly carrying and warning rioters to leave the area, could be deliberately misconstrued as hostile aggression. This is why it is vital to never taunt, tease, insult, or unnecessarily engage while performing neighborhood protection.

A Portland area journalist, Mike Strickland, was convicted of a felony for brandishing when he was surrounded and threatened by an Antifa mob in 2016. Strickland had a history of repeated harassment from Antifa who did not like his coverage of their protests and vandalism. Despite credible evidence Strickland was acting in self-defense, charges were stacked against him under political pressure and his appeals were denied. What was either not a crime or a misdemeanor at worst made a man into a felon because of political persecution.

Depending on the politics of the area where you live, this is a real danger to citizens who attempt to protect themselves from politically favored groups. Therefore I highly recommend that, except in a life-threatening situation (meaning you *will* die if you don't act) or a WROL scenario, that you remove yourself from the crowd and get inside before things get violent. If you remain impassionate, decline to fight, and retreat it will make it hard for prosecutors to press their case.

Use lethal force

- You may use lethal force to prevent a murder or a violent felony like rape, robbery, or mayhem.
- You may use lethal force to protect your home against anyone who is attempting to commit a violent crime inside.
- You may use lethal force against someone who is breaking in and you reasonably assume they are doing so to commit violence to someone inside.

Do not use lethal force

- You may not kill someone just for stealing, vandalism, or a non-life threatening assault.
- You may not kill someone breaking in to your home or vehicle unless they are a threat to your life or may inflict a serious injury.
- You cannot kill someone unless you have an actual fear of death or serious injury; not just a theoretical one.
- You may not kill someone if you started the fight and have not tried every reasonable means to stop fighting and get away.
- You do not have the legal grounds to suppress a riot with lethal force.

No duty to retreat (stand your ground)

The duty to retreat is different in each state. Most states do not require you to try and get away before resorting to force, however, some do. Other states have specific laws that enumerate no duty to retreat in different ways and to different degrees. Readers will be familiar with Florida's strong protections. Your state may require you to retreat if in a public place, but not at home.

For example, California has a statute of "no duty to retreat" inside the home, known as Castle Doctrine, where "a man's home is his castle" and he has the right to defend it. However, in *People v. Hatchett* the doctrine was expanded to everywhere in the state, but this is case law, not hard statute. In neighboring Nevada and far away Florida, the doctrine is split between two different statutes with one specifically mentioning homes and vehicles while the other is general. Check your state laws for specifics.

Again, politically favored persons and groups may be your undoing if you are politically prosecuted (or persecuted as it were). The more you can do to convince a jury you were just trying to protect yourself and were the "good guys" by backing off, trying to avoid the fight, etc. the more likely an acquittal is. You are the victim so act in a way to make people sympathize with you.

As a rule of thumb, if on the street, retreat whenever you can into your home where you are protected. You will look better if you declined a struggle when you didn't have to and will have additional rights and protections in your home (if not avoiding a confrontation entirely). A fight is not worth the trouble and risk, even if you are 100% legally justified and live in a self-defense friendly state. Only in a true long-term WROL situation would you want to draw a line in the sand or go on the offensive.

Property

In most states, you cannot use lethal force to protect private property. Even where you can, the details are more complicated than that. There is also the moral issue of whether or not you want to shoot someone in the back as they run away with your TV. Even in a WROL situation, there could be repercussions such as retaliation or being ostracized for killing over theft, vandalism, etc.

A pawnshop owner in Minneapolis was arrested for shooting a looter in his business during the initial Floyd George riots. The charges were later dismissed against him, yet he still had to deal with being arrested and charged.

For property crimes, you are expected to use reasonable force that is just enough to stop the crime such as grabbing a shoplifter by the arm to detain him. If resistance increases, you may be justified in using additional force, like hitting them, using pepper spray or a Taser. One might construe this to using paintballs or a hose against vandals.

Some states may allow you to defend your business against an intruder while other states specify just homes. I highly recommend you do not attempt to use lethal force or amateur crowd control in defense of a business. In today's fractious times and twisted legal/political atmosphere, it isn't worth the risk.

Roof Koreans and riot suppression via lethal force

If you remember the 1992 LA riots or have seen the photos of Korean shop owners with openly carried weapons defending their property, you may be familiar with the term "Roof Korean." This term refers to people defending their property at gunpoint. A lot of the open carry of weapons in these instances was just a bluff. If the looters called it, shooting wouldn't be justified unless the looters began to physically assault the defenders.

You are not a cop and in most states the ability to use lethal force to suppress a riot is not yours. Even so, police can't just shoot into a riot to stop it. Except in a WROL situation, openly carrying a weapon is often enough a deterrent against those stupid enough to think it is legal to kill looters and rioters on sight.

Don't think you are going to show up tough and armed like a Roof Korean and the rioters, looters, and mob will leave you alone. Deterrence is half luck anyhow. Don't bet all your chips on hoping your opponents are dumb cowards. Woe betide you if the crowd understands that you can't legally shoot them and won't shoot them.

Furthermore, there were incidents of arrests of Roof Koreans for various violations (loaded open carry and brandishing). Police may choose to arrest you because you did something technically illegal in the heat of the moment, like brandishing, and feel that your possession of weapons is escalating the situation. Police may target *you* because they know *you* won't shoot them if they arrest you.

W R O L

In a true WROL situation, defense of property may be different. Here, in the absence of police most crimes will carry the penalty of death, as the saying in the prepper world goes. This is because there are no police, no courts, and no jails. With no threat of punishment for the shooter, and no punishment for the criminal, thieves will likely be shot rather than taking the risk of having them return and in lieu of having them punished in other ways.

In only a true, long-term WROL situation, one could justify shooting a thief who is for instance stealing food. If the thief who stole your tomatoes last week comes back for the potatoes this week, you may very well starve to death without that food. The mortal threat is not in the immediate term but exists none the less. It will be interesting to see what kind of moral and legal doctrines evolve after an extended lawless famine.

Brandishing

Brandishing is drawing or exhibiting a firearm (or weapon) at any person in a rude, angry, or threatening manner not in necessary self-defense. Basically you can't pull a gun on someone because they made you mad or you want to intimidate them. Note the elements of the crime: drawing a weapon or calling attention to it while being rude, angry, or threatening. "Self-defense" and "rude, angry, or threatening" behavior may be stretched by the courts if there is political pressure to prosecute you.

St. Louis, Missouri, 2020: An angry mob broke down a gate and entered the lawn of a wealthy couple's mansion. The group was loud and threatening the homeowners, the McCloskeys. Fearing what the mob might do, Mr. and Mrs. McCloskey came outside and pointed and waved two unloaded guns at the crowd, while yelling back. Despite Missouri law permitting the homeowners to do exactly what they did[14], they were still charged with a crime.[15]

The husband of former Los Angeles District Attorney Jackie Lacey was charged for pointing a gun at an angry mob outside his home months prior to the 2020 unrest. The incident was used in his wife's re-election campaign against her. While strictly not a legal use of force, it could be said that Mr. Lacey was not overreacting or acting immorally.

Whether or not the law is on your side, do you really think it is a good idea to go out and yell rudely and angrily at your opponent while pointing a gun at them? Taunting a crowd and pointing guns at them is a recipe for getting shot by someone who will pull the trigger over words when you won't. Then you will be in the position of having to explain why you *aren't* the aggressor and how your self-defense claim overrides that you were angry, rude, and pointing a gun at people.

The Catch-22 of brandishing is that pointing a gun at someone who has malicious intentions will often get them to run the other direction, but for it to be legal self-defense, the bad guy must already be presenting a deadly threat. So preempting a potentially deadly situation before it even gets there is kinda tricky unless you can articulate why you were in fear of death or serious injury. Now WROL, brandishing with the will to back it up with gunfire may, in some cases, be the only way of deterring someone with the tools you have at hand.

In the meantime, you should never draw a firearm (or point it at someone if it is already "out" like a rifle or shotgun)

---

[14] May not be legal in your area or circumstances. The tactical decisions made by the McCloskeys were poor, in part because they left their house, which provided them safety and greater legal protection, and by their account the guns were illegal.

[15] They eventually took a plea bargain for a minor misdemeanor.

unless you intend to use your firearm and can legally kill someone. First off, unnecessarily drawing your gun and threatening someone is illegal. Second, pulling out your gun like that may cause the situation to escalate to deadly force. Deadly force encounters are to be avoided at all costs. If you do happen to shoot someone, you may be accused of a crime because your words and actions were inappropriate.

Warning shots

Do not fire warning shots. Not only are they illegal practically everywhere, in an urban area a bullet could miss widely and hurt someone. If you are pulling the trigger of a gun, it should be because it is permissible to shoot someone as justifiable homicide and you are shooting them to stop a deadly threat. Issue verbal commands or use sirens to give warnings. If warning "shots" must be fired, use less-than-lethal munitions or sprays, but typically "rubber bullets" are *not* within the purview of civilian use.

Less-lethal used against you

Law enforcement officers will often use deadly force against a suspect who uses or attempts to use an incapacitating agent against an officer. Plenty of people have been shot for trying to Taser or pepper spray officers. The theory for using deadly force against less-than-lethal force is that pepper spray and a Taser temporarily incapacitates the victim who is then unable to defend themselves effectively. Such an attack on an officer usually precedes an attempt to disarm the officer of his handgun.

The difference between you and an officer is that the officer is being paid to place himself in that situation. Almost by job definition, the officer cannot be considered the original aggressor in the fight as he gets involved to keep the peace (hence *peace officer*). You are not.

In a strictly legal sense, you cannot block your street and keep strangers off it anymore than an angry mob can walk out into and stop traffic. Without legal authority, you can't move a protester out of traffic or shove a rioter back from your barricade. You technically become the aggressor and the other person may then defend himself against *you*. So at that point, if he pepper sprays you, technically you can't argue it was legal to shoot him because you were openly carrying and you were afraid he would disarm and kill you. Unfortunately, you were in the wrong because you had no authority to use physical force to bar them from whatever they were doing.

In an October 2020 protest in Denver, an unlicensed security guard for a local news crew, Matthew Doloff, shot and killed another protester who was armed with pepper spray. Video and photos show Lee Keltner in a verbal exchange with protesters, then Keltner and Doloff struggle. Keltner hits Doloff's head with an open hand. The two separate and Keltner has not raised the pepper spray.

Doloff then reaches for his concealed handgun. Keltner raises the pepper spray. Almost simultaneously, Keltner discharges his pepper spray at Doloff as the latter fires his gun, a photo catching Doloff's pistol just after it fired as the slide recoils and a cartridge ejects (probably just as the bullet struck Keltner). Keltner was killed and Doloff was charged with second degree murder, but the defendant claimed self-defense.

What exactly lead to the Kelter/Doloff scuffle is still not clear. The photos and video do tend to show that deadly force was not proportionate. Doloff seems to have fired using the law enforcement reasoning of gun versus pepper spray. As of this writing, the case has not gone to trial yet. It will be interesting to see what the outcome is.

Again, in a non-WROL situation, the best defense if the outer perimeter is forced is to retreat into the home. In the middle ground a less-than-lethal response would likely be proportionate. In a WROL situation, use your judgement for what is the *best* outcome, which may be the discretion to back up and separate yourself to avoid being incapacitated.

Tasers follow the same principles closely along with pepper spray, but a Taser incapacitates someone for 5-30 seconds (depending on the model). It is designed to interrupt the person's ability to resist and will do just that if the probes make effective contact. During this time, your attacker could easily seriously and fatally assault you. In this case, the police officer's argument about pepper spray and lethal force *might* apply to you using lethal force against a Taser attack.

A Taser attack can be mitigated by wearing thick clothing. Often when a Taser is ineffective the probes can't penetrate the clothing or only one probe hits correctly. When and if you can move, thrash at the wires violently and pull the probes loose. Remember if you can fight effectively while being shocked, you probably have one probe in. For Drive Stun mode or a stun-gun, just keep the person far enough away so they can't touch the device to you.

Should you be attacked with pepper spray, shield your face with a hand or arm. Half a face full is better than a full face full. Don't panic. Fight to open your eyes and continue to run and fight. If you can run screaming to the bathroom after getting jalapeño juice in your eye, you can run away from a pepper spray attack and fight back. Use the appropriate amount of force for whatever the attacker is trying to do to you.

If you expect a pepper spray attack, wear a mask and eye protection (goggles preferred). After an attack, force your eyes to tear up and self-flush. To clean up, use cold water and cool, fresh air. Do not use warm water as this will open the pores and make you burn again. Washing with soap to remove the oils from the skin is good and saline solutions or even eye-safe shampoos can be used on the eyes.

Tactically appropriate vs. judicially appropriate

I had the opportunity once to watch SWAT training as it took place in a fire department's training tower. The entry team came in, "shot" the armed dummy, and the instructor threw it to the ground. When the second team made entry, the gun was still attached to the dummy and each member of Team 2 muzzled the dummy and "fired." The instructor commended Team 2 that the dummy was "dead," but their procedure was correct.

He explained that the Israelis fire a "confirmation shot" into possibly dead terrorists during assaults, just to make sure that the terrorist is dead and not just wounded. The last thing you want is a terrorist who will pull the pin on a grenade or detonate his suicide vest. The instructor said that sometimes each member of the team fired a shot into the terrorist, just to make sure.

The idea of a confirmation shot immediately makes sense. Sometimes you aren't sure if you have truly incapacitated the guy you shot. Is he still a threat? You aren't sure. This is where sound tactics of combat conflict with self-defense jurisprudence.

The law wants you to be able to specifically say why you took the shot. Unless you can argue that you shot the man, who had already been grievously wounded, in the back as he lay on the ground because he was still reaching for a gun, you may have problems. It may be very hard to convince a judge and jury that since you couldn't be sure you neutralized the guy, you fired a second shot just to be sure. You didn't want him to pop up again and start shooting at you.

Reasonable people might understand that, in a flexible and chaotic situation where amateurs are forced to operate beyond their training and experience without a police response, such things might be necessary. The attacker might be feigning death or disablement until your attention is diverted by another threat.

What is prudent in combat may be regarded as overkill and unjustifiable in "peacetime." If you take necessary "excesses" in order to protect yourself, courts may not agree. In infantry tactics, overwhelming firepower is often necessary to crush enemy resistance, such as an ambush. In a civilian context, this would be like firing rapidly and inaccurately into the proximity of an armed roadblock and driving through. Such tactics may get you through alive and may be your only chance of defeating the bad guys with guns, yet a hostile court could portray you as the bad guy.

Mob (multiple attackers) self-defense

Some case law and theories hold that because of the nature of a mob, the mob is acting as one. Thus, if one person in the mob becomes violent and it is necessary to use deadly force against them, because of how the mob could/does react, the mob is as valid a target for self-defense as the individual. Your actions should be directed against the most immediate and deadly/dangerous threat rather than indiscriminate.

I would say that in a situation where you have to shoot, say the front member of a line of rioters, if you miss and hit someone in the mob, it is still justifiable because the mob is in a sense one entity and the rioters all chose to be in that place and egg each other on. The doctrine is predicated more on the idea that you are surrounded by a group that is beating you, etc. and you start shooting members of the group, even though certain members may be more violent than the others.

This following quote from a Texas opinion explains the doctrine:

"The theory behind the multiple assailants

> charge is that, when it is clear that an attack is being conducted by multiple people as a group, a defendant is justified in using force against any member of the group, even if the recipient of that force is not engaging in conduct that would, by itself, justify the use of force (or deadly force as the case may be)."
>
> For example, if a defendant were trapped in a house with several hostile individuals, some of whom were brandishing firearms and threatening the defendant, the defendant may be justified in using deadly force against a different person who was blocking an exit that would otherwise be a viable path of retreat. The use of deadly force against the person blocking the exit would be justified, even though that person possessed no firearms and made no threatening moves, because of that person's complicity with those who threatened the defendant's life. The rule concerning multiple assailants is essentially an application of the law of parties to the defendant's assailants."[16]

The above only applies to Texas law, but the general nature of the principle holds in many states.

As far as misses are concerned, if a member of the crowd is shot when you were intending to hit someone else, the totality of the circumstances would be weighed. In a fair trial, if you had the right to use deadly force and did your best to hit the correct

---

[16] *Dickey v. State*, 22 S.W.3d 490, 493 (Tex. Crim. App. 1999).

assailant, but missed, chances are the shooting would be found justifiable. I'm not a lawyer so I'm not sure if there is any case law to support this, but if a gang member shoots, misses, and kills an innocent person instead of a rival, they are still charged with murder because the intent was to take *someone's* life maliciously.

Assuming the legal speculation is correct, this is not to justify shooting indiscriminately into the crowd. Unless it has *truly* come to that as the only way to stay alive, the consequences will be severe if you survive. Non-lethal means are much better than bullets to disperse a mob. A legal defense against a thing like that would be nigh impossible and even if the rule of law has collapsed, the mob or heavy hitters from the other side may retaliate.

Video recording

Some may want to have their own body cam to document the incident so that edited video can't be presented to support one-sided testimony. You will have to be your own witness. Your friends and neighbors may not have seen the same thing you did. They, like members of the riot mob, may testify against you. A body cam can be your only witness that you weren't in the wrong.

I have mixed feelings about this. If you record your own video and are involved in a critical incident, that video then becomes evidence. If you made a mistake or had to do something of questionable legality, though morally acceptable and necessary, do you really want to be the one who created the evidence that might be used against you?

What about "forgetting" to turn on the camera or "losing" the memory card? Ask yourself, are you comfortable lying, potentially perjuring yourself, and/or committing the crime of destruction of evidence? It is a double-edged sword, so whatever you decide, be careful.

In any scenario that isn't a total grid-down collapse you must assume that you are being video and audio recorded. Anything you say and do can be used against you. A mob will be recording you to have evidence of your "crimes." Any video they do share will inevitably be purely in their favor and exonerating video will never get the same media treatment as "guilty" footage.

Most neighborhoods now have some form of video surveillance, from wide area cameras to Ring doorbells. Cameras that just catch a snippet of the public areas like sidewalks and roads can be canvassed over an entire city to track your movements, should law enforcement want to. Get a night vision scope or a cheap night vision camera and drive around the neighborhood at night looking for lights that are only visible in infrared. That will give you a good idea of where the cameras are and what they can see.

Retreat is not cowardice

Your number one way to surviving a self-defense situation is to avoid the situation entirely; in other words, don't be there. If you can withdraw from danger, do so. What is the first goal of self-defense? To survive; so why engage if you don't have to?

It is not retreating nor is it cowardice, it is *avoidance*.

- As a general rule, avoid violent confrontations whenever possible unless violence is unavoidable.
- Avoiding a violent confrontation is not cowardice.
- Unnecessary violence entails physical and legal risks.
- You may be prosecuted for your crimes or persecuted by the "other" side if they have power.
- The situation may not be morally loose as you think it is.

Taking combative action against anyone is physically and legally dangerous. If you engage with rioters, looters, or even a common criminal, you stand the risk of being injured, killed, and jailed. Especially in today's world, our concept of justice and fairness isn't a guarantee that if you survive the fight, you'll survive the outcome. Even if you are objectively acting in your defense against people caught on video trying to murder you, the messed up legal system may prosecute you.

In everyday life, I personally practice and advocate for simply walking away. I don't allow myself to be drawn into arguments or road rage because of the risk of the other guy escalating things. Someone else's fight or even a robbery isn't your problem. That gun you carry is to protect you and your loved ones, not some stranger. Even in a mass shooting, you shouldn't be a hero but use that gun to shoot your way to safety, if necessary.

Some find it hard to walk away from insults or conflicts. I tell my friends I'm much more likely to shoot someone than fight them because my entire adult life has centered around conflict avoidance. Even if I have the right to physically defend myself, yell back, or shove someone, I'd rather not. I can't tell you how many hours I stood stoically listening to verbal abuse secretly wishing cops could still crush skulls in with impunity.

Some of you may find it humiliating to walk away, but you're not the jerk trying to start problems. Let that guy live his life getting arrested for fighting. You have a family to protect and life to live. Don't make your lot worse because you don't want to back down in front of a bad guy or an idiot.

Legal problems in a WROL scenario will probably be the least of your worries. Your rules of engagement will open up in that time, but I still urge restraint. How do you know that the situation is truly without the rule of law and not just a temporary absence of law and order? Can you guarantee that some authority won't rise up and punish you for your "crimes" in the name of self-defense. Not that you will commit crimes against humanity, but the genocidal killers and war criminals during the Bosnian war never thought they would be brought to justice, yet many were.

Whether the law is in effect or not, let morality be your guide. Just as you may choose to intervene in someone else's violent attack because you could not live with yourself if you did nothing, you will need to decide what you can live with. This isn't a glib time to say, "Better judged by 12 than carried by six." Maybe you could just suffer a little embarrassment or anger and avoid either possibility.

If a rape-pillage gang comes down your street, you may want to just mow them down, but can you live with that? And if you can live with that, what are the odds that tomorrow night a bigger gang comes and burns you alive in revenge? Will things go back to normal in a couple months and you'll have to explain to a jury why you felt it necessary to shoot indiscriminately?

What if evacuating or ignoring the rioters by sheltering in your house for a few hours keeps you safe *and* out of legal troubles? As much as someone of us want to see the mobs get their comeuppance, and WROL that may be in your power, is that the best course of action?

- Can you avoid trouble now and in the future through avoidance?
- Is your intended response appropriate and proportionate to the threat?
- Will your intended response only further aggravate your opponent or his allies to retaliate in the future?
- If you exercise avoidance, will it be seen as weakness only to place you in jeopardy in the future?

When violence is unavoidable

There may be times when a situation can be resolved by backing down or giving in. However, you must strongly consider what the implications of *not* dealing with the situation then and there will be. If the threat will simply repeat itself and possibly with greater menace because your non-confrontational solution was misinterpreted as weakness, avoidance may be a mistake. There is no guide to when to stand up and when to avoid. All I can offer is that sometimes you have to take your chances and standup to a bully before it gets worse.

Always fight on your terms. That may mean that "here and now" is where you have the best odds of success. On the other hand it may mean retreating and setting up an ambush later.

Restraining yourself

Refuse to engage a verbally hostile person as long as in doing so you are not endangering yourself or others you care about. If someone is trying to bait you, ignore them and leave. You can't be sucked into a fight if you don't involve yourself. Yes, if someone is harassing you it might be embarrassing and infuriating. Immediately get up and leave the area without a word.

Don't argue back. These people are looking for a reaction; don't give it to them. You are not going to verbally de-escalate a situation with these people. Shut up and leave. If this means taking a few nasty words, or even objects thrown at you, leave. Decline any challenge to fight physically, even if you have to retreat.

Carefully control what you do and say; act as if everything is being recorded. These days, it likely is. We've seen stupid arguments escalate into hate crime charges because of racial differences between the parties or people running their mouth and uttering some unmeant racial slur. Be restrained and polite, 100% of the time, and only do things within the law. Act in recognition that whatever you say or do is being captured on video and will be used in court against you.

Give up your ego. Yes, some of these people need smacked down repeatedly and taught a lesson, but legally, you can't do that. Even if you want to do it extra-legally, you will not get the same favors the politically favored ones will.

Do not draw a weapon, use a weapon, or engage physically until you absolutely have to. Drawing a weapon prematurely may escalate the situation. Turning the other cheek is a good tactic here. Unless you are going to be seriously injured or killed, I would say not to resist and run away. In short, get the heck out of there and do as little as possible to make the situation worse.

Avoid the fight

Avoid the fight if you can. Stay away from riots and protests. If a violent confrontation breaks out while away from home, go home. Don't go sightseeing or try to protect a friend's business. Retreat inside your home and let the storm blow over.

Why risk your safety, life, and freedom by trying to do battle or score some morale points? This is why I recommend withdrawing back into your home and battening down the hatches if trouble comes rather than duking it out in the street. The first rule to surviving a dangerous encounter is not being there.

Weapon seizure after a shooting

It is commonplace for police to seize a firearm used in a critical incident as part of the investigation. In some jurisdictions, you may be cleared of a crime quickly and the weapon returned. In others, it may be near impossible to recover the weapon. A politically motivated investigation may limit your ability to defend yourself in the future if other weapons are seized.

When police serve a warrant in cases like this, they will typically seize anything related to weapons or self-defense. Use a shotgun to shoot a rioter? If you are politically unfavored or the local authorities are unfriendly to self-defense in the crisis, you may lose much of your gear. Judges will sign off on search warrants for just about anything and the items to be seized can be extremely broad. Assume that a warrant will result in the deprivation of anything you need to protect yourself.

After a shooting, (if you have time) get any extra *uninvolved* weapons, ammo, special gear, etc. out of your home. There may be little time before police arrive and secure the premises before they obtain a warrant, so quickly remove anything they might seize. You don't want police seizing your backup weapons and having to fight to get them back. Remember, they may seize guns and ammo never used in the incident to "punish" you for resisting violence or just to cover their asses.

Offense

If an offense is legally justified (preempting an attack), lethal force is rarely legally justified. As discussed earlier, imminence is a major consideration in the validity of justifiable fear. A future threat of harm isn't good enough to kill someone. If law and order totally collapse, you may need to consider proactive defense, or limited offense. **Disclaimer:** if you do this now, you will probably be on trial for murder. Tactics used in "wartime" are *not* those of normal law and order, even if both are temporarily absent.

If freed from the duty to let the other guy start the fight (such as WROL), persons who you can actually say are going to attack you can be engaged preemptively. If it's your life or theirs, seize the advantage and take them out. An example is that now, under the law, if a man approaches you aggressively says "I'm gonna kill you," you can't just shoot him. He could be bluffing. In WROL, waiting could unnecessarily expose you to danger, so you would be morally justified to shoot him.

The "just f***ing shoot everybody" approach

So many people assume that when SHTF, they will "just f***ing shoot everybody" who appears to be a threat. That is a terrible and unrealistic approach. The only scenarios where this is remotely near a good idea is when an intruder manifestly intends to do harm and violence, such as a small armed gang sneaking in to burglarize a house. If the rules of engagement permit, it may be prudent to shoot them *before* they break into a house, rather once they've entered and begun terrorizing the residents.

Just shooting is a really bad and lazy defensive plan. Many other situations can and will happen that could be better handled than with bullets alone. Pelting someone with paintballs and spraying them with pepper spray might solve the problem without legal complications or fear of reprisals. Do you really want the only tool in your tool box to be a gun?

Shooting on sight will mean that innocent people can get killed. What if you shoot a man openly carrying a rifle only to find out he was from six blocks over coming to warn you about a looting gang? Just killing people right and left because they "look" (subjectively) suspicious or threatening can become justification for thrill killing. This is how places like Sarajevo's "Sniper Alley" happen.

What will your neighbors think of you if you kill a kid for graffiti? Are you cold hearted enough to do that and not care what the neighbors think? You may be feared and shunned after, losing any ability to get help or cooperation when you need it. Neighbors may consider *you* a loose cannon and might have to make plans to neutralize you.

- How do you know the social, legal, and political situation will allow you to get away with excesses?
- Can you deal with the psychological stresses of killing? Does your morality permit you to easily kill? Can you handle the social blowback, like ostracism and fear from your neighbors?
- What if someone decides to retaliate or fight back? Are you willing to accept that brutal reprisals against you, your family, or your community may happen in revenge?

Living the gray zone; warning about self defense

Note: I write this at the risk of editorializing too much, which I have tried to avoid elsewhere.

We live in a disturbing time where self-defense is being delegitimized. Those who use force against rioters and mobs have faced prosecution. Political differences only makes this more fraught as some prosecutions may be politically motivated against ideological opponents or in a mistaken move to appease parties critical of the criminal justice system or politicians. De-policing and orders not to engage mobs has created a trend where police are seen to be "on the side" of the rioters.

In a lot of cases, officers are afraid of being charged or punished with a crime themselves. So police are in a place where they can't protect you and won't stop the rioters, but it is easier and safer for them to arrest you. This is a mistaken appeasement of the "mob" where justice is sacrificed for political expediency. Political views may also slant how a prosecutor handles a case and we are certainly headed into a time where that will become a common way of suppressing ideological enemies.

Several incidents in April of 2021 involved police arresting innocent motorists who were surrounded by a mob rather than targeting the crowd. In Oregon, one man was surrounded and, in fear for his life, brandished a firearm. He was detained then released after police dispersed the crowd. What if the crowd had the numbers, weapons, and intent to lynch the motorist at that point?

Again, it is easier for police to arrest you, the law-abiding, compliant citizen with no grievance than it is for them to disperse or arrest the mob. The rioters and protesters are politically favored; in many cases politicians openly approve of this behavior. In the other cases they are too afraid of criticism and the effects of rioting to do anything about it. Instead, they turn on the good citizen who defends himself. Some sort of perverted logic tells them that if they prosecute the good guy, the mob will relent.

Individual citizens have stepped up to protect their communities and have found themselves painted as aggressors or criminals. That is a risk you will face if you stand up for yourself, but the alternative will be worse if you do nothing. Weakness is *always* exploited in the long run.

Kyle Rittenhouse in Kenosha, Wisconsin, shot three men who were attempting to kill him. Rittenhouse was separated from his group and assaulted by several rioters. Two were killed and a third grievously injured. One man was a sex offender and wanted for domestic violence. Another was a felon who strangled someone and was also accused of domestic violence. The third had been arrested for prowling shortly before the shooting.

The incident was captured on video and any sane person would conclude that Kyle was acting in self-defense, yet he is being treated like a terrorist notwithstanding the fact he was targeted for murder by those three. Despite clear video evidence of the attacks and the shootings being done in obvious self-defense, Rittenhouse was charged with murder.

You may be overcharged in order to try and appease the mob. My department turned a road rage incident from a simple Vehicle Code misdemeanor into a hate crime and felony. Based on this guy yelling a racial slur and throwing something, detectives got a search warrant and seized his guns. I seriously doubt being a jerk justifies going that far. Politicians and police today are so utterly terrified of being called racists, justified or not, that they will not defend you. I think seeing law enforcement take a knee says it all.

If you are forced to defend yourself, expect the full

weight of the hate mob against you. Sure, you may be arrested, booked, and bailed out, but expect your personal information to be found and leaked. Angry people may try to get your employer to fire you. Persons may come to your house to intimidate you or vandalize your home. Don't forget the death threats. All it takes is one loony unhinged enough to follow through with murder.

It doesn't take violence to ruin lives. How many stories have we heard that someone did something that the rage mob didn't like, so the mob got that person fired? People will destroy other's livelihoods for perverse fun. You might survive the shooting, but can you survive the court of public opinion?

An army sergeant who confronted a suspicious man in his neighborhood, after an incident of sexual harassment and other concerning behavior, was slandered as a racist by the sheriff. The person the sergeant accused fit the suspect description. All it took was a video without context and idiots on Twitter calling the Internet rage mob to show up. The army opened an investigation. This man lawfully confronted someone in his neighborhood who didn't belong and, without the formality of a trial, is being tried by opinion simply because the suspicious man was black. Never mind the fact that race had nothing to do with it and the sergeant never used a racial slur.

In 1992, LAPD officers arrested Korean store owners who tried to stop their stores from being looted and burned. Videos still exist of officers disarming and cuffing up these store owners while the same officers do nothing to stop the rampant crime. Do not assume that police are on your side and expect that your actions, legal and moral as they may be, will be twisted to be used against you.

Citizen defense groups (opposite from the groups fomenting the unrest) have been formed in several areas to protect businesses and residents, with varying effects. Coeur d'Alene, Idaho, made national news when the downtown area was protected by an ad-hoc group of open carriers when rumors of a looting mob were circulated. Video of a neighborhood group guarding the entrance to their subdivision in Washington was also making the rounds.

This is not without danger. Those Koreans in 1992 were detained improperly by LAPD, who did not understand the open carry laws (at the time) or were uncertain of what was occurring. For instance, Washington has recently criminalized open carry within 250 feet of a protest, making armed self-defense with a long-gun possibly illegal.

To conclude, our system of law and order is being perverted in many cases to punish the people who try to stop crime. Whatever you do, be cognizant of this fact and circumspect about your behavior. "Better judged by twelve than carried by six," may indeed prove to be prophetic.

CCW/legal defense insurance

Practically every concealed carry instructor will tell you that "every bullet fired has a lawyer attached to it." That is a euphemistic way of saying that whether you are charged criminally or not, expect to go through some part of the criminal justice or legal process. This may be an interview at a police station (where you should have a lawyer present) up to a criminal or civil trial. All of this is for an ordinary self-defense shooting where the defender (you) were acting responsibly in good faith to save a life.

From the law enforcement perspective, it's far more complex. An officer who shoots someone will be interviewed after the incident. He will have the benefit of an attorney and a union representative. He will be given the Lybarger Warning, a sort of Miranda warning for government employees. His Miranda rights will be specifically violated so his statements then will be inadmissible in court. His defense, if he is sued or charged, is paid for by his union or employer.

You do not have those benefits. You may not even get the benefit of the doubt that you were acting reasonably or legally. This is why I recommend concealed carry insurance, which is really legal defense insurance and often civil liability protection, to help with legal expenses. Don't rely on a public defender whose job is mostly to get plea bargains. Can you afford a top-notch legal defense out of pocket? Remember you may be prosecuted by overzealous prosecutors who are out to score political points against you, a politically unfavorable person.

Hardening the Home

American suburbs are just the kind of thing any army of bad guys would want to see from the Romans tearing Carthage down to Genghis Kahn and the Mongols sweeping into Europe. Freeways turn into wide, arterial streets that feed neighborhoods built mostly on a grid pattern. Our streets, let alone the individual lots, are very rarely defensible.

Our modern homes are flammable, not bullet resistant, weak, and filled with lots of easy access points. Examine the structure of your home. Bullets easily penetrate most suburban construction. Homes aren't bulletproof. See the chapter "Fighting and Combat in a Suburb" for a more detailed examination of bullet penetration of homes.

Your defense is like an onion; one layer after the other. The first line of defense is the neighborhood, or street itself, covered elsewhere. The second line of defense is your property line or yard. The final line of defense is the house itself.

For most Americans, anyone can simply walk up to your door without any sort of gate or other obstacle stopping them. Layered security is the key. Your yard is the outer perimeter, the exterior doors and windows are the inner perimeter, and your weapons are the final defense. You are much safer *not* having to do combat inside and instead keeping bad guys outside entirely.

Passive defense is anything that makes it difficult or less desirable to enter your property. Examples:

- No trespassing signs;
- Video cameras;
- Lights;

- A barking dog;
- Fences; and,
- Sharp or thorny landscaping.

All of these things discourage entry. Signs just keep people honest but can add legal "oomph" in court. Video cameras say, "we see you," while lights say, "you can't hide." Fencing, shrubbery, and landscaping that funnels people into one entrance is a way of denying people the ability to easily approach your house by any way they choose.

Creating a physical and psychological boundary is important. Physical boundaries are barriers that have to be traversed to cross. Fences are obvious and if tall and sturdy enough, serve as a strong physical barrier. Psychological boundaries are things that break up public spaces from private ones like decorative fences, hedges, or even landscaping that most people wouldn't want to walk through or across.

- Make your perimeter uninviting to cross.
- Make your perimeter hard to penetrate.
- Make your home difficult to enter.
- Make your house and property easy to defend.

Vulnerable locations

Accessibility to your street and neighborhood are a concern. How easy is it for someone to exit a freeway and get to your neighborhood? Easy road access is great during normal life, but in periods of unrest it makes rapid vehicle-borne attacks very easy. Today outlying suburbs often see criminals commute from the inner city to burglarize suburban homes while the residents are off working in the city.

Now you can't just up and move, but if you can, select a home that is well off the beaten path. The further away from a freeway or main highway the better. Try and get deep into your suburb or rural community, far away from the main roads. Pick a house or a lot at the end of the road. Let other people be the easy pickings.

As for your home now (or ones you're vetting), look at the area around it; how could a bad guy use the terrain to attack? Is there a treeline bad guys can hide in? Do you have flammable brush a tossed road flare could ignite and burn down your house? Is there a secluded avenue of approach like an alley or brushy gully behind you? Maybe there is a hill where people can shoot down on you.

For tract homes, houses that are located in the middle of a block with another house behind them are in the strongest position. Think of the other homes as insulation against danger. Another house means more sets of eyes and ears, more obstacles for intruders to get past, and other targets for bandits to hit before your house. What is behind your home, and the homes on the street behind yours, is just as important as your own street. You want to be invested in the defense of the surrounding streets.

The deeper down a street or into a neighborhood you are, the better. Cul-de-sacs are great. Vulnerable homes are those on corners, those with a perimeter shared with a street, or any home that backs up to an alley, bike path, walkway, or open space.

Vehicle or pedestrian access are places where intruders can pretend to be something they're not to enter backyards quickly and more discreetly. Similarly, parking lots, streets (notably arterial streets), shopping centers, businesses that are often unattended or are open 24 hours, or apartment/condo complexes can have a lot of unwanted spillover.

Also consider the socioeconomic makeup of your area. Do you live near an impoverished neighborhood with high criminality? Is that apartment complex behind your house a Section 8 slum? Perhaps there is a halfway house down the street. Low-income areas will see increased violence and instability in times of crisis or economic hardship, meaning that higher-income areas nearby will be targeted for crime first.

Class trumps race every time. Poor neighborhoods tend to attract more people who are criminally inclined, lack poor impulse control, or those who consider themselves a politically disadvantaged underclass. While these people are less likely to be restrained, historical examples tell us that underclasses (whether actual or perceived) are most likely to protest or steal from those who they consider to be better off than they.

Outer perimeter, the yard

Keeping them off your lawn, the front yard

Someone who lives on a prepper's dream property well out into the country might have their acreage surrounded by a five-foot fence of barbed wire and a ditch that'll stop vehicles. A stout gate may bar the driveway. Hundreds of feet of open ground between the property line and house makes for a perfect field of fire. Any hidden avenues of approach are filled in with dense, thorny brush, like an out-of-control blackberry patch. Not only will the homeowner have plenty of warning, but there are many things an attacker has to contend with before reaching the house.

In the suburbs, a porch pirate can walk up to the front door and grab a package. Some homes have gates between the sidewalk and the front door, but these are rare. Look at homes in the third world, like South Africa or South America. Front yards are fenced or even walled off. Most American cities and HOAs would have a fit if someone raised a fence higher than three and a half feet in the front yard. It is mainly in the inner city does one regularly see fenced front yards.

Securing the perimeter of the home will do two things; first, it keeps any mobs on the street/sidewalk. If you have an open lawn up to your house, anyone fanning out across the street will treat the open ground as a thoroughfare. Even if the person/group is just passing through, wouldn't you rather have them do it thirty feet away instead of just outside your windows? What kind of mischief might they get up to if they had the temptation of the home so close?

This is basically crowd control. People take the path of least resistance. If cops don't want people walking in an area, they put up those metal barricades. For parades or other peaceful things, people don't want to deal with jumping the barricades.

People tend to stick to paths even if the adjoining ground is just as easy to walk on. It serves as a guide for them. They might not even be aware of the effect it's having on their subconscious navigation. Angry mobs might unconsciously pass by and target the house with no protected yard and not even realize that they made that decision.

Deterrence is easy and mostly psychological in many cases. One house on the corner on the way to my elementary school had a problem with kids cutting the corner and walking on the golf course quality lawn. Eventually one section of picket fencing, just enough to reach the planter on the corner of the lawn, was enough to force kids back on the sidewalk. The kids with parents who didn't teach them to stay off other people's lawns couldn't cut the corner anymore.

Unless someone wants to be a jerk, they aren't going to jump fences, walls, or trample landscaping. Take a look at some of the yards in your neighborhood. Which ones would be easy to walk through? Forcing one's way through a rock garden filled with plants is how people break ankles; casual trespassers aren't going to do it.

Defensive landscaping doesn't even have to be ugly. Ideally, you would want to set up a sturdy fence with thorny plants (like roses) for several feet in front so no one can just jump over it. That idea might not work due to design, space, taste, or local codes. You can keep your lawn, but maybe if you don't want a fence, rip up a two-foot section of grass along the sidewalk, put in some large decorative rocks, and then plant roses in between.

Using the idea of psychology, you could build a landscaped funnel through a path to the front door. Instead of someone cutting up the side of your yard, give them the obvious path where it is to your advantage (where you can see them from the window or where your cameras are). That way, if someone wants to sneak, they'll have to navigate the landscaping and will stick out like a sore thumb going through the roses for no good reason.

While we're on the topic of landscaping, don't create areas for bad guys to hide. Rose bushes are great because generally you can see a person hiding behind them. A dense hedge could entirely conceal a bad guy who could be crouching on the sidewalk with a rifle ready to shoot you the moment you open the front door. You want to be the guy behind the bushes ready in ambush.

Securing the driveway is more of a problem. The new trend in superdense housing tracts are driveways too small to actually park in. In older homes or pricier developments, the driveways can actually park cars. Some homes have yards where a simple chain can be stretched across the driveway. Other tracts were built so the only way to secure the driveway would be to build a fence and install a long gate across the two-plus car drive. Again, not something you really see outside of the inner city.

Hardening up a front yard isn't an easy prospect and is going to depend a lot on your home, your property, your neighborhood, and until things really fall apart, your city codes or HOA. Someone serious about turning their front yard into a perimeter should study up on CEPTED, or Crime Prevention Through Environmental Design. Your local police department *may* have a program or officer who can advise on such things. Otherwise, information is available online.

The basics of CEPTED in layman's terms is to make your home less friendly to people trying to hide, keeping bad people out, and establishing your property as "off-limits." This "off-limits" approach, or territoriality, we've already discussed.

If you mark an area as private through subtle psychological barriers, you've won part of the battle. The second consideration is access control.

Low fences are about deterring people; not keeping people out. Fencing and landscaping can funnel people into areas where they might be faced with a real gate. This gate might secure your front courtyard or it might be your security screen on your front door. An open lawn creates a wide path to the front door; a single gate from the driveway to the front walk makes only one access point.

One final tip for keeping people out of "denied" areas: motion activated sprinklers. Usually these are to scare deer out of gardens, but just imagine the surprise a miscreant would get when suddenly, out of the dark, there is a hiss and a jet of water soaks them until they run away. The sound of the sprinkler or a surprised yell might also alert you. It's a great prank and enough to either buy you a few seconds or convince the unserious to go elsewhere. In-ground sprinklers can also be turned on as a mob approaches to create a soft denied area.

If you are concerned about vehicles driving through your yard, several different approaches can be adapted to stop them. Strategic placement of decorative boulders of several hundred pounds about two feet tall will stop most cars, assuming they can't squeeze through. The same applies to concrete filled flowerpots. Block walls that have a concrete foundation and are rebar reinforced can also stop vehicles.

- Install a fence that encloses your front yard or plant landscaping that has the same effect. If a physical barrier can't be placed, design flower beds or shrubbery to create a psychological one.

- Narrow the approach to your front door to make it look less welcoming and easier to barricade.
- Plant thorny shrubs or cactus, or at least very dense bushes, to create denied access zones or make jumping over a wall/fence hazardous.
- Ensure that your landscaping choices and any natural foliage does not give a bad guy a place to hide.
- Gate your driveway or have a chain and bollards you can place to create a psychological barrier.
- Remove large rocks that can be thrown to break windows or hurt you.
- Place a motion activated sprinkler or turn on in-ground sprinklers to create a soft denied area.

The backyard

The front yard is problematic because of aesthetic concerns. From the days the Indians stopped attacking settlers through now, no one wants to live next to Fort Apache or a home that seems to be styled after a prison. The backyard is something else. Building codes and aesthetic issues are less to the rear of the home.

Suburban backyards are usually surrounded by a six-foot fence or wall. This extends to the front of the house where the side yards end. Your side gates should be locked already. If not, get on it. A padlock is best, but even a deadbolt that someone can't reach over the gate and undo will help. Also make sure that gate is stout; you don't want it kicked down.

Remove anything from the gate/fence/wall area that someone might use to jump over. This includes garbage cans, junk, rocks, or trees. If you have a utility box there, see if the company will move it. If you can, make sure your fencing or wall material is such that it doesn't create an easy foothold, like rough textured stone will. If you have the space, plant thorny shrubs in front of the fence so no one will want to approach to jump it.

Houses that are on corners are in a tough spot. A lot of homes in suburbs have sidewalks just outside the property line. That means strangers are just that close to hopping the fence. There might be no room for those thorn bushes and installing a taller fence might violate local ordinances. You have to make any fence jumper immediately regret any attempt.

We've all heard about broken glass set in concrete on top of walls, but that could get you sued if some idiot gets cut. Sure, when SHTF, you can put up concertina or barbed wire, but what to do right now? (If you are desperate and don't care about some ambulance chaser suing you, a discreet solution would be to tack in a single strand of barbed wire just on the backside of the fence slats where a jumper's fingers would land.)

Bird spikes are a great idea. These are plastic strips of spikes that keep birds from landing on the fence. Take a look at them and imagine someone in a hurry putting his hands, then his weight, on those. It will be unpleasant and should cause minor injuries if anything. Best of all, you have plausible deniability. You didn't want to hurt trespassers, but you wanted birds to stop landing on your fence and pooping on it. You even installed the warning signs about the spikes on the street side! These are common in South Africa where even razor sharp metal spike strips are used.

"What if I live in a neighborhood without fences between the houses?" Time to get a fence and encourage your neighbors to do so. For the rest of us, have you considered what might happen if things get so bad fences are torn down to be burned as fuel? That roll of barbed wire isn't looking so bad now.

Advanced: Keep a roll of barbed wire at home. Include stakes if you have room in your stash. You will also need strong cutters and pliers designed to work with barbed wire. A two-man team could string up a fence relatively quickly, especially if posts don't need driven.

Barbed wire could also be used to "harden" brush, bushes, and any other concealment a bad guy might try to hide in or penetrate. The wire can also be used for trip lines or strung up haphazardly as an obstacle. Barbed wire, especially if hidden, should only be put up in a WROL situation.

- Lock gates.
- Remove anything that anyone could use to jump walls/fences.
- Install plastic bird strips on the top of a wall/fence to keep people from jumping easily.

Dogs

A dog's bark is an alert to you and a warning to trespassers that the dog might bite you. Even small "pocket dogs" can work as an alarm, although they may intimidate no one.

Dogs should be encouraged to bark when intruders are around. Praise them for alerting you. Rather than train them *not* to bark, train them to be quiet on a command to hush. One trick for testing your dog is to have someone the dog doesn't know too well to pretend to prowl around outside. The dog's reaction can be learned and you can train them to alert to prowlers.

- If you don't have a fence in your rear yard, put one in.
- Lock your gates.
- Remove anything from fence lines or walls that could be an aid to a jumper.
- Install plastic anti-bird spike strips on top of a wall or fence to defeat handholds by jumpers.
- Avoid usage of textured stone walls and maintain fences so they are not easy to climb.
- Use dogs as a deterrent or intruder alarm.

Surveillance and observation

Physical deterrence is great, but psychological deterrence is important too. Light is not the friend of the criminal. Most crooks fear being seen and caught, so they try and operate in the shadows, literally and figuratively. Take those shadows away with lights. I'm not going to go into great detail; you can find info on security lighting elsewhere, but it is a very important consideration. Use light to create denied zones for people *who want to hide*.

Motion lights aren't magically going to scare away criminals. Plenty of vehicle burglars can be seen on video footage ignoring the light and going about their theft. Motion lights are so common now that the homeowner and neighbors practically all ignore them after decades of innocent activation by people taking a walk, animals, or the wind.

Lights need to be used to deny darkness to ambushers and the kind of criminal that wants to hide in the dark (area denial). You will need to pay attention to why the lights were activated, investigate, and act as necessary.

Use light to your advantage. Cops use spotlights and takedown lights to blind you. This is why traffic stops at night look like a TV studio pulled up behind you. Not only is the cop illuminating you and your car to see what you might be doing, but if you turn around, all you will see of the cop is a silhouette. Not being able to see details and being blinded by the lights makes it more difficult to aim a gun.

This is where a handheld spotlight could come in handy. Staring into something with 100k or more candlepower is not fun. These kinds of lights aren't like your driveway floodlights or your porch light that will also illuminate you. Not only will you see a suspect character clearly, but he will also be disoriented, and he will be in the literal spotlight. If you were trying to be stealthy to do something bad, wouldn't you change your mind if someone was challenging you while you were lit up in a circle of light?

So far, we've mostly been talking about warding people off. The whole idea of hardening your home is to send a signal that says, "Go somewhere else." Criminals for the most part like easy targets. They'll find a house without an ADT sign in the yard, without a gate, and without cameras or lights. But not all criminals will be like this, especially if the world figuratively ends.

Security cameras are obvious solutions. Now pretty much all of us have Ring doorbells or Wi-Fi cameras that will alert us to a person's presence. These depend on the Internet, which may not work in a serious situation. Also, we've all noticed latency with these alerts. A ten-second delay for the signal to go from the camera to the hub, to the router, to the server, then to the cell phone company, and finally from the tower to your phone before you get the notification might be too late if the attack is fast.

One consideration for blind spots or even front walkways are wireless alert systems that will chime if someone walks there. These are very cheap systems and will work instantly without the internet. Yes, your front porch might start sounding like a convenience store every time your family comes over, but it beats your sole warning being pounding on the front door.

For security cameras, consider a hardwired system with cloud integration. Not only do you have a stand-alone system you can watch from a TV or computer even if the Internet is down, but you can get cloud storage (off-site) in case the local hard drive is stolen by bad guys, and notifications on your cell phone. If you have a large property that you maybe don't regularly patrol, remote areas where someone might be creeping around could benefit from game cameras. Traditional models must have the SD card downloaded and newer ones can send real time feeds to your phone. Even with the old-fashioned function, you could see if someone is scouting your property.

Use camera placement to your advantage. Point cameras at the street so you can see what's going on and possibly identify vehicles. Use them to cover dead zones. Read up on security cameras and placement. Don't forget infrared lighting at night for night vision mode and don't entirely rely on Internet connected cameras.

Motion activated alarms can be installed all over the

place to cover blind spots and dead zones. These can take the form of motion alarms on gates, sonic trip alarms, or infrared monitors. The noise could scare and deter an intruder as well as alert you.

- Cameras and lights increase your observational abilities.
- Consider using very bright perimeter lighting to blind attackers in an emergency (not all the time, your neighbors will hate you).
- Install motion lights to alert you and light up areas where there is movement.
- Light dark areas to deny the concealment of shadows to bad guys.
- Cameras are a force multiplier allowing you to monitor blind spots and more area than just your eyes alone from one static location. Motion activated cameras with real time alerts are even better if you aren't actively watching.

Inner perimeter, the house

Windows

Keep your public-area facing windows closed when you are away or during times of trouble. Only upstairs or barred windows should be opened for ventilation. Ground floor windows can be opened during troubled times as long as they are under direct observation from an armed individual. Remember the Night Stalker came in through a lot of open windows. Close stuff up if you aren't prepared to immediately defend the opening.

Windows are your weak spot, ripe for a bullet, rock, or baseball bat. Now for gunfire there isn't much you can do unless you want to get really spendy and even then your wall will be as weak as the non-bulletproof window was. There are some things you can do to make your house more secure. First step; take any throwable rocks out of your front yard. Why give the bad guy ammo? Get crushed rock or gravel instead.

Deny the area outside below the window to the intruder. Keep them as far away as possible to make breaking, tampering, or climbing through hard. Plant thick bushes, preferably with thorns, below them. Cactus, thorny roses, and other "sharp" plants are a good way of creating standoff distance from your windows.

Back in the 1980s and 1990s the big thing in So Cal were window bars. This was mostly an LA thing, but out in the suburbs they were pretty uncommon and out of place. Most people don't want bars on their windows, period. Plus if there is a fire it's a bad idea because you can get trapped, even with quick release functions. What are your options?

Most homes don't look good with functional hinged shutters. If yours would, get those. Hurricane zone folks may already have storm shutters in storage. One long term solution that isn't too ugly are rolling shutters. These operate just like metal roll-up doors and store above the window in a projecting rectangular box. It is possible to match the shutters to the house paint. The shutters aren't too obtrusive either deployed or retracted.

Typical suburban homes have usually one or two big windows on the front of the house facing the street. That big picture window in the living room is a great target for a rock.

A broken window then might invite a firebomb. The easiest solution is to board it up before it is broken. Buy and precut the lumber now, stash it in the garage or in your side yard, and it will be ready when needed.

Cut viewing slits at eye level to see out. An alternative is to leave a gap at the top or bottom of the window to still see out, get daylight, and maybe catch a breeze. Another idea is nailing up wooden bars (at least 2x4s) in combination with chicken wire (to deflect thrown objects). To deter pull-down attempts, the bars (or any boards) can be studded with nails or screws pointing outward. Barbed wire could be stapled on.

Know what it will take to mount your wooden window shield to the house. You don't want the mob to be coming down the street when you realize those wood screws aren't going to punch through your stucco. Have the wood ready to go and the hardware already at home so it's a ten minute matter of mounting.

The wood solution can be used for all major ground floor entrances or windows that someone could access. Second floor? Maybe if you're not home, but if some dude climbs up my balcony or on top of the patio cover to try the window, he's getting shot.

Another worthy idea is to use chicken wire, wire netting (the kind often used in home concrete work), or chainlink. This will allow visibility and deflect objects that would break the window. "But what about bullets?" you ask. Remember, anything short of a pallet of plywood in front of the window won't stop bullets.

These wire products have flex in them, which will absorb impacts and move with the blow. On the plus side, this will mean less resistance that could shatter a Molotov cocktail but if up against a window, could give enough that the rock or whatever still hits the glass. Any wire barrier over a window would need some stand-off distance, like its own little 2x4 frame to allow some give for flexing.

The permanent solution is security film, particularly the 3M brand. This is a clear plastic laminate that goes over your window and makes it harder to break. It is not impossible to break through nor is it bulletproof, but it will take a determined attack for the window to be breached. Filmed glass and all of the foregoing can be broken by a determined attacker with tools, but that is why you have guns to shoot them if they try to cut their way in.

Check out the videos online. Several versions of film are offered and you can double layer both sides of the glass with it. By the way, you do have double-paned windows already, right? Ideally you would have plenty of time to hear an attempt to break in and respond before the window is broken. You may have a messed up window, but at least it won't be open and exposed to the elements in a time when glass companies are booked up.

My advice is to put film on all ground floor windows. If you have windows on the street without screens or something that could take a rock, but are on the second floor, consider it there. If you have rear sliding glass doors, get the film! Those doors are extremely vulnerable to regular burglars. Keep the boards handy in case things get really stupid.

- Install security film or rolling shutters.
- Board up the windows or make homemade wooden bars and/or chicken wire lattice.

- Have boards prefabricated and ready to be installed in minutes.
- Keep your windows closed and locked when trouble approaches.
- Use dowels or thumb locks to keep windows from being slid open.
- Landscape with thorny plants to deny easy access outside the window.

Doors

All doors need to be locked at all times. Although this is asking much, the front door and any door you're not using at that time needs to be closed. Sure, during gatherings or while you're doing something outside, you will probably leave the backdoor unlocked or open. However, if danger threatens or prowlers are likely, an alert intruder could be watching for those 30 seconds you are taking the trash out to jump the fence and get into the house.

American doors suck. Burglars kick them down all the time. The deadbolt extends into the doorjamb usually less than an inch. Get a deadbolt with a longer throw. Drill out the hole it goes into. Add cane bolts at the bottom of the doors. Replace the short screws in your hinges with 3" long ones that go deep into the wood.

Make sure you have two locks on your door if possible and that neither can be unlocked by someone breaking a window in the door or a sidelight. Deadbolts should be present on every exterior door (not just the knob locks). For doors with windows or sidelights, double-keyed deadbolts (both inside and outside need keys) should be installed to prevent a burglar from just reaching through and twisting the lock open.

You need to make sure your front (or other) door can't be battered open. One option is outward opening metal security doors that are like reinforced metal screens. These have the advantage of opening outward so they cannot be kicked in. Most lock and many versions have provisions for deadbolts.

You can install a horizontal 2x4 bar like you live in a castle or fort. I opt for those levered bars that wedge against the door. They are easy to deal with in "normal" times and are not too ugly or obtrusive. They will buy enough time to keep the door from being forced. Couple this with a 2x4 in bad times and you're doing alright.

If you can, replace the doors entirely with steel or even bulletproof ones and have the frames reinforced or replaced with steel as well. Solid hardwood doors are a minimum; steel doors with a steel frame are the best. Yes, they are pricey but you might as well pay the cost now before inflation gets too high, things become too dangerous, or there is no supply. Remove any sidelights. Install a peephole if you don't have one.

- Reinforce your door latch, the deadbolt, and the hinges.
- Replace the door and doorframe with steel security models.
- Make sure that sidelights and doors with windows can't be exploited.
- Construct or buy bars for the door so it can't be kicked open.
- Buy and use doorknob motion alarms.

Garage

If you park your car outside, don't leave the garage door opener in the car. A vehicle burglary might turn into one of your house. Garage door windows also need security film and preferably covers so no one can see in. Your side garage door with a window is very vulnerable; consider losing the window or using security film on it. Also get rid of your remote keypad or at least put it behind the fence if you must have it. Remember to lock the door between the house and the garage, especially at night or in times of trouble.

The emergency door release mechanism also needs to be protected. A simple wire tool, which can be just a coat hanger, can be slid between the weatherstripping and the frame from outside. Then it is used to disengage the manual release by pulling the red handle. Then the door can be lifted up by hand. The easiest way to remedy this is cutting the emergency release handle's cord.

The second easiest way to fix it is by inserting a zip tie in the top and bottom holes of the release mechanism. Standing inside under the rail your bodyweight will be enough to break the zip tie and open the door, but from the outside not enough force can be exerted to break it. You can also install a furring strip or other piece of wood just above the top door gap to change the angle that the burglar's tool has to enter from to complicate their effort.

- Remove rocks or other objects from the yard that can be used to break windows.
- Replace single-pane windows with double or triple panes and install security film.
- Consider installing rolling shutters or security bars.

- Pre-cut and store plywood for boarding up windows.
- Store chicken wire to create anti-object shields to stop any thrown objects from breaking windows.
- Secure the garage doors (vehicle, outer, and house) and make sure the emergency release mechanism can't be tripped from outside.

Misc.

Don't neglect mail slots. The last thing you want is someone to toss a lit road flare in your mail slot or to start shooting through it. Consider a locking slot or a way to block it off.

Remove any ladders or tools from your yard and store those items indoors. The principle is the same as removing window-breaking rocks from the yard; don't give bad guys any help getting in.

Consider door alarms, like you would use for teenagers who might sneak out. Put one on your front or other vulnerable doors. Maybe even your bedroom. These or other similar devices can be placed on your gate. Alarms exist that can use trip lines as well. Blank cartridge/shotgun shell trip alarms work.[17] Not only will this alert you to an intruder, but it might scare them off.

If you really want to go all out or have no other option, turn the bedroom areas into a citadel. Many homes in Zimbabwe (the former Rhodesia) and South Africa have gates in the hallways to the bedroom. The windows are

[17] Do not use live cartridges. Booby traps can kill or injury innocent people and are illegal in most places.

reinforced in that part of the house as well. Anyone who gets in the front door can't just come into the bedrooms at night and attack people while they are sleeping.

A less expensive and odd looking version of this would be solid interior doors. Again, they are more expensive than typical hollow-core doors, but combined with a good lock and stout frame, the door will not just open at the turn of the handle or with a kick. Ensure that your walls aren't a weak point; drywall can be kicked through. If you have a wall like that adjoining a bedroom, tear it open and reinforce it with plywood or OSB to give additional anti-kick protection.

Be vigilant about reducing the flammability of your home. An old wooden shake roof needs to be replaced ASAP. Tiles or metal are the most flame resistant materials for a roof. Vents, eaves, and soffits need special attention to be fireproofed. Any flammable plants or materials need to be removed from near your house. Brush clearance needs to be done as well. Don't let a deliberate fire or Molotov cocktail take everything from you.

When crime becomes rampant or the security situation trends toward SHTF, someone should always be home. Get a house sitter you trust to stay in your home if you need to be away for a long time. Use timed lights, turn a TV or radio on, and all the standard anti-burglary tricks to make it look like someone's home.

Bulletproofing

There isn't much you can do about your outdoor walls.

Rifle bullets will go right through. In fact, a rifle bullet might go through the *entire* house. Pistol bullets are a danger for at least the front rooms of a house. There are lots of videos and studies about bullets penetrating various housing materials (see the "Fighting" chapter). Bullets penetrating barriers lose a lot of energy and tend to be deflected by stuff. You might as well assume that anywhere in the house, not underground or protected by concrete, is vulnerable to gunfire.

If you don't care about appearances, you can place sandbags below window level and people can take refuge there. Forget about adding plywood; bullets will go through whole trees so a sheet of plywood isn't going to help you against high velocity stuff. This is where body armor might come in handy. Remember, cinder block will crumble under gunfire unless it is filled in with concrete.

Should someone start shooting at your house, pray it is with a small-caliber pistol with cheap ammo and they are too stupid to aim for where people might be. Hit the deck and then return fire if you can. Hopefully, you have a basement.

Drive-by shootings may become a problem. Sleeping away from the street (back of the house) may be a good idea. For those who have no choice, consider bulletproof glass for front windows and having a contractor reinforce the wall with bulletproof materials. A brick exterior veneer or steel plating inside the wall are cost-effective and easier to obtain than bulletproof wall panels. A sandbag wall can be emplaced as well with everyone sleeping down low, below the top of the sandbags.

If it hides you, but won't stop bullets, it's concealment. If it stops bullets and hides you, it's cover. Concealment are things like bushes, cars, tall grass, shrubbery, trees, and residential construction. Yes, bullets will go through your house, most thick trees in residential areas, and even cars. Only the engine block will stop *most* bullets. Remember bullets can skip over the hood or trunk of cars, so try not to use them as cover.

You can install cover now. Get man-sized decorative boulders you can duck behind. Erect cement or solid block retaining or decorative walls. Build and landscape a berm. Dig a foxhole if it comes down to it.

- Upgrade doors and windows to bulletproof when possible.
- Place sandbags below windows.
- Take cover underground or get low to the floor in a part of the house further away from the threat.
- Cars and tree trunks won't necessarily stop bullets.

Be discreet

In America, until recently you could be as open with whatever belief and ideology you had and little to no repercussions would come of it. Sure, your neighbors might shun you for flying a swastika flag from your front porch, but no one was going to burn down your house for being even the vilest racist on the planet. Today, people have faced vandalism, arson, and physical violence for their choice of presidential candidate.

We have entered a time where political violence and harassment are becoming excusable and it will only grow worse. There have been thankfully few cases of persons being attacked or their property damaged because of political or ideological affiliation, but in every revolution or civil conflict, opposing ideologies attack each other.

In your neighborhood, your home may be identified because of the flags or signs you have posted. In your purple neighborhood, your candidate's flag or sign could be a "reason" to target your home. Even an American flag in the midst of a riot, fueled by anti-whatever hatred could be a problem. True, we shouldn't have to worry about such things, but here we are.

Keep a low-profile in your home. If your political opinions and orientation differs significantly from that of your neighbors, I would advise you to begin keeping a low-profile *now*. No matter how ideologically homogenous your area is, when trouble shows up in your neighborhood, anything the least bit controversial needs to come down. Do you really want to be facing off against a mob because of your flag?

The same way one would be a "gray man" out in public, be a gray man at home. Right now, I wouldn't advise anything beyond an American flag. When trouble comes, that Gadsden Flag might be more of an invitation to fight than you want it to be. Be the house that is so unremarkable that the mob passes it over. I'm aware that voter registration information is public, so it might not matter if you advertise your politics, but we're talking about random protests and riots. If someone is picking specific voters out of the rolls and targeting them for violence, odds are things have gotten so bad you're better off making yourself an overtly dangerous target.

Real SHTF scenarios have shown that hardened homes that appeared as a hard target were the first to be attacked. These homes only held out if they had the men and guns to defend it. Attempt an approach that makes your defenses and hardening appear to be slapdash. Be the ugly, rundown house that doesn't look like it is protecting something.

Operational Security (OPSEC)

OPSEC is a term that applies to all aspects of keeping your plans and preparations secret. This includes not telling the police you have a defensive plan or sharing with the neighbors that you're part of a team of five men who plan to form the nucleus of a defense group. For you and your family, this means keeping mum about what food and supplies you have.

A civilian acquaintance of mine, who is not at all on the prepper spectrum, said to me his neighbor had large numbers of MRE cases and other supplies in his garage. My acquaintance said to his neighbor "Man, if the world ends, we're coming over here." I can assure you my acquaintance will do just that if his family begins to starve, knowing already what is next door. Loads of preppers have heard the same kind of thing from other family and friends. That will present a problem if you are not in a position to support them.

Concealing your food and supplies is vitally important. Do not just stack food openly in your garage so that anyone passing by when the door is open can see tubs of Mountain

House freeze dried food. Re-package it into discreet cardboard boxes, put it in cabinets, or onto shelves that are covered with a sheet. With guns and ammo, discretion is even more important. Someone looking to score points with the government in a time of tyrannical gun confiscation may rat you out.

Having more than your neighbors will be a cause for division. They are going without and you are not. You may wish to create the appearance of want, for instance by eating one meal a day to both stretch your supplies and lose weight like everyone else. If you dole out "extra" supplies, your neighbors may begin to wonder what else you can spare and bleed you dry. People will resent you for having food and the foresight to be prepared. Theft, robbery, or even murder is a possibility as people grow increasingly desperate. Eventually, this will happen.

- Don't tell the police about your plans.
- Don't start knocking on doors and asking neighbors to join your defense group until things deteriorate and such an idea isn't crazy anymore.
- For any small group of like-minded individuals, keep any plans within the group until it becomes necessary to bring others in.
- Wear your ordinary clothes as much as possible, especially when in public, and save tactical gear and clothing for active responses to violence.
- Conceal your extra food and supplies from prying eyes and do not discuss what you have with anyone outside your family.
- Do what the unprepared are doing: ask the same worried questions they are asking. Go out and look for food and supplies. Accept charitable distribution if everyone else is. Don't act like you are better prepared, informed, or supplied than they are or they

may start asking questions why you are behaving differently than them.

- When in public among a large crowd, act like they do to behaviorally blend in. Avoid confrontation, conversation, and eye contact.
- Conceal your extra food and supplies from prying eyes and do not discuss what you have with anyone outside your family.
- Avoid talking about contentious political or religious beliefs.
- Do not display flags or political signs, etc. on your home or vehicle.
- Make your home look run down and avoid the appearance that you have something worth protecting.

Defending Your Suburb

This section is not intended to be a guide on shooting people on sight just for walking down your street without permission. Much of this is intended for a time of ineffective policing, but a functioning judicial system. While some of this can be used for more kinetic times, this chapter is aimed at keeping people out to be used in combination with less-lethal methods.

What this is, *is* an analysis of the suburban neighborhood and a discussion of ideas on how best to protect it. Fighting in a modern American neighborhood has unique considerations that have not been encountered in warfare. Police have always been able to handle civil disorder (for the most part) keeping residential areas safe from marauding bands.

Remember, whatever your plan is, two immutable truths of combat apply: 1, hope is not a plan; and 2, the enemy gets a vote.

Civilian defense works; the psychological presence of firearms

A friend in the Las Vegas area told me that in the upscale, westside area of Summerlin (about ten miles from the Strip), residents thwarted a planned riot/looting spree at a large mall by organizing an ad hoc armed defense. In Boulder City, home of the Hoover Dam, when residents learned of a planned BLM protest in the city, they organized via social media to patrol the city with firearms. When the protest organizers learned this, they cancelled their plans saying "Boulder City is off. They got guns."

In Montecito, California, after the 2019 mudslide, some residents began openly carrying firearms after looters were reported casing the evacuated homes. Law enforcement took no action against these citizens[18] and looting was not a problem. Video emerged from Washington state as predominately black protesters passed a small neighborhood where residents stood outside with firearms. Not that anything was going to happen, but the protesters just walked by.

Often the presence of a firearm is enough to ward off trouble. Open carry supporters are unable to provide statistics on how often open carry prevents crime because the weapon doesn't have to be drawn to provide a deterrent effect. If a criminal sees a gun on someone's hip, and chooses not to act, almost always no one knows but the suspect. It is hard to prove a negative.[19] Although one should never assume that firearms have magical properties to ward off crime like it's some kind of amulet.

It is interesting that the mere presence of firearms or the plan to simply stand around with them openly halted these planned protests. Persons who are unacquainted with

---

[18] Though there is some conjecture, open carry is not necessarily prohibited on private property in California. Information is based on ham radio reports, so I'm unclear if the armed persons left their property or not. The point is, in extreme circumstances law enforcement often does cut residents and good people slack to bend laws for self-defense out of necessity, even in a very liberal, wealthy part of California.

[19] The same theory goes for police patrols; a cop driving around neighborhoods may generate no "statistics" to support his activities, but he may deter crime. You can't document what doesn't happen because the bad guy is scared off.

the reality of firearms and don't understand that looters simply can't be shot on sight are susceptible to this kind of superstition. In many subcultures, restraint with firearms is unknown and the idea that someone who has a gun might not use it, despite heaping on a stream of invective and even actual criminal acts, is unthinkable to them.

This superstition can be used to your advantage by exploiting the primal fear of firearms. For the same reasons animals have bright colors, puff up when angry, or old fashioned armies wore big hats and "tough" looking uniforms, you too can appear to be a hard target. Having the means and ability to backup appearance with performance is a requisite.

If you have no illusions that you aren't a super soldier, you can at least get the stupid, the lazy, and the cowardly to leave you alone if you do look like Delta Force or the meanest SOB in the city. Maybe even smart bad guys who want a weaker target with less risk. However, you must also never let your equipment or appearance create false confidence in you.

On a long enough timeline, you will meet someone who knows what your limitations are or has no fear of your guns. Just standing around with guns will not solve your problems. You might run into someone who will call your bluff or you will find yourself facing circumstances that require force, but not gunfire. **Have the equipment and plans to resolve things without bullets.** This chapter deals with warding people off and creating defenses. Later on we discuss riot control measures and fighting in these spaces.

Basic concepts

Your defense is like an onion; one layer after the other. The first line of defense is the neighborhood, or street itself. The second line of defense is your property line or yard. The final line of defense is the house itself. Passive defenses deter problems and active defenses are reactionary or proactive towards threats.

Reactive response: Looters are breaking into the house next door, so you grab your gun and go outside to scare them off.
Proactive response: A looting mob is getting ready to come to your neighborhood, so you and your neighbors arm up and start walking around while openly carrying.

Passive defense: Security cameras, alarms, fencing, and locks.
Active defense: Fighting off or shooting a burglar, robber, etc.
Proactive defense: A security force that patrols or mans a post, looking for threats, and actively engages the threat.

First line of defense: the neighborhood.
Second line of defense: the street.
Third line of defense: your yard.
Final line of defense: your home.

All of these concepts work hand in hand. Strategy entails things like not being there in the first place, such as choosing to live in a middle class suburb with a low crime rate, far from the metropolitan area. Your safety starts with passive defense to stop intrusions and alert you to them and in normal times goes to active defense, such as having to shoot a burglar. Proactive defense is reserved for untypical times such as trying to catch looters before they break into your house or fend off a riot.

Your first line of defense is your neighborhood. Many of us are tied to where we live and can't move. Rural retreats are not an option for most and for some, even small cities are out of the question. Strategy when things go south are about avoiding conflict altogether. Tactics are how you respond to conflict when it arrives.

If you can't keep people out of the neighborhood, your next chance to stop them is the end of the street. Think of intruding bad guys as a water leak; if you can't stop the water flow, at least make it go somewhere it will do the least damage. Stopping a crowd at the end of your street gives you far more advantages in dealing with them than if they are only stopped by your fence or front door.

Perimeter

What is your defensive perimeter? The short and obvious answer is the outer line of the area you want to protect. Pull up a satellite view of your neighborhood. Most residential streets are houses on both sides of a street with the same thing right behind. Some streets will back up to a natural break, like a geographic feature, an arterial street, or a park. We aren't lucky to live in Europe where your city or district just might have a medieval town wall.

Your defensive perimeter includes the boundaries of the entire area you want to protect; not just the intersection at either end of the street. This includes monitoring the streets around you. Perhaps the street behind you is undefended and intruders can just hop the fence from one house and suddenly be inside your perimeter. Road entrances to your neighborhood will be the primary entry points and where your team focuses itself, but don't let that be your only focus.

How exactly you define your protective perimeter depends on the character and design of your neighborhood. Where are the weak access points? Is the big field or geographic feature next to the neighborhood an asset or a liability? Sure, that boulevard behind the houses may be a great "firebreak" from the run-down neighborhood, but could intruders enter your neighborhood off the boulevard? You may have to expand your defensive perimeter to control strategic points.

Outer perimeter: the natural boundaries of your neighborhood. This may be the back fences or walls of homes bounded by arterial streets or you may have geographic features like gullies, hillsides, or woodland. The access points for most people would be the ordinary street or pedestrian/bike entrances.

Inner perimeter: your street and the barricades at either end. Your neighborhood geography might be different, so if you are defending more than just one block, consider creating secondary defensive positions within each block with barricades.

Final defensive perimeter: the yard of your home or a fortified group home. You would typically fight from the yard and fall back inside if the yard became indefensible.

Sneaking in

It's easy to identify the main entrances to your neighborhood; they're all streets. Some communities have secondary entrances like alleys, pedestrian walkways, or bike paths. All of these need to be identified for closure as they are the paths with least resistance. Open spaces, even if they are brushy or densely wooded, need to be considered an avenue for approach. Your average, lazy outrage mob looking to destroy things and make noise might not cut their own path through the woods, but in a desperate scenario, a determined bandit would.

Walk around your neighborhood. Where could someone sneak in? How about a pedestrian bridge over the creek that no one really uses? Identify holes in fences, broken sections of walls, gaps in fencing, or places that are easy to climb. Is there a culvert or drainage ditch that goes under a wall that someone could crawl through?

Things like culverts and storm drains can't be overlooked. A storm drain through your neighborhood is a perfect path for someone to have access to all the backyards. In California, most of these drains are concrete lined, with ladders or sloped sides, and access roads alongside the channel that make it easy to traverse them. Low chainlink fences and gates often are the only thing keeping people from getting into them.

Few people would expect an attack to come from the

wash behind their house. Usually no one is back there except for irregular maintenance. Storm drains can't be easily closed. Debris flows will wreck any barbed wire obstacles in the channel. It would be best to reinforce any gates with locks/chains and put barbed wire at the ground level access points (usually where streets cross). Installation of motion detectors in these areas could be a good way of keeping tabs on movement back there.

These lesser known areas have to be repaired, closed, or hardened. All members of your neighborhood security team have to patrol it routinely. Neighbors should be reminded to immediately make a report if they discover someone in these areas who doesn't belong. Persons staying inside homes (spouses, the children, the elderly, or non-combatants) need a way to contact and alert the defenders if someone enters from another yard. Utilize non-combatants to watch weak points where people can sneak through.

Surveillance

The utility of drones should be apparent to anyone who has ever seen a shot from a TV news helicopter. You too can have an eye in the sky. This will allow you to make remote patrols of your neighborhood and the outlying areas. You could fly a drone several blocks away to see what a mob is doing and monitor their progress. They are also fairly cheap as well. Neighbors using drones should communicate so that "friendly" drones are not mistaken as enemy reconnaissance.

Drones can also be used by sophisticated enemies to

spy on you, so beware of any drones overflying your area. Do not attempt to shoot down drones. Bullets fired upwards will return to earth and can injure or kill innocent persons. Shooting up at an angle accurately is difficult. At low altitudes, specialty shotgun rounds that tangle the rotor blades can be used, but results may vary. If you *must* use lethal shot against a drone, employ birdshot as it will do less damage on the ground. Drones will likely be invulnerable to fire above altitudes of 100 feet.

Open areas and hidden areas

Consider using barbed wire obstacles and "tanglefoot" trip wires in hidden areas. Trip lines with noisemakers (electronic alarms, bells, tin cans with pebbles inside) can be strung across entrances, gaps, or dead zones. Blind zones at night can be covered by a solar powered motion light that can deny darkness to an intruder in that area and possibly alert you. Areas that might be under visual surveillance during daytime may require night vision, a patrol, or area denial.

Barricades

A barricade is your way of drawing a line in the sand to would-be interlopers and to stop assaults. This will also function as a checkpoint for people entering your neighborhood. Another important function is stopping unwanted vehicle intrusion. No barricade will be impenetrable, but an obstacle has the purpose of delaying an attacker and diverting his course to give you an advantage when interdicting them.

Your goal when installing a barricade is to keep the enemy outside, stop any vehicle attacks, and focus any penetration attempts to where it is easiest for you to defend against them. Obstacles are only effective if they can be enforced. This means someone is there to stop someone, physically or verbally, or if you have it covered (with a gun)[20] and can interdict someone trying to negotiate the obstacle. Enforcement can be done three ways: psychologically, physically, and kinetically. Each is a gradual escalation of force in and of itself.

Psychologically: Conveying the impression that any attempt to be passed will be stopped. This can be done by simply being visible (people like to do bad things unseen) or communicated visually. In ancient times, dead bodies were often strung up as warnings. We're a little more subtle today and have the ability to make excellent signage.

An example is caution tape. So easy to step under, but honest people will stay on the other side, especially if coupled with other warnings. Traffic cones also work wonders. "Road closed" type signs on portable A-frame folding barricades should be used in combination with cones to close roads to traffic. The A-frame barricades should be plastic; I've seen a man hack his way through a windshield (he did penetrate) with a leg of a metal one.[21]

Physically: Shoving or escorting someone away or preventing

---

[20] Known as "covered by fire."

[21] He later died from excited delirium after being shot with a less-lethal bean bag shotgun.

them from entering. Think of a bar bouncer chest bumping a line jumper, grabbing them by the collar, and tossing them into the gutter. This would also be something like a wall that "can't" be negotiated.

Kinetically: Using weapons to keep someone away, either lethal or non-lethal. Militaries describe shooting people trying to cross barriers as "cover by fire" as in gunfire. Soldiers kill enemies trying to climb obstacles. You are more likely to use pepper spray, paintballs, or water hoses against crowds than bullets, but using less-lethal projectiles or means has the same essential meaning.

Your neighbors are not going to tolerate living in a place that looks like it was lifted straight off a World War I battlefield with trenches, pits, and barbed wire everywhere. This might be a temporary thing, but daily living will make it impossible. That is why I suggest portable or at least relatively easy to assemble/disassemble barricades. Life must go on and the odds of things being so bad everyone is going to spend a long time "behind the wire" are low.

Consider constructing your barricades to leave openings in the daytime. Perhaps you can set it up and tear it down quickly at dusk and dawn. Certain elements (the heavier ones) can be left in place and things like gates or fencing can be removed when the security situation doesn't require it. However, keep in mind that you may not get advance warning of when an attack comes.

This section will discuss items you can purchase in advance, could scrounge, or what materials you might have on hand to adapt for expedient fortification.

Purchased barricade items

There are purpose-built barricades intended to stop vehicles from ramming through available for purchase. Heavy and stout barriers have the ability to halt vehicle attacks. Indeed, almost any foot-mobile force can be scattered by a vehicle attempting to ram through a soft barricade. Thus, these items are heavy and difficult to move. They are semi-permanent in nature and would need to be guarded or combined with sturdy fencing for anti-personnel use.

Concrete K-rail (Jersey barrier) is the gold standard of temporary vehicle barricades. Four foot sections are sold that weigh about one ton and can be moved with a standard pallet jack. One or two men could move these in and out of place and the short length means that the rails can be easily stored in a yard. Poles can be inserted and several men can lift them as well. These will stop most vehicles or at least badly damage and slow down a heavy vehicle trying to batter through.

Water or sand filled plastic barriers can be used in a similar manner to above. These weigh 400-600lbs when filled and can be purchased in short sections. Because of the weight, resistance to vehicles will be much less. When empty, they are much easier to move than K-rail, but water may be in short supply. Removing sand or soil could also be problematic. Both the plastic and concrete ones can also be chained together with *very* strong chain.

So let's say you have access to a construction site.

Those temporary chainlink fences that sit on their own bases and interlock with each section would be perfect to fence off a street. The bases, or feet, would need to be weighted down with something like sandbags or other heavy objects to avoid them being easily overturned. Since the sections can be disconnected by lifting them apart, wire or chain the sections together by the vertical poles so cutting tools are needed to separate them, frustrating any quick-lift attempts by mobs to tear down the fence.

Homemade wooden fortifications

Barbed wire is an easy and cheap static defensive item to have on hand. Its uses are varied and makes lots of things more "exciting" for an attacker. If barbed wire is available, use any lumber stout enough, plus any existing objects, to make an improvised fence to string the wire up.

How about a portable cactus? A hedgehog is six pieces of wood arranged in a x-shape strung with barbed wire stretched along each axes. This could form the posts of a fence line with barbed wire strung up from hedgehog to hedgehog.

Have no barbed wire or portable fencing? Construct from lumber a *cheval de fries* or an *abatis*. These are access denial devices, just like razor wire obstacles would be. They cannot be surmounted easily as you would probably attack anyone trying to force their way through. You can make one of these using common tools and lumber sold locally, even scrap or salvaged lumber, or tree trunks and limbs cut by yourself.[22]

In the days before firearms (and even after) these obstacles were intended not just to keep enemies out of an area or channel them but discourage jumping or charging over them. A failed attempt to go over the top (or bash through) is likely to impale someone or a charger horse. Intruders would be picked off by infantry or bowmen (later with muskets or rifles). No one is just going to run through these but will have to go around or be slowed down enough to be interdicted.

The *cheval de fries* could be described as a sawhorse that took defensive lessons from a porcupine. This is a large wooden barrier with multiple axes of legs and spikes that can't be climbed over or under. It stands on multiple legs set at a 90 degree angle, that if they were continued upward, would form an X by sharpened tips facing outward. Both the legs and the spikes are connected to a central spine.

For the *cheval*, its central spine is made up of a tree trunk, telephone pole, or stout beam, such as a 4x4" or larger. The heavier the better; you don't want someone trying to lift it up out of the way. The legs need to be stout to support the weight and prevent being easily knocked down. You could mount the legs in concrete, add steel weights to the bottom, or bury them. For the spikes, stout wooden dowels (probably 1-2" minimum) sharpened and set in the wood make up the spikes. A hole could be drilled and rebar set in, then sharpened.

You can also adapt some snow fence designs. One simple version is an A-frame of poles that can have additional

---

[22] For more information, see: War Department, FM 5-15 Engineer Field Manual-Field Fortifications, 1940, pp. 42-43

longitudinal rails set on the sloping axis. Be careful not to put too many rails in place so it becomes easy to climb. For this reason, barbed wire should be strung up to fill in the dead space.

Another variant is an *abatis*. These are sharpened pieces of wood (often small tree trunks) that stick out of a slope, or out of the ground at an angle, closely placed together. Think of the butt of a spear jammed into the ground at an angle with the pointed head at the top. Attackers can't just squeeze through the gap or run over them. Fence slats could be cut down into points to serve as the *abatis* poles using salvaged material already on hand.

This is best suited for a natural slope, but if they can be driven deep enough to stand at a 45° angle, they could serve as a type of palisade fencing. The "feet" of the poles could be set in concrete and placed in, say, six foot long sections, so that they face outward like an angry rake.

Several of these barricades could be placed in a street in place of barbed wire. These can be relatively easy to move out of the way, like cars. Unless these are made of steel, they cannot be used as anti-vehicle barriers, although well-constructed models might cause most small vehicles a serious problem. Access to large pieces of steel, like I-beams, and a welder can make really strong, anti-vehicle defensive obstacles (the Czech hedgehogs recognizable from many D-Day photos). The only limit is your imagination and materials.

Caltrops

Caltrops, those four-pronged spikes that Batman shoots out of the Batmobile to flatten the tires of someone chasing him, are a bad idea. Boards with nails driven through and placed upside down go in the same category. They are too easy for someone who isn't paying attention or is walking in the dark to step on and be seriously injured. Like landmines injuring innocent people, it's not worth the risk to your neighbors, your fellow defenders, or the poor hapless person that might come across them months or years later.

A less-dangerous anti-vehicle caltrop barrier can be constructed if you really need to deflate tires. This would best be done with sturdy steel pipe and sharpened metal spikes. The spikes could be bolts driven through or welded on and then ground sharp. Another alternative is fitting caltrops to a chain. Such a defense might not only pop tires but could get lifted up by the tire and tangled in the wheel-well or under the car.

To mitigate the risk of injury or accidental punctures, one should paint the tire deflator in a bright color, like yellow, and should place cones or other warning devices to keep people from stepping on it. Caution tape is an excellent way to create both a psychological barrier and a safety line.

Booby traps and ideas

Anything that a bad guy can step on can hurt a friendly neighbor or an innocent civilian, especially if you forget to pick it up. No booby traps for the same reasons, plus they are illegal in most places. An alarm (siren, shotgun shell blank) serves the same purpose as a lethal trap. Do you really want someone's kid to accidentally be shot in the face by a shotgun with a string around the trigger or fall into a pit of spikes?

Cars as vehicle barriers or people funnels

If you can't just erect vehicle-proof barricades on your street, how about some illegal parking to stop anyone from just driving right in? In a perfect world, the local transportation department would just drop off some K-rail. You aren't going to have access to that and few people are going to want to sacrifice their RV as a barricade. But every neighborhood has plenty of superfluous vehicles or junkers that can be used in a pinch. Cars actually are far from perfect barriers (look at how much cars move or are damaged in collisions), but they can seem formidable.

The heaviest part of the car is always the front end where the engine is. If you need to ram a vehicle to move it, hit the trunk/bed and the car will pivot on its center of gravity up front. That's why anti-terrorist driving courses (or in the case of law enforcement, the PIT maneuver) focuses on the comparatively light rear end. Hitting a vehicle in the rear causes it to pivot in the front.

Place two vehicles along the curb or edge of the road facing nose out towards the cross street along the side of the road. Put two more nose to nose, or staggered, perpendicular in the road. A V-shape (nose to nose) is the easiest car barricade to make.

Make sure that the middle-of-the street vehicles are on

the *threat side* of the cars parked normally along the curb, so that if hit in the rear, the rear end pivots and hits the curb cars at a 90 degree angle. If space or willing car owners are a problem, make do with less—this is where the two-car V-shape comes in handy, although someone willing to damage their own vehicle could simply muscle through, which is why I suggest the four-car solution.

If parking the cars side-by-side, you can place three to four together (or more or less, depending on the width of the street) with room for the doors to open, but not enough for a car to pass through. With the engines in the front, someone will really have to be going fast to get through them. The delay will likely be enough for you to start shooting if things are at that point.

This barricade should be manned and placed at a point where someone can't just drive across a lawn or empty bit of space to get around. Be creative and thoughtful. Maybe you need to expand your perimeter. Even if the barricade can't be manned, with the street blocked off like this any vehicle-borne bad guys have to get out on foot at the end of the street.

Keep in mind that vehicles may need to be moved for residents to get in and out of their homes or if there is another emergency.

Engagement areas

Let's face it, most people only see one way into a residential street and that's using the street/sidewalk. Jumping over walls and fences is alien to us. This is why we are focusing on barricading the end of the street. A mob of rioters or looters isn't all going to come charging over the back fence en masse. That's the attack for a lone wolves or small groups looking to hit and run. These principles can be applied to alleys or other channelized accesses.

The barricade at the end of the street allows you to focus your defensive efforts on one or two locations and hopefully lure bad guys into that area. For a mob, that's almost certainly where they'll go. Your job is to clear the area where the bad guys will be (and site your barricade location appropriately) so you'll have a clear field of fire.

For an engagement area or "kill zone", you want an environment where there is little cover for the bad guys to hide behind and shoot back at you. You also don't want innocent people, like neighbors in houses, in the line of fire (**both your fire and the bad guys' fire**). Ideally, the engagement area should keep the bad guys as far away from you as possible. Despite the "deadly" terminology, this doesn't mean you have to kill people.

It's also a safe area to contain your enemy and the safest area to deploy lethal and less-lethal weapons. A group of people running through a narrow gap, or confined in a section of street, are easier to deploy pepper spray or a fire hose on, etc. Surveillance is also easier if there is just one access point.

A funnel is any area that forces someone to come through a certain area where their passage will be predictable and it is difficult for them to easily run away or take cover. If you have a deeply set front door between two rooms of the house, like an outdoor hallway, this is a funnel.[23]

Your barricade design (if you fall back or have multiple ones) should concentrate any attackers into a narrow area, like three feet between two parked cars. As engineers deliberately build in failure points to lessen damage, you want to do the same thing to put anyone who gets through where you want them. Make the path of least resistance be to your advantage. This allows you to bottle them up and concentrate force in just one area.

People tend to move like water in a crowd. Design your barricades and obstacles to funnel the crowd where you want them to go. If you have to have openings, make it one you can control. Should you have the ability, there is nothing wrong with finding a way to shunt rioters away from your neighborhood to another one. Make sure that you have an outlet for retreating attackers to take so they flee when routed, rather than fighting you like a caged rat.

Manning barricades

A manned barricade without the legal authority to enforce it is just a threat to the stupid and a warning to the would-be tough. Legally anyone can walk down any public street they want. Barricades are meant to be kept impenetrable by force; either you have people there to physically shove off anyone trying to get through or you can shoot them with lethal or less-lethal munitions, depending on the situation.

---

[23] This situation is frequently called a "fatal funnel" by SWAT teams.

Always consider where you will go when the shooting starts. Remember, cover is something solid that will stop bullets while concealment just hides you from observation. What wall, hill, or building could you hide behind? Do you need to build a sandbagged position or dig a foxhole? Where would an attack come from? If you were a sniper, where would you hide? Consider places where you might want to be visible and places where your backup might not be so obvious.

Standing around in tactical gear or with long guns openly carried will be handled differently from place to place. In most of California, you'd probably be arrested. In urban Arizona, the police are familiar with open carry and would probably be quite blasé. But you know your area; will your cops freak out if they see people with guns standing around, even if it is perfectly legal? You may want to openly carry handguns (if possible) to serve as a deterrent and keep the rifles discreetly at hand.

Don't automatically challenge people walking through unless they are actively up to no good. You never want to start with anyone on the defensive. Why make enemies of a fellow neighbor you don't recognize? If someone you don't know approaches the barricade, greet them politely. Don't move to stop them. Ask them a question like "How is it out there? See any troublemakers?" Or introduce yourself; that's a subtle way of saying "Who are you?"

If they ignore you and keep moving, turn and keep an eye on them. Don't kettle them up or follow them closely. They may be a scout for the bad guys, but you aren't at the stage when you can use force on people for being unfamiliar and suspicious. Simply acknowledge them and let them go; don't create a confrontation that isn't needed.

Remember your legal limitations. You can't detain someone for being out of place. If you do and things go sideways and you use physical force, that may be deemed false arrest, kidnapping, or may escalate to battery or even murder depending on the use of force.

The idea behind a manned barricade, sentries, and roving patrols is about observation and deterrence. You want to know what's going on, who is out there, if bad guys are about, and for people to see that you are prepared to meet any threat.

Vehicle checkpoints

Vehicle checkpoints for residents will be a necessity. Your barricade isn't always going to be up and people will still need to come in and out. Your neighborhood might even turn its entrance into a full-fledged gated entrance. Entry will be controlled by the threat at the time. Here are some suggestions on how to manage a vehicular checkpoint.

Entry/access

- Place stop or warning signs out and designate a stopping place.
- Stop vehicles away from the barricade with room to back up or turn around.
- Keep the anti-vehicle barricades in place until it is clear to let the vehicle in; an easy to move low vehicle stop or tire flattening device can be used in lieu of moving heavier obstacles.
- Keep the security team under cover if the threat is high.

- If there are multiple vehicles waiting, clear all vehicles seeking entry before letting one car in (do not let one car in so the others can tailgate through).

Identification and searches

- Ask the name of the driver and who they are visiting. Get photo ID to confirm their identity. If they are not expected, contact their host and confirm they are expecting this person.
- Consider identifying everyone in the vehicle, at least by name, if they appear suspicious.
- Ask the driver to turn off the vehicle.
- Be polite and do not raise your voice unnecessarily.
- Only one person should be the point of contact and should speak primarily to the driver.
- Never argue back and forth; either stay calm and don't bicker or deliver your commands and stick to them.
- A second team member should be on the passenger side of the car while others maintain security overwatch looking in through the windshield. If shooting has to occur, it should be from the front security team shooting through the windshield to avoid friendly fire.
- Refrain from aiming weapons or drawing handguns unless necessary for self-defense.
- Suspicious vehicles should have at least their trunk and cargo area searched for suspicious items. If SHTF, assume everyone is armed and the presence of firearms and related equipment will not be unusual. An extensive vehicle search should be unnecessary; you're not a cop.
- Remember a negative encounter while on patrol or manning your checkpoint could turn a neutral person into an enemy or give someone who doesn't like you a reason to become violent.

Restraint

A major challenge you might face defending your neighborhood is if someone calls your bluff. What if the angry mob of rioters turns down your street and suddenly you are in a standoff with them? You have rifles and pepper spray, they have bats, clubs, cameras, and bad attitudes. They will try to provoke you.

Look at how they treat cops, trying to blind them with lasers, throwing objects that could cause head injuries, even trying to burn officers alive. Imagine some emboldened jerk trying to beat you with a stick or something to provoke a reaction so they could escalate into lethal force against *you*.

Even the slightest use of force by you could be considered criminal. Shove a guy who tries to break the barricade? Assault. Pepper spray him? Battery. Now maybe he's black, you're white, and your sheriff is a coward, so now you're charged with a hate crime and violating his civil right to march down your street and threaten to kill you for being a "white capitalist pig." Don't do it if you can help it.

Also put yourself in someone else's shoes. Say there is a black or Hispanic friend visiting in a predominately white, upper class neighborhood in the South. This friend (Bob) parks around the corner because he doesn't want to try and parallel park on your street to visit your neighbor Steve. Sure, you might be worried about radicals who happen to be whatever race, but it is immoral to just call out Bob because he looks out of place.

Why piss Bob off or risk going physical with him? At best, Bob is now alienated and maybe Steve too. Instead, you could greet Bob, who explains he's a friend of Steve, and mentions that he's here to help Steve finish off the preparations for your group's water cannon or something. Judge people on their actions and beliefs, not their appearance.

Many would love to put a bayonet into the belly of the first punk that dares cross the line in the sand, but that is not going to happen in our world. Political prosecutors will crucify you for using force to stop "peaceful" protesters from coming down your street. You can't just start shooting because they disregarded your warnings. Hopefully, most of these jerks will be total cowards, but eventually, some of us will have to face the determined ones who want to be thugs.

If you have to open fire, be prepared for the consequences. You may rout the crowd and win the battle, but they could quite probably be back with a vengeance. Let's say you are out on bail, with your guns confiscated, and police arrive to arrest or threaten you anytime you show up on the street to defend your neighborhood. Maybe when the mob comes back, they want to burn down your house or break in to beat you to death. Eventually that will be a possibility.

My advice in a dysfunctional world of law-and-order is stay inside. You may want to conduct a tactical retreat, all while showing you are armed, until you're back on your front porch. Don't breach your perimeter. Suck it up while the idiots have their day. Don't ruin your life over ego or petty vandals. Don't be the guy to fire the "shot heard 'round the world."

Always be disciplined and restrained. Take nothing personally. If things escalate to arson and personal violence, then you can get involved. At the extreme where the police no longer can/want to protect you, you must decide what to do. This is an individual choice before and after things "go kinetic."

Unhappy neighbors

Just because a number of neighbors or even a majority of them agree that the street/neighborhood should be secured doesn't mean that everyone is going to agree or even go along. This is why, if you have the choice, living in a neighborhood that aligns with your beliefs is very important.

You may have unhappy neighbors for reasons of noise, disruption to their daily life, outright opposition to your cause, existing feuds, down to a displaced reaction of fear. "Displaced fear reaction?" Yeah, they are afraid of the chaos going on, they see you out in the street, which disrupts their illusion of normality, so they become angry at you over the pretext of blocking or guarding the street.

Always accommodate the unpleasant neighbors. Don't block the street in front of their house or even park there. Try and stay out of direct sight of their windows. Let them and their guests come and go as they please. Be welcoming and polite to them. Don't pester them about getting on board with the defense plans.

Whatever you do, don't engage in arguments with them. Don't try to sway them to your side. Remain neutral and uninvolved. Give them no reason to be an enemy. You don't want to piss them off so they call the police or worse, call in the mob that they might identify politically with.

Access control

Legally, you have to let anyone onto a public street who wants to go down there. Until things get to a point where the risk of allowing strangers or rioters/protesters into your neighborhood is greater than the risk of arrest or lawsuit, you have to keep your neighborhood open. Your options will be tied in with law enforcement's capacity to maintain law and order and also respond to calls such as armed people blocking a street.

When figuring out what to block off, take care of the obvious places first. Don't just block the end of the street but consider walkways that cut from one block to the other. How about alleys? Do you have a bike path that divides the tracts? Don't forget about empty lots or user created paths. If you can't guard them, close them.

At night or during times of unrest, everyone should stay home and stay inside as much as possible. The last thing anyone needs is the confusion that someone might cause by being out and about in the dark. Also having people come and go from the neighborhood when you're trying to blockade it will create hassles. Only active defenders should be on the street during night or red alerts. Just imagine the tragedy if someone gets spooked and goes trigger happy on kids playing hide-and-seek in the dark or if your neighbor, who ran to the store for milk, forgets to stop for the checkpoint.

Commands and challenges

- Issue commands from a position of strength; i.e. you are armed, you outnumber them, you are behind cover, etc.
- Have your weapon either out or pre-deployed, or at least be ready and willing to use it, as the rules of engagement may dictate.
- Give your command before the other party can make his own. Being the first to speak can give you a psychological advantage and also serves as "fair warning" for whatever measures you may have to take next.
- Additional psychological benefit can be gained from calling out an individual through a particular description: "You in the black jacket with the red cap with a gun in your hand, drop the weapon!"
- Commands should be very simple and be restricted to necessary information only. Such as: "Stop now!"; "Go away!"; "Drop your weapon!;" "Who are you?" Use a firm, but polite tone.
- Tell; don't ask. Let your actions, your posture, your demeanor, and your tone be your emphasis.
    - It is not "Please stop," but "STOP NOW OR I'LL SHOOT!"
    - The above latter command indicates seriousness by its tone, says what you want the person to do, and what the consequence is for failing to obey.
- Profanity or threatening language can confuse and potentially escalate a situation.
    - Do not use profanity unnecessarily; some persons may mistake polite firmness for weakness, so occasionally it takes profanity and tough talk to reach violent, low-class individuals on a level they understand.
    - Don't make vague verbal threats, i.e. "I'll blow your head off." Instead: "If you pass those cars, I will shoot you."
    - Do not make insults or make comments like "make my day." A number of fatal shootings

occurred because the victim said something like "You don't have the guts to shoot me."
    - Over-the-top language could lead a suspect to believe (perhaps correctly) that you are desperate and terrified, thus the tough talk instead of action.
    - Do not engage in an argument or allow yourself to be baited into one. Remove those persons from a situation who are vulnerable to running their mouths.
- Remember what you say can be used against you. If you are overly aggressive or foul mouthed, that may be used as evidence that you were the aggressor in the situation.
- Reasoning is off the table. You are not going to be asking a bandit "Please don't make me shoot you." Asking and trying to reason will only make you appear weak.
- If a subject complies with you, do not let your guard down.
    - Watch their hands. Make them take their hands out of their pocket or from behind their back. If they are armed, order them to drop their weapon or set it down slowly.
    - Do not have them remove a weapon from a holster.

Incident response

Mob arrival: Close any openings in your barricade and reinforce the guard. Consider early crowd dispersal options. All homes lock down.

Police response: If feasible and safe to do so, lay down or sling any long-guns. Keep your hands visible, away from any weapons, and potentially put your hands up. Step into lighted areas so the officer can see you. Comply with all orders; do not resist or argue. Give as little information as possible to the police when asked. (See "Dealing with Police in a Crisis Situation").

Barricade breach: Deploy less-lethal force at the start of the attempt to cross the barricade (unless a lethal threat exists). Continue to apply force as needed while an apprehension team moves in. Restrain the intruder and remove him from the area. Disperse any other attempted intruders or the crowd as the situation dictates.

Flank attack: Rapid reaction force responds to the breach elsewhere on your perimeter. This may be distraction for a mass breach of your barricade checkpoint. Stay alert and prepare to repel a mass breach.

Projectiles being thrown: Don helmets if not already worn. Back away from the barricade to outside throwing distance. Ensure the barricade is covered by firearms and less-lethal weapons to prevent penetration. Attempt to disperse the crowd if possible.

Brandishing: All team members take cover. Less-lethal weapons may be deployed. Lethal force may be used according to the circumstances and self-defense laws.

Shots fired: Take cover and move to a safer position, using smoke to camouflage movements as necessary (usually for a sniper). If the shooter is a sniper, identify their location and return fire. For a drive-by shooting, take cover and respond with a high volume of fire. Suspicious approaching vehicles should be aimed at by a **concealed** shooter in case an attack occurs. Attempt to move the wounded to safety.

Apartment Complexes

A low-rise apartment or condo complex is just a bigger, denser neighborhood with more complex considerations and many others who may be unwilling, or unable, to participate in the defense. The "geography" is going to be different as well, making things a bit more challenging. Yet the right complex may actually offer more security than a housing tract.

This is not meant to address the situation of those living in dense, downtown area high-rises (this is *Suburban Defense*, after all). If you live in a high-rise, you need to plan to evacuate in a catastrophic situation. High-rises are easily surrounded and even if you barricade the ground-level entries, all it takes is one resident trying to get in or out to let bad guys slip in. Additionally, the building type and surrounding city makes an excellent target for snipers and arsonists.

Downsides to surviving in an apartment

- You cannot make permanent modifications.
- It is difficult or impossible to board up.
- Your avenues of retreat from your unit are limited.

- There is a much larger number of people in a smaller area.
- Your fellow residents could be a danger because:
  - They oppose you on ideological or political grounds;
  - They disagree philosophically on how to deal with the crisis; or
  - They may ignore or circumvent security procedures.

Conflict points

- A wide variety of people, who likely have no investment in the property, may have differing ideas of what should be done and may work at cross-purposes.
- Your neighbors may be too cowardly to take action, hoping to give in and make the problem go away.
- It is possible that the consensus of your complex is to side with the antagonists, or in a worse situation, they empathize with a faction that you are worried about.
- Management or the owner may resist your organization attempts, interfere with erecting defenses, or limit security actions.
- People coming and going may complicate security control.

Organization

Organizing a defense group and hardening the property will be a lot easier if troubled times have already arrived and especially if the owner or management have abrogated their duties. In a functioning world where you are still paying your rent, management buy-in will be required for most things. Depending on the situation, the manager may be more receptive to certain ideas, especially if the suggestions resolve an immediate concern they have.

Management of a corporate complex will always be a thorny spot. It is more complicated than having a majority of homeowners agree since the entire property is owned by someone else. A single owner of a complex is likely to be more amenable to defensive preparations than a corporation or board. HOAs and big corporate apartment companies will naturally resist anything that takes the complex away from the status quo and creates potential liability issues for them. If you live in an HOA, consider getting on the board and encouraging other like-minded people to join it now.

Granted, none of us want society to collapse, but once it does, everything will be much easier. As long as the courts are still effective, you can always be evicted or have your defenses torn apart. When SHTF, the apartment manager won't be coming to the complex unless they live there. The owner won't be maintaining it and the residents probably not paying rent, so you're on your own. That nasty Karen that sits on the HOA board who thinks that open carry and barbed wire is "excessive" won't have any authority anymore. Until then, make do with what you've got.

Perimeter reinforcement

On the surface, an apartment complex seems easy to defend, especially if it is walled and gated. Usually access points are limited for gated residential communities.

Ideally, management would ensure that the complex is

walled or fenced and all entrances gated. If you don't live in a fenced complex, good luck. Move if you can. For the walled complexes, if the city security situation begins to gradually deteriorate, see if you can encourage management to harden the perimeter with anti-jump devices on the perimeter walls.

I lived in a complex where one side was a storm drain (behind a shopping center) that had a four foot wall, but the other side, which backed up to a strip mall, had a six foot wall and was lined with "decorative" wrought iron spikes to keep people in the parking lot from hopping over. I would have liked the storm drain wall to be topped with something to keep people from jumping it since the drain itself was easily accessible.

In a catastrophe, security will be up to you. This may entail buying barbed wire or snipping sections of it from other sources, like a freeway right of way. You top off the wall yourself with whatever you can. The same goes for barricading gates with expedient items like dumpsters or vehicles.

Short of a true grid-down WROL scenario, your physical hardening of a residential complex will not be easy or even possible. Concerned residents will have to content themselves with situational awareness and security patrols.

Access control

Lots of people constantly come and go in apartment complexes. Getting several hundred people to agree on an access control plan will be exceedingly difficult, if not impossible. Working class people who don't have the luxury of working from home or the ability to simply stay home when things are really bad will need to come and go. Other residents may often have guests over and they may not be happy with the complications to get in or out.

Remember, there may be hundreds of people living in your complex. You can't know them all, so it is important to be polite with everyone just in case they do live there. Never alienate a neighbor or a potential ally if possible. This is why a list of residents or maybe some sort of identification (i.e. issued parking passes) is smart to have.

- Only one entrance/exit should be used unless there is manpower to man both. Other exits should be locked or barricaded.
- Gates should be closed at all times and opened either by the resident directly or buzzing a guest in or by a guard.
- If gates cannot be closed at all times, they should be closed during the hours of darkness and monitored at all times.
- Guards should have a list of residents and residents should be made to inform the guard of any guests or deliveries.
- Unexpected deliveries (i.e. not your regular UPS driver) should be cleared with the resident and/or the vehicle inspected and all occupants identified.
- If guests or delivery drivers won't identify themselves, turn them away.
- Secure all weak points or pedestrian gates.

Hardening your apartment

If you live on the ground floor, move to the second floor so no one can just creep in your window. Replace the screws in your front door hinges with long screws, like 3" ones. Consider replacing the deadbolt with one that goes deeper into the doorframe (drilling required). Get an anti-kick bar for the front door, thumbscrew window sill locks, and a sill lock for any sliding glass doors (wooden dowels work for windows too). Now, if you're home, someone trying to break in will need to use a lot of force or shatter windows.

Most likely case best practices

- Get everyone to agree to use one entrance/exit and to not go out after dark unless absolutely necessary.
- Create both a volunteer gate guard team and a security patrol team/response force.
- Establish a robust means of communication (not just an app) to notify everyone and the security team of a threat.
- Everyone needs to notify the gate guards of expected visitors.
- Get management to ensure all security cameras and lights are working.
- If management won't do it, secure any obvious weak spots in the perimeter to the best of your ability.

Dealing with Police in a Crisis Situation

If you've ever been arrested, you know that arguing with the cop isn't going to help. It'll infuriate the cop and might erode any goodwill he might have given you. Instead of perhaps getting a citation and being told to "scram," you might get a trip back to the station. Nothing you can say is going to change the officer's mind once he's established he has probable cause to arrest you. Only in situations where you truly are the victim and can immediately and politely make that apparent can you change an officer's course of action.

Law enforcement in crisis situations is often just as stressed and worried as the public is. Take those underlying mental factors and compound them with officer safety concerns, exhaustion, and often conflicting information or orders and a cop might not be the same Officer Friendly he would be on a regular day. Sometimes we have to be hardcases.

Sometimes intentions can be misunderstood and civility goes a long way. During a forest fire when my father lived in the mountains, he tried to bypass a road closure by talking to a highway patrolman. My father thought the officer was giving him a wink and a nod to drive past when the officer turned away. When my dad got a few hundred yards down the road, he was chased down by the officer. It turned out to be a misunderstanding by my dad and poor non-verbal communication by the officer.

My dad got it all straightened out by being polite and explaining that he thought, given the officer's casual denial of access, followed by his action of walking away and turning his back, as an "okay" sign. The officer quickly realized how that could have been misinterpreted and both of them laughed at it. My dad's property survived the fire unscathed.

Should you "work with" your police and inform them of your plans?

Inform them of your plans, no. Use their public programs or public record requests (FOIA) to get information and intelligence? Yes. You don't need police approval to do this. Are you really going to go pull a city permit to block the street or something? You also don't need a police officer's official opinion either. The less they know, the better. If you are doing something that might be slightly illegal (though morally acceptable) or possibly politically incorrect for the government's taste, they may be obligated to stop you.

Police reaction to individuals planning to defend their own homes or neighborhoods will vary widely. Enclaves of minority politics exist in states where the police might listen more to the local X Party mayor than their own conscience. You might have one officer in your local agency that is a true believer in X ideals and would love to make an example out of you to further *his* personal beliefs.

It's great to be friends with cops and like the idea of police serving the role for which we intend them for, but you have to acknowledge that the idea of "The Police" will be against you in principle. Lots of people want to feel special by establishing some sort of pleasant relationship with policed.

Don't go seeking their approbation. Officer Friendly isn't such a nice guy when he is writing you a ticket or arresting you.

You may have a really pro-Second Amendment sheriff, but do you want to bet when the chips are down that he, or maybe some deputy you confided in, won't arrest you for a weapons violation if the law or attitudes change? Do you really want a copy of your defensive plans you left with the community resource officer to be entered in as evidence at your trial for shooting a "peaceful" protester?

Unless you personally know the officer and can count them as a close, personal, and trusted friend, do not tell police of your plans or try to "work" with them. They have their job which may one day be to wreck you. Under pressure of losing their job, an officer who may privately support you might arrest you or turn you in to some special squad to save his own butt.

Why police do the things they do

Police often unreasonably "hold the line" or follow orders in an emergency. This can be anything from keeping a road closed, even though there seems to be no reason for it, to illegal gun confiscation as happened in New Orleans after Hurricane Katrina. For better or for worse, here's my explanation as to why cops do what they do.

Police have a mission and a desire to protect. That often means protecting you from yourself. Most traffic tickets are issued because of what could theoretically happen if you keep speeding, etc., not what actually did happen. So if something is or could be dangerous, an officer is going to stop you from doing that thing, going to that place, or might just strongly recommend otherwise.

"Someone could get hurt," is what an officer might say about your barricade. The logic behind that is that it could be *you*, the good guys, who get hurt and he doesn't want to see that. Or he doesn't want to get you in trouble for fighting back, even though you may have been morally correct.

Liability is another motivation. If a cop fails in his duties to keep bad stuff from happening, or lets it happen, he can be disciplined by his superiors. Legal liability is not the issue, but the political fallout and the heat politicians or department brass might dump on an officer can be hot enough for an officer to stop what you're doing.

Law enforcement is also a paramilitary organization and officers must follow orders or they can be fired. These orders can be questionable even without being outright illegal and immoral. Thus we saw cops confiscating guns in New Orleans under some combination of poor briefing, subordination, and a weird need to protect people from themselves. You might live in a small town where there is an attitude of blind "respect my authority" among officers.

So be aware that a cop who vetoes your self-defense activities may sympathize with you but is acting under external influences. It is better to feign compliance than force the issue and *really* be disarmed.

Dealing with an upset officer

Arguing with police is pointless. I don't mean reasoning, like presenting an argument, I mean a loud oral disagreement. Anyone who has seen *Cops* or *Live PD* knows what I'm talking about. A suspect who is dead to rights going to jail will try to yell, scream, debate, threaten, or whine their way out of trouble. Once a cop has made up his mind, it is noise. He isn't even listening to you at that point. All you are doing is aggravating him.

Reasoning implies both parties are trying to achieve a compromise. An officer's line in the sand command isn't a compromise; it is a demand to comply or face an even worse outcome. I personally never had my mind changed by someone's argument. It is tiresome and annoying, like a young child who won't listen to reason and has every excuse in the book.

Attempting to argue with a cop is a pointless endeavor and is counterproductive. You will only annoy him, meaning he is less likely to do you any favors or cut you any slack. There is nothing you can say to persuade him to change his mind once his mind is made up. No cop will want to, or have any reason to, be reasonable if you are foaming at the mouth.

My advice is to always be polite and respectful. Never insult the officer or his agency. Stay calm and realize you won't win an argument with him. The more intense your language or behavior the more likely the reaction will be to your words or behavior rather than the substance of what you are saying.

Realize that the officer is operating under his own emotions. He may be afraid and exhausted in a very fraught and dangerous situation or feeling guilty because politics are making him treat you like the bad guy. He may respond emotionally based on what he is feeling and not what you are actually saying or doing. If you understand this, you can empathize and stay calm, even perhaps address his unconscious concerns.

Heated arguments create an emotional response and stimulate the flight or fight hormones. The flight or fight response decreases one's ability to reason, which is something that officers annoyed with a suspect's or violator's diatribe are vulnerable to. Their willingness to be persuaded can literally shut down.

Do not get angry and yell back. When on the receiving end of an angry person people will feel their flight or fight response hit. Never curse or insult. Becoming angry will only spiral the interaction into negative emotions. Getting "loud" yourself may turn you into an aggressor in the cop's mind.

Officers who are frustrated are more likely to be aggressive, which means your verbal obstinacy can be taken as non-compliance. A frustrated officer is less likely to grant you any leeway and will be quicker to exercise his authority punitively against you.

Have a friendly and witty person talk to the officer, one that won't get flustered and yell back and might even deliver a well-timed joke to break the tension. Don't deliver ultimatums or threats. The officer is highly likely to respond poorly to those and his response comes with the full force of the government.

Cops and armed citizens

In nearly all jurisdictions, if you have a negative encounter with the police, i.e. they are detaining you, expect to be disarmed. A cop just driving by who disapproves of your legal carry of firearms might run off at the mouth, but if he has authority to detain or arrest you, he is taking the guns. If you use force against the crowd, be prepared for a worst-case scenario from police; that is being arrested and losing your guns.

Plan for a search warrant and/or "red flag" gun confiscation order to be served. This may also be a tool by corrupt police or local politicians to try and placate the mob or simply a totalitarian tactic to disarm opposition. Hide and bury extra guns.

Weapons will provoke varying reactions from police in emergencies. If you're lucky, the cop will praise you off-the-record. Others will try to convince you not to openly carry, etc. and might even be a bit of a douchebag about it. On the worse end, some legal authority or simply naked power might be used to disarm you, harass you, or send you away.

Police attitudes will vary from location to location and situation to situation. Cops might be antagonistic to openly carrying citizens one day, but on day three of the rioting, they might give a "thumbs up" as they pass by. But let's assume the worst: the cops are in a foul mood, people are being killed, there is chaos all around, and they roll up to find your group with AR-15s, dressed in cammies, and have the street blocked off. How will you react if the cops are pissed?

During Hurricane Katrina, police confiscated firearms that were legally owned and carried. This was a huge mess and completely wrong morally and legally. A lot of the people who lost their guns were also minorities. Don't discount tired, harassed, and scared police doing the same thing again in your town. I would think this behavior would be more common in big cities where guns aren't usually openly carried and where there is a big gang/drug problem (where police usually encounter criminals with guns).

From a safety standpoint, assume police will always disarm you unless the encounter is purely positive and consensual. Yes, some cops don't care that you are carrying concealed legally, but others go all "officer safety" and take your gun until the traffic stop, etc. is over with. It is legal if they are detaining you. It sucks, but work on educating your local department rather than fighting. All this unrest is over people who fought cops when they shouldn't have, remember?

Should a cop want to disarm you, don't fight. Have someone video the interaction and comply with the officer's instructions. Don't try to argue in the moment, he's not listening. It would be helpful to have a print out of statutes and/or case law at this time. If you fight, the officer will just fight back. Are things really at the point where you want to escalate stuff until you're shooting it out with the cops? When the disarming, pat-down, and cuffing is done, then politely and calmly speak with the officer.

Police interactions go sideways because people don't listen to the police, whether the cop is right or wrong. Many cops have a chip on their shoulder and want you to "respect my authority" whether they mean to or not. Some won't be able to disconnect their ordinary reaction of "don't block the street" from the reality that the city is falling apart.

As we discussed in group dress, look and act professional. Police will react to you as concerned citizens, rather than wannabes or a new threat if you don't look like a militia from a bad 1990s "60 Minutes" documentary.

Compliance

I just recommended using discretion in suggesting that sometimes the better option is feigning compliance. It could be that an officer just wants you to go inside long enough that he can honestly report that everyone was dispersed and was compliant. It's not his fault you came out again after he left.

Reasoning with an officer is different. An officer may be willing to reach some sort of compromise with you or could help mitigate your problem some other way. In these situations, you may bargain for an increased police presence, which a good cop should feel honor bound to provide. You will have to feel this out to know when compromise is viable.

Non-compliance has to be backed up by force. Are you ready if the cop calls *your* bluff? Remember, he has virtually unlimited resources to take you into custody. You can't legally use force back against the officer. Even if this is legal in your state, who says he's going to comply with you or his partners won't get involved? If the police are operational and *want* to, they can and will arrest you.

Unless they are totally corrupt and the alternative is worse than arrest and prosecution, de-escalate the situation and comply until you can get around the police problem. In a very tense situation, such as when guns are out, compliance is absolutely vital. Comply immediately and fully.

Shut up, listen, and do. Drop your weapon and comply.

Police interaction considerations

- Your appearance and attitude influence police reactions.
- Police will treat neat, well-dressed and professional looking people more seriously than a rag-tag bunch.
- If you are aggressive and hostile, police will reciprocate the attitude and be disinclined from doing you any favors.
- You may receive a negative reaction based on the perception you are usurping police authority or causing more problems for officers.
- Police may have no idea who you are and may treat you like potential threats.
- Just because you may regard police as "the good guys" they may not be.

If you are detained by the police:

- Do not reach for your weapon. Do not touch your weapon unless given explicit instructions to put it on the ground, etc. and only do so slowly and while announcing what you are doing.
- Comply with all orders and do not resist. Have your day in court.
- Do not attempt to argue with a cop; he's not listening and it won't help you.
- Do have copies of relevant statutes, ordinances, or regulations handy.
- Give as little information to the police when asked and only for the purposes of allowing them to catch a criminal or stop someone who is a threat. Never volunteer details about your plans.
- If asked what you are doing, make a simple statement that you have formed an ad hoc neighborhood watch.
- Never, ever make statements to an officer if arrested, detained, or you think you may be in trouble. You aren't talking your way out of it.

Do you need police approval for your plans?

- No.
- The police are not your friends.
- You do not need their permission or approval of your plans.
- Sharing your plans with the police could result in them stopping you or later using such plans as evidence against you.
- You do not need a police officer's opinion of your plans, nor do you need their consent. If you want someone to give you an "attaboy," ask your father.

Should you be a police volunteer?

- Yes.
- This includes helping out at the station, being a member of the citizen's patrol, or at a minimum, taking a citizen's academy.
- Being a volunteer allows you to obtain inside information about the department's operation, the crime situation in your area, and insights into how you can improve your situation.
- Having a relationship of trust (being a part of the department) can go a long way with your own plan and survival. Cops tend to treat you better if you are a known quantity and see you as one of their own.
- Volunteering at the department can actually help your community in the traditional sense, which is good if your area has not succumbed to stupidity.
- Working with your department will give you a huge insight into their attitudes.

Dangers of police cooperation

- You might give your plan away to people who could later use it to stop you from protecting your neighborhood or use it as evidence against you if you do.

- Police may be downright hostile as often they see it as their job alone to protect the public and community, with you being untrained, idealistic interlopers.
- Officers, or more likely management and politicians, may actively oppose your ideas.
- Sharing information, your views, or plans with police may put you on a potential "list" radicals could later use against you.

Riot Basics

How riots start

Riots provide a form of anonymity through strength in numbers. The risk of arrest is inverse to the number of participants; more people, less risk. One or two people on a street smashing windows and stealing things are gonna get rolled up by the boys in blue quickly. Make it several hundred and the cops will watch helplessly from down the street. Police can't arrest everybody, arresting anyone other than the absolute worst of the worst is pointless, and attempting mass arrests of a violent crowd is just too dangerous.

Large crowds provide anonymity. Anonymity encourages violence because the risk of being identified and caught is low. Violence increases the risk for police and ensures an atmosphere of low consequences because being stopped or apprehended is unlikely. This leads to an accumulative effect as more people join the riot; for instance looters taking advantage of the "cover" provided by the rioters engaging with the police.

The anonymity of the crowd and the free-for-all attitude leads people to do things they otherwise wouldn't. An average person takes on the identity of the crowd. They are part of a large entity, which causes them to displace their morality and restraint. This is the "mob mentality;" everyone else is doing it. When a crowd begins to take action, it becomes a mob.

The mob attitude has a disinhibiting effect. Someone

who ordinarily wouldn't steal or beat someone up will loot a Nike store or attack the guy in the MAGA hat because they are anonymous in the crowd and there is little danger of being caught. Peer pressure is one factor in the crowd breaking down morality/restraint, but an atmosphere where one can behave badly without judgment or worrying about the consequences is highly likely to lead someone to act on what's in their heart, which could be theft or physical violence.

In short:

- Police intervention is inverse to the size of the crowd.
- Crowds provide anonymity and a disinhibiting effect.
- Disinhibited people who are unlikely to get caught act on their impulses.
- Large amounts of unrestrained lawlessness tend to escalate acts to the extreme.

Who, what, when, where, why and how? 5W1H

Identify the nature of the event and what is likely to occur. How have these events developed and how have the organizers or participants behaved in the past? Where is this happening and how could it affect you?

Know your enemy and their goals. For instance, a protest group that just wants to march, make noise, and feel good should probably be ignored so as not to give them any reaction to feed upon. A marauding mob might need to be driven off through a show of force, whereas a bandit attack needs to be fought with lethal force. Intelligence can allow you to prepare an adequate and appropriate reaction.

Types of unrest

There are three levels of disobedience or disruption:

Passive: loud, raucous assembly to make a point and cause non-harmful disruption. At worst, minor vandalism or spontaneous fights may occur. This includes *demonstrations*, *protests*, and *affrays*.

Active: intentional violence, vandalism, or looting. Typically characterized as a *riot* or *looting*.

Anarchy: widespread violence, theft, vandalism, and looting. Authorities are absent and out of control. This could be a temporary (near WROL) or long-term (WROL) condition. This may be a major disaster situation, an absence of police control during massive, citywide riots, or an *insurrection* or civil war.

Demonstrators and picketers often want to be seen and heard. Demonstrations are usually political in nature or stem from social, religious, or racial grievances. Their goal is to spread a message, gain public awareness, and get media coverage. There can also be a personal component that demonstrating or protesting satisfies an urge to "do something" and "be heard" or even annoying ideological opponents.

Many demonstrations are peaceful in nature but can be exploited by agitators or an unfortunate chain of events may turn them into a riot. Small-scale instances of injury or destruction are affrays. An affray is a breach of the peace, typically by a small group and is self-limited in nature. This could be kids blocking a highway and banging on cars or counter-demonstrators getting into a fight during a protest.

A riot is a large event with many people engaged in personal violence, looting, or property destruction. You know it when you see it. Looting and riots can begin over economic problems such as a collapse of the EBT system, a supply chain disaster emptying grocery stores, or a bank run. A failure of government authority may allow these underlying causes of unrest to explode into anti-social violence.

An insurrection is generally the overthrow of legitimate (or putatively legitimate government). For our purposes, an insurrection is basically a civil war where government (police) institutions are incapable of keeping domestic peace. A state of war, whether between rebels/government or civilians on civilians, may exist locally.

All of these things may be spontaneous or pre-planned. Even planned peaceful protests can inadvertently turn into riots if things go wrong. The 1967 Detroit riot was spontaneous to a police raid on a background of racial tension. It was not a pre-planned protest like today that is often intended or exploited to leave the territory of free speech and become civil unrest.

A disturbance (for our purposes) is any protest or assembly of a group causing disruption of civil order and may cause death, serious injury, theft, or damage to property. Once widespread personal violence and vandalism begins at large by members of an assembled mob, I'm referring to this as a riot.

Agitators

Consider who the crowd is composed of. Mostly unarmed young people without any equipment are likely going to be on the lower end of the threat scale. Use your powers of observation to identify troublemakers and potential special threats early. Look for people who are staring intently at you "mad dogging" or display other behaviors typical of aggressive, violent types. Anyone in the crowd is capable of intentionally or unintentionally inciting a riot.

Watch out for agitators before things turn ugly. Ordinarily, every civil disturbance turns into a riot because of individuals with few moral compunctions who like to stir up the pot. For instance, the violence in the 1992 LA riots were incited when individuals decided to loot a liquor store. Recently, we've been seeing an influx of semi-professionals who travel to potential hotbeds to inflame things for their political goals or as part of being paid by dark sources.

Pay special attention to any semi-pro agitators. You can recognize an agitator by their clothing or equipment even before their behavior makes things apparent. Clothing is usually all black ("black bloc") or red (for communism/anarchy). Symbols may include the anarchist "A", the iconic Che Guevara T-shirt, and images of Marx or other socialists. Equipment includes backpacks, ski masks, gas masks, shields, bludgeon weapons, fireworks, or firearms.

Semi-pro agitators are specifically there to inflame a situation. They may work in teams communicating by radio (proven in a few cases and easy to monitor). Their goal is to cause destruction and violence. As things in the country destabilize, these people will be ever more dangerous and be the initiators of arson, infrastructure damage, serious injury, or even death.

In a justified use-of-force situation or WROL, one may consider targeting agitators to take them out before the situation devolves further. Early identification allows you to monitor and intervene proactively to your advantage. Stopping agitators helps take fuel and heat away from the fire of a disturbance.

Escalation of violence

Mobs usually operate through escalation. As their size grows and authorities' control over the situation slips, the mob's actions get worse. Often they begin with yelling, noise, and verbal abuse. Vandalism for destruction's sake happens often before the attention is turned from property to people. Individuals may be shoved or beaten. Cars can be swarmed, carjacked, or vandalized. Objects are typically thrown before other forms of violence begin, like shooting. Arson and Molotov cocktails (and now laser or firework attacks) also preceded shooting. Shootings in most events have been between rioters or limited attacks on authorities.

Rioters and agitators will use chaos to their advantage. This can be used to distract police or defenders from a particular target. Snipers often shoot at fire fighters so that burning buildings can't be extinguished. Driving crowds or fleeing people in front of or between police or defenders as human shields can happen. Panic and terror can be used to further accomplish political ends or merely clear out an area for theft, etc.

Crowds v. mobs

While "crowd" and "mob" are used interchangeably with other nouns describing an assembly of people, there is a distinction.[24]

A crowd is just a group of people assembled over a common cause. Crowds become mobs when that common cause turns into a purpose to achieve an outcome with the intent and ability to do so. Agitators or a leader can motivate the crowd to engage in violence or destruction. Mobs may have different motivations. Terror mobs want to inflict violence and destruction while looting, or acquisition mobs, want to steal things. The two can overlap.

Goals of your anti-riot/anti-mob efforts

Your goals in any effort to keep riots or mobs from causing havoc in your neighborhood or on your street should be:

- Deter any acts of destruction, violence, or demonstrations in your neighborhood;
- Restrict, delay, or prevent entry to the street or neighborhood by troublemakers;

---

[24] I may use "protest/protester" and "riot/rioter" the same way.

- Prevent damage to property or injury/death to your neighbors;
- Stop attacks against personal property or violence towards persons; and,
- Disperse mobs from your neighborhood to end the danger they are causing.

It should never be to take revenge, cause harm to a group you don't like, or for personal gain.

Riot and Crowd Control

Crowd control measures

Crowd control (versus riot *suppression*) is limiting the growth of the crowd, controlling its geographical spread, and dissolving it. These three means are **isolation**, **show of force**, and **dispersal**. Arrests are not included as you will not be making them since you have no where to "drag" arrestees to (see *dispersal*). Dealing with the crowd (making the bad people go away) comes before using force (riot suppression) on violent/destructive mobs.

Isolation

Isolating a crowd will be difficult for a small team to do. The goal is to prevent new additions from joining the group to stop or slow its growth. This can be done by creating physical barriers or having a second team isolate newcomers from the main body. This can be risky for the defenders as rioters may react when boxed into a corner. If possible, leave a route for them to escape from where it is unlikely reinforcements would enter from.

Show of force

A show of force is essentially a warning and a threat that destruction and violence will be met with force (not necessarily kinetic). Crowds may be deterred from their propensity to become rowdy if they are faced with a large number of opponents who may use force. We have seen plenty of instances (discussed elsewhere) where open carry groups have caused rioters, protesters, and looters to pass by simply by standing ready.

Place armed people at your perimeter; this is to intimidate the crowd and ideally deter them from choosing your neighborhood. Hopefully their "protest" continues by or they stand a good way off jeering at you until they are tired or bored.

However, one should never assume a show of force alone will be effective. Individual antagonists and the group itself may be willing to escalate. They may have their own ability to react violently to a use of force, which we have seen to some extent already (particularly in the Portland area). You must be prepared to back up your exhibition with actual and sufficient force to halt any resistance.

In the civilian's case, a small number of armed defenders and limited barricades may be enough to persuade a gun-shy mob to pass by. They may not be seeking any real trouble. Others may seek undefended targets. Whatever the case, be prepared to react and do not bluff. Much of a show of force for civilians is a gamble. The fallback is not arrests and dispersal like police, it is using force or taking shelter until the attack passes. Nonetheless, in many cases involving less-aggressive groups, a show of force may be entirely effective.

See also: "Defending Your Suburb" chapter.

Dispersal

Dispersal (without force) is not the best tool in the toolbox of the civilian defender. Rioters are removed from the scene by police through two methods: **drive** and **drag**. *Dragging* them away means that they are arrested, handed over to the booking team, and transported to jail, thus removing them from the area.

Driving them away involves the suggestion or the actual use of force to get people to leave. This can be physically encroaching on the crowd so they feel uncomfortable and move away, hopefully dispersing entirely. Or it can be by application of force to dispel a crowd to make them run away out of fear of being subjected to the pain of riot control weapons.

Civilians will rarely have the numbers to effectively move rioters away. Leaving one's defensive perimeter and pushing a crowd away is dangerous. Should you need to use a human formation to push rioters away, attempt to do so by moving your defenses outward. A heavy barricade can be lifted and pushed outward into the crowd, forcing them back, while the defenders stay behind the moving barricade.

Alternatively, vehicles can approach in a line abreast and drive at the crowd, but armed defenders have to be able to stop anyone attacking the cars or trying to sneak through. This is far more dangerous to the driver, the crowd, and for liability reasons (a vehicle vs. pedestrian collision).

Dispersal orders and warnings should be given. Make multiple warnings from as close to the crowd as possible and in multiple locations if necessary. Use a megaphone to ensure everyone hears the order in a noisy environment. Do not bluff. There is no need to read "the riot act" or say something specific, but I would make it clear that this order is to be obeyed immediately and force will be used to disperse the crowd if it is ignored.

Keep your distance from mobs. Never wade into the crowd or let them mingle among you if you can at all help it. Physical barriers help maintain this distance. Don't let rioters get behind you or your group or between members of your group. We've seen too many images of someone trying to plead or negotiate with rioters only to be bushwhacked from behind and killed.

Tips

- Order the crowd to disperse;
- Always try to leave as much open and defensible space between you and the crowd (such as behind a barricade);

- Allow the crowd clear avenues of escape or retreat;
- Try to focus the crowd into an area that benefits your defense most or is an otherwise open, unobstructed area;
- Allow the crowd to disperse down its escape route;
- Remain behind a barricade, do not let rioters get in between your individual defenders;
- Always protect your rear and sides from rioters attempting to attack from your flank; and,
- If the situation devolves into violence, escalate to using force as appropriate.

Rescues

Should a member of your defensive team or a non-defender neighbor be surrounded or attacked by the mob, an immediate rescue has to be mounted to limit the chance the mob has to inflict injury on that person. Depending on the precariousness of the situation, this could be serious injury, death, kidnapping, or rape.

- Be assertive and aggressive, force your way in hard and fast;
- Keep your weapons secure against snatching;
- A minimum of four people is ideal, two to lift and drag and two others to shield/shove/fight, although six—two fighters, shielders/shovers, and draggers each—is better;
- Attention has to be paid to a 360° area around the team at all times;
- Push the crowd away with shields, body or weapon strikes, or even bayonets if justified;
- Use of shields to protect from thrown objects or blows of impact weapons may be necessary, especially when stooping to lift a fallen friendly;

- Use distraction devices or area pain compliance weapons to create an opening and/or get the attackers off the victim;
- The people behind the defensive line should cover the advance and retreat while the fighters should cover the retreat from within the crowd; and,
- Remember your use of force could potentially injure the victim.

Avoid

Avoid engaging in verbal altercations. Yelling insults or waving political flags or signs won't help. Be quiet, be impassive. The only communication with the crowd should be stern, but polite, commands necessary to keep the peace. Remove any loudmouths on your side from contact with the crowd.

Don't bang on things like cops do with their batons against shields. Ancient people (and remote tribes today) used the rhythm of drums to stir up morale before a battle. It will probably be incendiary rather than intimidating.

Non-kinetic riot control

Many of the characteristics of a riot can be exploited to break them up before they get out of hand by disrupting the growth process. Unfortunately, politics is such now that protests that start as loud and only blocking traffic serve as a catalyst for worse because police can't intervene (legally or politically) at that point. This is why early intervention is your best policy. If you can break it up early, you will disrupt the catalyst for the protest to turn into a riot.

- Make a show of force when the crowd is small. Openly carry weapons, outnumber them if possible, use megaphones or other loud noises to your advantage. If you can do so and the legality of the situation permits, disperse them yourself.
- Deny the crowd anonymity with lighting and video cameras. If you can identify people, call them out by name or at least by what they're wearing, i.e. "I see you with that brick, Mr. Blue UCLA Sweatshirt!"
- Challenge people who don't belong in the area who commit small wrongs, like walking across a lawn or jumping a fence. Set the tone that they are not welcome and you care about small infractions of neighborhood decency. This also has the effect of showing determination and resolve to someone who might be testing whether or not you are confrontational.
- Deny the area to them using creative means, like sprinklers, intolerable smells, light, etc.

Use of force

Use of force continuum

Law enforcement uses a concept known as the "use of force continuum" that serves as a guide of what force to use against a suspect for a given level of criminal resistance and how that force should escalate. It is a kind of rules of engagement. The continuum starts with no application of force up to deadly force. It is modeled as a gauge or stepped spectrum, although based on the circumstances changing levels of force may not be a linear progression. That is to say someone who needs only a verbal command at first may suddenly pull out a gun, requiring a lethal response.

Law enforcement uses the following categories: officer presence, verbal commands, empty-hands/physical control, less-lethal, and lethal force. At the low end, the fact that most people will comply with an officer is coupled with verbal commands to keep most people under control. The implied threat of arrest, citation, or force and the fear of the same for the majority of the population is what makes the lower tier effective.

When a resisting suspect ignores what he has been told to do, an officer will begin to physically restrain the suspect. This may be handcuffing them, grabbing, or shoving them to physically stop the escape, assault, or make the person sit still. The continuum has considerable variations. An officer might use martial arts or standard fighting techniques to subdue a suspect who is physically assaulting the officer or someone else.

When there is no threat to life (or serious injury), but the suspect is assaultive or offering physical resistance, less-lethal weapons can be used. Batons might be used to strike at this level, depending on how the department classifies usage. This includes Tasers and pepper spray (OC), escalating to bean bag shotguns or police canines. The last level is lethal force.

Police endeavor to use the least amount of force to control a non-compliant suspect. Thus, the reasonable amount of force that is comparable to the resistance being offered is used. For instance, passive resistance may see an officer haul a suspect to the back seat of his unit. A suspect who is fighting may be tackled, hit, or may face a Taser or pepper spray.

Civilians also owe a level of reasonableness when acting in self-defense. For instance, it is legal to use force to prevent a crime being committed against one's person or property. Thus, hitting someone back after they've assaulted you, in order to stop the attack, is legal. You may also be able to physically restrain (arrest) someone who is stealing or damaging your property or use non-lethal means to get them to stop.

Suburban defense continuum

For the private citizen, in a non-life threatening situation *reasonable self-defense force* is that which ends the criminal action. Using the standard of reasonableness, this would mean the least amount of force necessary to get the person to stop is used. Therefore, if you are physically able to grab and escort a vandal off your property, that would be far more reasonable than pepper spraying them in the face. Of course, legal standards and laws vary from jurisdiction to jurisdiction.

In this chapter, I make suggestions that would be appropriate for a civilian engaging in suburban defense during a time when police will not or cannot control the situation. Note that "aimed weapon" means not just a gun with sights, but any weapon or device, lethal or not, that is targeted against a specific individual." "Area weapon" is also not a gun (although it *could* be) but is something that affects a specific area and multiple individuals in that area, such as tear gas would be.

Passive measures

These aren't force at all, but things that might keep an interaction from occurring. Such things would be fencing, barricades, and security cameras. The defender doesn't have to interact with the aggressor at all.

Deterrence and warnings

Threat: none specific, but the possibility trouble could develop.

This includes non-kinetic forms of crowd and riot control, like setting up barricades, openly carrying weapons, making your presence known to the crowd, and issuing warnings. Your goal with this method is to make anyone who does not want trouble to pass by and those who do want trouble to think twice and remain peaceful.

Shows of force will probably be the best tactic in times of a functioning legal system as it is hard to screw up and do something illegal just standing there. A lot of potential troublemakers expecting no resistance will be headed off if they know they will face resistance.

Defensive physical force

Threat: small-scale criminal acts occurring or the threat of escalation to greater crimes.

Physical contact with a mob should be avoided unless no other option exists. Using physical defensive force would be with your body to stop a crowd from crossing your defensive line, entering your yard, etc. In extreme situations physically dispersing the crowd may be called for. Non-contact forms of less-lethal force to stop criminal acts or interrupt things before they get worse could be used like megaphone sirens, bright lights, laser intimidation (not blinding), or stink bombs.

Less-lethal force

Threat: someone will sustain less-serious injuries or major property damage.

Anything that could potentially cause injury, but not death, should be placed in this category. This would include airsoft "sting" grenades, paintballs, flashbangs, pyrotechnics, Tasers, fire hoses, etc. In non-WROL situations, this would be to immediately overcome physical force to prevent injury or damage to property in-line with your state's self-defense laws. In a WROL situation, less-lethal force could be used to disperse a crowd before it reaches critical mass or to break up an attack.

Lethal force

Threat: someone will be killed or seriously wounded if you do not neutralize the aggressor immediately.

Use of firearms will be the most likely threat and the reciprocal use of force in this category. Remember, lethal force is typically permitted in most places to stop an imminent fatal or serious injury, something horrific like rape or kidnapping, or forced entry to a home. This may apply from a lone shooter in a mob to an armed bandit attack on the neighborhood.

Lethal and non-lethal force

Non-lethal

- Make a lot of noise; yell back, deploy flashbang grenades, firecrackers, etc.
- Cause pain/discomfort; throw airsoft pellet grenades, spray them with pepper spray, shoot them with paintballs or airsoft pellets, turn on your fire hose.
- Use light; blind them with spotlights, turn on disorienting strobe lights on your flashlights or weapon lights, or use fireworks (if you must).

Intermediate less-lethal

- If this is a WROL situation or lethal force is justified, using shotguns to fire less-lethal projectiles like rubber slugs or shot and bean bags can be used.

- Shotguns are lethal weapons and less-than-lethal rounds have been known to kill.
- Aiming guns as a bluff (not their mere presence) is not recommended if you can't legally shoot someone.

Lethal

- Use all of the above methods, particularly flashbangs and pyrotechnics that make a lot of explosion sounds in combination with gunfire.
- Mixing in less-lethal with lethal force amplifies the effects of gunfire. Example: a bad guy who hears gun shots, gets hit by a paintball and feels the wetness of the paint might run away and not stop to check to see that it is not blood.
- Try and take aimed, accurate shots at close and imminent threats if possible rather than shooting into the crowd en masse.
- In a WROL overrun situation, fire rapidly at the front row of the crowd to knock down as many as possible to stop their momentum.
- An old tactic is to skip buckshot (or birdshot) off pavement and into the legs of a crowd by firing at the ground a few feet in front of the people. Israeli troops used Ruger 10/22 rifles to fire .22 LR bullets into the lower legs of rioters. Both of these methods are lethal force because both the weapon and the ammunition are lethal. Projectiles can ricochet to cause lethal injuries and the legs also contain major arteries that if severed can lead to death.

When do you use force on members of a mob (lethal or non-lethal)?

- In a direct response to a use of force against you or the imminent, threatened use of force.
- On any attempt to break into a house or set it on fire.
- If the crowd attempts to break through a hard barricade to commit acts of violence or major destruction against the neighborhood.

- Indiscriminate fire should only be used as a last resort when the entire mob is likely to overrun you and most defenders are going to engage in life-threatening violence.

Considerations

Before using force, consider the following:

- Is the crowd mostly peaceful and behaving? Can you legally use force to stop what they are doing, even non-lethal force?
- Is the crowd tending towards personal violence or just property destruction and what is the likelihood that they will retaliate if you use force?
- Will the wind blow pepper spray or smoke back in your team's face (back across your "release line")?

Using force may not be the proper thing to do at that moment given the circumstances. One type of force may be better to use than another. This is not a decision to make reflexively or take lightly.

Best practices

- Self-defense and justifiable homicide laws should be obeyed as much as possible.
- Force should be proportionate to the threat and used sparingly as a last resort.
- Aimed weapons should be used directly against specific persons who are engaged in actions that pose an immediate threat of death or serious injury.
    - In WROL, this could be expanded to agitators and serious property damage.

- Aimed weapons (lethal or not) can be used judiciously to discourage certain individuals from crossing barricades or engaging in actions that may escalate the risk of death or injury.
- Firearms used indiscriminately should only be used against crowds as a last resort.
- Area weapons should be used to disperse crowds, stop rushes against barricades, defenders, and victims, or in concentrations of rioters who are presenting the greatest threat.

Riot control (suppression) devices

Grenades generally

Here we're discussing civilian legal (and easy to purchase for non-law enforcement people) grenades, mainly from the airsoft world. Odds are you won't have fragmentation grenades (I pray we never get that far) or military/SWAT grade flashbangs.

When using a grenade, tape the pin and safety handle (spoon) down until ready to use. Store them in an area safe for flammable materials, in an ammo can or something similar, and keep dry. When holding it in your hand, place the spoon against your palm, not your fingers (opposite of what you'd assume). Your hand will hold the spring-loaded spoon with greater strength that way.

Carefully research the appropriate standoff and

deployment distance (the effective radius) of the device so you know what the right deployment distance is. Pick where you want the grenade to land before throwing and focus in on the area like a pitcher. If you can't pitch, have someone else throw. Remember your follow-through.

Do not attempt to "cook off" the grenade by holding it after the pin has been pulled and the spoon released for a second or two before throwing. Nor should you attempt to airburst a grenade over the crowd. Some airsoft grenades are pyrotechnics so be mindful of any flammable material in the deployment area.

Smoke

Smoke grenades are available to civilians, but sourcing can be difficult. Military issue or civilian versions of military smoke grenades are hard to come by, but not impossible. The easiest sources are airsoft supply stores. Models that have about the same burn time and create a large smoke cloud, like military models, exist. Smaller ones exist as well. YouTube has lots of videos by airsoft enthusiasts discussing the pros and cons of each.

Smoke grenades can also be used for concealment. "Pop smoke" is slang for running away because a cloud of smoke can obscure your movements. Watch the videos of the smoke clouds; how much smoke you get (and how much "area" is obscured) varies by model and also depends on the wind. A high wind may quickly disperse the smoke fast, no breeze may cause it to rise vertically, while a light breeze may cause the smoke to lie low and spread far, perfect for concealment. Several grenades might need to be used.

These grenades come in several colors of smoke. The color doesn't really matter unless you are using it for signaling. Remember that tear gas is white smoke (although the crowd might not know that) if you want to simulate tear gas.

You aren't going to get tear gas. The closest you can come is pepper spray. Smoke grenades will work better if the crowd is stupid, panicky, and it helps if you yell "gas, gas, gas" before lobbing the smoke grenade (while you wear gas masks for psychological effect). Once the crowd realizes the smoke isn't an irritant, you will lose the advantage of confusion. A helpful addition to the white smoke might be pepper spray, which will cause irritation, and the combination of the two may enhance the illusion.

Flashbangs and pyrotechnics

Also from the airsoft world are flashbangs. Flashbangs, also known as stun grenades or distraction devices, basically make a deafening boom and a bright flash of light to disorient and distract bad guys. Military/law enforcement models will not be sold to you, even if they are legal to possess.

Airsoft versions come in two models; CO_2 and pyrotechnic. The CO_2 models are basically a small BB gun CO_2 cylinder in a grenade body. The gas expands a plastic "balloon" that pops very loudly. The pyrotechnic versions are basically firecrackers in a grenade shaped cardboard carton. These are louder and do produce something of a flash (nowhere near the brightness of a real one) and also blow apart the carboard container. I would *highly* recommend this latter version.

Flashbangs would be used to startle people. This might get a crowd to disperse or could induce a panic that may disrupt a rush of your barricade. Don't overuse them or they will lose their impact. These models don't have that much of a lasting effect of hearing impairment or tinnitus. Be aware though that the explosion (the sound or the flash) plus the body of the grenade blowing apart could make people think it was a bomb. Slight injuries or risk of fire could occur.

Yes, you can use firecrackers and other fireworks based items, including smoke. I would advise against those as they need to be lit with a match or lighter versus most of the airsoft models that work like a regular grenade. Just pull the pin and toss. Fireworks, especially the ones that shoot colored sparks or explode, carry with them an extreme risk of injury or fire. Don't use them against people. The same goes for shooting flares at people.

At the end-of-the-world extreme, shooting aerial fireworks into the crowd can be a devastating tool. We're talking about the kind of fireworks that are illegal in a lot of places and that people out west have to drive to Indian reservations to buy. Safe and sane; not! There are lots of videos from recent riots showing just how loud and disorienting these things are when exploding at ground level.

What you're doing with these is lighting the fuse, putting them in the mortar tube, and angling the tube down to fire the shell into the crowd. Some experimentation will be necessary to ensure you can fire horizontally instead of vertically with some accuracy. I'm sure Antifa has documents online somewhere.

Again, using fireworks this way is a last resort when all laws enforcement has disappeared. If the shell detonates in contact with someone, they could be killed or seriously injured. The burning metals in the exploding stars could cause major burns or start fires. In a sane world we're talking criminal charges up to possible mayhem to murder if someone takes a direct hit.

37mm flare launchers and specialty 12 gauge ammo

37mm flare launchers resemble the slightly larger 40mm M203 grenade launcher (which is why California and other states ban them; they look scary). These launchers are not capable of firing grenades. Instead, they fire large marine flares or other ammunition.

One common type of cartridge is a pyrotechnic round under various names that is essentially a firework; a loud bang and lots of "stars." A variation is a flashbang type that bangs and flashes, but without the star effect. Some just make noise. Smoke rockets are also available, allowing you to deploy smoke out to 50 yards, further than you can throw. Tear gas and baton rounds are not commonly available to the public (law enforcement only).

The advantage these devices have is that if a firework effect is desired, using the launcher is much safer than lighting a firework mortar and holding it horizontally. The flashbang types can be fired into a crowd to disperse them or at an attacker who is behind cover to flush them out. Just imagine what a sniper would think if a pyrotechnic round exploded around him after hearing the grenade launcher like "bloop."

Similar cartridges exist for 12 gauge shotguns, though their effectiveness is questionable. Flashbang shotgun shells are very short range and detonate just past the muzzle. These are usually used by entry teams firing through a gap into a room. Door breaching rounds are not going to help you either.

"Dragon's breath" shells should *not* be used. These expel burning metal particles for a long distance, creating a spectacular effect at night, but are very prone to starting fires. Anti-personnel use could set a human's clothes on fire and any dry vegetation or flammable materials hit could easily ignite.

Stink

Stink bombs just smell bad but are a non-force option to disperse or move a weak crowd. These wouldn't be targeted at anyone, just thrown so as to stink up the area the crowd is or where you don't want them to be. Don't put much faith in this working.

Pepper spray

Pepper spray, also called *oleoresin capsicum* (OC in police parlance), is everyone's favorite spicy spray. It burns when on your skin or in your eyes as if you splashed yourself with hot sauce or rubbed a very hot pepper on your face. When inhaled, it causes a burning sensation in the lungs, coughing, copious snot, and occasionally respiratory distress. Older chemical formulations that act in a similar fashion are "Mace" and CN sprays.

Pepper spray would be employed in a situation where it would be legal to use force to resist a crime. Less-than-lethal force is typically justified to protect property and persons from non-fatal injury. It becomes extra legal if you start spraying widely into a crowd that is trying to intimidate you or force its way down your street (discussed elsewhere).

Your typical discount store "impulse shelf" purchase of a pocket or purse sized canister is worthless. It doesn't have the range or capacity to help you. Those are designed to blast a robber or rapist in the face so you can run away. Get a Mark III 1.5oz canister. These are standard belt-sized cans. Larger models exist up to the Mark IX "riot size" ones that come with a pistol grip, which you will recall from "bear Mace" products. Always buy OC that is formulated for humans, not bears.

I would carry a Mark III or Mark IV canister on my body for limited use. For riot control, I would have *several* Mark IX canisters ready to douse the crowd. Once you start using the canister, it won't last forever as pressure will leak out. Your mileage will vary between products. When selecting a product, check the formulation (percentage of the active ingredient) and the spray pattern. Do research on what kind of spray pattern and the exact product before you buy.

The *cone* spray pattern is like that of most of your aerosol home sprays. It covers the most area but creates a cloud that is prone to blow back in your face (ask me how I know). *Stream* jets are the most accurate, less troubled by wind dispersion, and have a greater range than the cone. This is due to the fact that the stream is concentrated. *Gel* products have further range than even streams and have the same accuracy, plus there is less risk of cross-contamination. Gels stick better to your subject. Cones require less accuracy while streams and gels need to be aimed directly at the face for maximum effect.

Pepper spray grenades are basically aerosol cans like the handheld stuff, but with a valve that continuously sprays until the pressure supply is exhausted. These are unidirectional cone sprays. Once you press that button, it starts spraying until empty, usually for about 10-15 seconds. Though pepper spray grenades are often sold only to law enforcement, some suppliers are willing to sell them to the general public. This is legal in most places. Whether or not the formulation or the size is legal in your area is for you to research.

These grenades are generally intended for throwing into confined spaces like a jail cell. The range of their spray isn't great. They obtain maximum coverage when placed vertically (like a bug bomb), but if thrown, will likely only spray in whatever direction they land. They also don't spin around and project the spray in a radial pattern. What it does do outside is create a direct line of spray and can form an irritating aerosol cloud.

Breathing in OC aerosol really sucks; I've done it before on accident. A small dose of it is like instant allergies. I coughed, sneezed, and felt kind of wheezy for a while. It is not even comparable to being properly sprayed in the face. Proper application of pepper spray feels like a much more intense version of the foregoing while having the hottest peppers rubbed on your skin and eyes. The videos of OC training are *not* an exaggeration.

Personal Protective Equipment (PPE), including goggles and masks—preferably gas masks—is suggested when using pepper spray. The area you deploy the spray (or gas) from is called your "release line" which should be *upwind* of the crowd so any wind increases dispersion on them. Check wind direction and speed indicators like flags or trees waving in the breeze to know which way the wind is blowing.

Note that with chemical/irritant agents, the crowd can avoid the affected areas if you deploy incorrectly. Perhaps the wind is blowing the spray the wrong way or the pepper spray grenade lands in an open area where the crowd can just move away from it. Smoke is a good precursor to irritant grenades or spray to judge the wind and the crowd's reaction. High winds will render area sprays ineffective.

My earlier advice was to deploy these with smoke grenades while yelling "gas" to give the impression tear gas was being used. You might gain a little something with the illusion of white smoke and the reactions of anyone exposed to the OC spray. A smart crowd will figure out it isn't true tear gas, but it's better than nothing. Just remember, what ever is thrown into a crowd can be thrown back on you.

Paintball, airsoft, and

Paintball guns can be a good crowd control weapon. The balls not only hurt to get struck with, but I have been unable to find any instance of anyone dying or having lasting damage done. The worst I can imagine is hitting an eye directly and causing major trauma to it. Paint can be used to "mark" certain individuals. Frozen paintballs have been known to cause a lot more pain. Even pepper [spray] ball products are sold, though bulk pepper balls may only be sold to law enforcement.

Firing paintballs into a crowd could be a good way to cause pain to a crowd and startle them enough to leave the area without causing serious injury. Hoppers of paintball guns can hold hundreds of balls. Specific individuals can be targeted and repeatedly shot until they leave or stop doing whatever bad thing they are doing. Fire could be kept up for a long time with trigger discipline.

Paintball guns may be ideal crowd control weapons. Airsoft guns would be a distant second contender. Airsoft guns often look like very close replicas of firearms and someone may not notice the orange tip, which could lead to a tragic misunderstanding. The pellets are also smaller (6mm), do not leave paint marks, and because of their velocity could cause more significant eye injuries (though any eye impact would probably be immaterial as to what hit it).

Air guns (gas powered weapons that shoot metallic pellets) and BB guns would also go in the category of airsoft guns, but with concerns about worse injuries and greater lethality. In fact, some airguns are powerful enough to kill outright; serious hunters use various calibers of airguns to take game. I would say that airsoft, airguns, and BB guns should *not* be used as crowd control weapons.

Tasers/stun guns

A Taser is not a crowd control device, the same for a stun gun. A Taser shoots two metal probes attached to wires that are supposed to stick into the skin of the subject. The subject then is incapacitated briefly by the electrical current disrupting their ability to move voluntarily (neuro-muscular incapacitation). A stun gun (or Drive Stun mode of a Taser) is just an electrical circuit making contact with a person and causing pain via electrocution.

Each of these weapons are intended for use on individuals or at most two (in two-shot versions). Frequently the probes fail to make proper contact resulting in the need for other forms of force. This is how people get shot after being Tased; the Taser doesn't work and the knife-wielding maniac doesn't stop charging. Both weapons have to make physical contact one way or another with a person's flesh.

Electrical conduction devices are not indicated for crowd control. For civilians, they are intended to either give the victim the chance to run away or cause enough pain to the attacker that the assault ceases. These are very niche weapons and are best left to persons who are unwilling or unable to carry firearms but who may be attacked in the course of daily life.

Lights and lasers

Bright lights work as non-lethal weapons by disorienting someone through temporarily blinding them and producing that deep sense of discomfort one gets when staring at the sun. Lights also have the advantage of aiding identification and denying the cover of darkness.[25]

When I say blinding lights, I mean super bright spotlights at close range, like millions of candlepower. The handheld spotlights that can produce truly blinding levels of light usually have to be connected to power, like a 12 volt socket. Of course, as a counter measure all someone has to do is close their eyes and turn their head, but the light can disorient someone.

Ever get approached by a cop at night and he shined his flashlight directly into your eyes? It's annoying, isn't it? That is deliberate. As the cop enters fighting distance, a quick blinding with the flashlight will disorient a potential attacker and may give him some sort of night blindness. If the guy is about to pull a weapon, the involuntary reaction to blink, look away, and shield his eyes could buy the officer some time.

Strobe flashlights can also be used to disorient people. The strobing effect of the rapidly flashing light produces disorientation, although I believe this effect is only good for a short period of time, such as buying you an extra three seconds to shoot an armed suspect in a hallway. The effect of the light throws him off so he has to react to that before he can press his attack. We've seen these lights in 2020's riots, on both sides, and I'm not really impressed. You need to be close

---

[25] See SINCC under the section regarding flashlights, described in the "Firearms."

and it needs to be very dark for these things to have maximum effect.

Lasers are another good tool. The little red dot of a weapon laser can be a persuasive tool when you can shoot but don't want to. To someone who sees the laser and doesn't have a death wish, it is a picture in a thousand words moment warning them "back off or die." For the best effect, the subject needs to believe you have a weapon pointed at them. If you want to bluff them, you can get a laser pointer and hope it works. Otherwise, it might serve as a final, non-verbal warning to "stop or get shot."

More powerful lasers have already been used by rioters against law enforcement, most notably in Portland. Law enforcement officers have sustained serious eye injuries and possible permanent vision loss from these lasers, usually high-power blue or green lasers. Class III lasers, high power ones, are typically not easily available to American civilians. While blinding lasers might have a place, remember blinding someone is mayhem which often carries a very long prison sentence in most states.

Be aware that the crowd could use these lasers against you. Damage can be done before you can close your eyes and turn away, so special laser protection glasses are required. These are expensive and have to be purchased for specific color lasers and wavelengths.

Sound

Major police agencies like NYPD have sound-projection devices call LRAD, or Long Range Acoustic Device. These are basically specially designed loudspeakers that send out a focused beam of deafening sound, an alarm like tone, to basically annoy a crowd and cause ear pain. You're not getting one of these. The best you can do is a megaphone or a vehicle mounted loudspeaker. You might be able to annoy a particularly unenthusiastic mob with a megaphone's siren, but I doubt it would do anything beyond that. The two advantages to a megaphone I see are the ability to give warnings to the crowd and alert your neighbors rapidly.

Fire hoses

How far do you want to go? Get yourself a fire hydrant hose adaptor so you can attach a fire hose directly to the hydrant without a fire pumper. Water pressure will be that of your underlying water system, which may vary. Hose attachments may also reduce water pressure. However, the stream will be far more powerful than your garden hose and reach further. Spraying down an unruly crowd will surely dampen their spirits (pardon the pun).

If you do this, learn how to use a fire hydrant, specifically the type in your area, and get the proper equipment, including wrenches, adaptors, hoses, and nozzles. All of this may come in handy in case the fire department is unable to respond to put out any fires.

This will not come without serious consequences. You will probably get in trouble for using the fire hydrant without permission and maybe even charged for the water used. Because of the brutal use of fire hoses in the South during the Civil Rights Era, you will be called a racist regardless of who you use the hose against. The comparisons to Birmingham will be inevitable. Make your decisions accordingly.

Shields and protective equipment

Wear a helmet of some sort to protect from thrown objects. A hard hat or bike helmet will do, but if it doesn't have a chinstrap, it can be knocked off. Don't forget ballistic rated eye protection. Consider that your enemy may be well-prepared with helmets, goggles, masks, face and handheld shields.

Shields can be used to protect from blows or flying objects when rescuing someone from the mob or when defensive activities require you to be in within range of thrown objects. You will not be using them to shove rioters except in an emergency, such as a rescue. The shields should be used by dedicated bearers to shelter a downed person or provide cover for weapon bearers against crowd-thrown objects. Not every man is going to, or should, have one. In the event you really need a shield, you should be taking shelter inside or returning fire (lethally or otherwise).

Makeshift riot shields can be made of plywood or OSB with the corners rounded down and a bin pull or other handle added. Sections of 55 gallon plastic barrels are also popular choices. Plexiglass is also sold by the sheet which can be made into a homemade shield. Proper use of shields should be learned and practiced; tutorials are available online.

Batons and melee weapons?

Going hand-to-hand with anyone should be a last resort. You are not a riot cop who is going to beat someone badly enough that they will want to run away. Chances are, if they are going hand-to-hand with you, they can probably kick your butt. Also, in the situations you might apply a baton or something to drive a crowd off, it would probably be illegal to smack the participants.

I see batons as something that can be easily snatched away and used on you. Using clubs or other melee weapons are suited for physically fit, trained fighters. Hand-to-hand combat is essentially individual combat, but in numbers, and your side will probably be outnumbered. Also using melee type weapons will likely cause serious or fatal injuries, so why not just use firearms or get out of there, if things are at that level? You're not a Viking.

Using handguns to pistol-whip someone or the butt of a long-gun to butt-stroke someone are both terrible ideas. If you *must* employ strikes of any type, save it for a last-resort in a dire situation and practice muzzle strikes with a rifle or shotgun instead. Bayonets can be used to move the crowd back in a life threatening emergency as well. All of this is a last-resort, WROL contingency.

Fighting and Combat in a Suburb

Cover vs. concealment

If it can be seen, it can be hit. If it can be hit, it can be killed. If **you** can be seen, **you** can be hit. If **you** can be hit, **you** can be **killed**. *Concealment* is something that hides you from view, thus the root word of *conceal*. Concealment typically does not provide protection from bullets. *Cover* is something that can protect you from penetrating gun fire.

Concealment examples: smoke, shadows, bushes, shrubbery, brush, trees (even if they are thick), vehicles, and most suburban construction. Concealment *can* deflect bullets, but it will not stop them. For instance, shooting through thick brush or foliage may cause bullets to miss, but if you are on the receiving end of fire, don't count on it.

Remember you can shoot (or be shot) through concealment. A bad guy may conceal himself behind a bush. Just because you can't see him doesn't mean that he isn't there or that your bullets won't hit him. If you need to kill someone and they are hiding behind something, odds are you can try shooting through it. Cinder blocks appear to be solid and capable of stopping bullets, but they aren't.

One example of this is from an instructor of mine who received a shot from a suspect from behind a cinder block wall. My instructor knew where the suspect was hiding and shooting from, so my instructor fired his .357 Magnum through the wall. His first shots cracked the hollow blocks and the remaining four hit and killed the shooter. Various sources have reported that anything smaller than 9mm will not seriously damage cinder block, but multiple shots from larger calibers may damage the block sufficiently to penetrate.

If you are shooting from inside a building, don't do it right from the door or window. Stand back a ways inside where you will disappear into the darkness or the shadows. Use the shadows inside the building to your advantage.

Cover examples: lots of earth, solid rock, reinforced concrete, solid brick buildings, and thick steel. In your neighborhood, this may be walls built out of solid brick or rock. Outside of things like ditches or other geographic features, there is very little true cover in most residential areas.

Your suburban home will not offer true cover. The best you can hope for in a stucco or siding and wood home is great deflection and energy depletion of bullets. That is why getting low and far away from where bullets might come from is vital. Luck plays a part here and anything in the way of a bullet before it reaches the cover you are hiding behind gives you a better chance of survival.

The Marine Corps has the following to say regarding weapon penetration in urban areas. The most likely threat will be from the AR-15's 5.56mm round.

b. Weapon Penetration. The penetration that can be achieved with a 5.56-mm round depends on the range to the target and the type of material being fired against. Single 5.56-mm rounds are not effective against structural materials (as opposed to partitions) when fired at close range—the closer the range, the less the penetration.

(1) For the 5.56-mm round, maximum penetration occurs at 200 meters. At ranges of less than 25 meters, penetration is greatly reduced. At 10 meters, penetration by the M16 round is poor as a result of the tremendous stress placed on this high-speed round, which causes it to yaw upon striking a target. Stress causes the projectile to break up, and the resulting fragments are often too small to penetrate.

(2) Even with reduced penetration at short ranges, interior walls made of thin wood paneling, sheetrock, or plaster offer no protection against 5.56-mm rounds. Common office furniture such as desks and chairs cannot stop these rounds, but a layer of books 18 to 24 inches thick can.

(3) Wooden-framed buildings and single cinder-block

walls offer little protection from 5.56-mm rounds. When clearing such structures, Marines must ensure that friendly casualties do not result from rounds passing through walls, floors, or ceilings.[26]

7.62mm rounds have greater energy and greater penetration, but at short ranges tend to exhibit penetration characteristics similar to 5.56. 9mm and other pistol bullets will have even less energy to penetrate. Regardless of the caliber, it should be assumed that all bullets will penetrate anything other than substantial cover or correctly rated body armor for that caliber.

Despite what movies show, vehicles will not protect you. Most automobile body panels are very thin sheet steel. 5.56 rounds will typically penetrate at least half of a vehicle (bad for occupants) and may penetrate out the other side. Only the engine block will stop bullets, with the area directly behind the wheels slightly safer than the rest of the car. If you are forced to use a car for cover, try and do so with the vehicle lengthwise so that the maximum amount of glass and body is between you and the shooter.

As little true cover there is in a neighborhood, use anything and everything to your advantage. We've heard stories about people being shot in their pocket Bible or whatever and surviving. Putting part of your body behind a fire hydrant is better than nothing. Put whatever you can in between you and the bad guy. Perhaps the bullet will be deflected by a bush or chainlink fence enough to miss you.

---

[26] USMC, Military Operations on Urbanized Terrain (MOUT), MCWP 3-35.3, 1998, pp. B3-4

Take the chance a doorjamb or heavy grill will deflect the bullet rather than nothing.

Bullet penetration of suburban homes

Several formal and informal studies of the bullet resistance of homes have been done. The results show that while homes aren't truly "invisible" to bullets, their ballistic resistance is not enough to provide comfortable protection against aimed fire or "lucky" stray rounds.

Gun bloggers performed tests with typical home defense weapons. This was against the individual construction elements (bricks and boards) and not an actual building or simulated wall. Tested against gypsum drywall (Sheetrock), .22 LR cartridges penetrated eight inches, while higher velocity and larger calibers, like .22 Magnum or 9mm and .45, penetrated up to 12 inches. Note that each panel is usually 5/8ths of an inch thick.

Against cinder block, only bullets larger than 9mm caused structural damage. It took multiple shots to crack the block. One .357 Magnum round would "chunk" the brick and multiple rounds caused the brick to fail.

Shotgun slugs easily penetrated drywall and destroyed cinder blocks; shot tended to ricochet off the blocks without causing damage. Buckshot penetrated 12 inches of drywall and birdshot penetrated two inches.[27]

---

[27] Gun-Tests.com, "Handgun Bullets: How Do They Penetrate in Home Materials?", originally published October 13, 2015, updated March 19, 2020, retrieved 06/15/2021. https://www.gun-tests.com/ammo/handgun-

Canadian researchers fired .38 Special, 9mm, and .40 caliber rounds from handguns and found a third to two-thirds loss of velocity after bullets exited a simulated stucco exterior wall. Wood and vinyl siding covered walls caused about a 15% loss of velocity after penetration. Stucco walls were the most durable, which would slow a standard range type bullet down to about half-velocity.[28]

However, bullets traveling at even 500-700 feet per second are deadly. Using the blogger's test data above, a .38 Special round traveling at 700 feet per second penetrated six inches of drywall; more than enough velocity to go through five walls. It is beneficial that interior walls do have studs and wiring inside as well as other household decorations and furniture that could further deflect or slow the bullet.

Rifle bullets, like the ubiquitous AR-15's 5.56mm bullet, actually penetrates less building materials than handgun bullets, due to the rifle bullet's unique characteristics; yet this is cold comfort. AR-15 bullets penetrated into ballistic gelatin (which simulates human tissue) about seven inches or a third of the distance that handgun bullets did after penetrating a typical interior wall. Pistol bullets went in about 20 inches.[29] Seven inches of penetration would easily cause serious injuries or death to someone on the other side of the wall.

The Blog *Box O'Truth* found that 5.56 rounds "deviated so much from its course after the first wall, that it was *almost* impossible to hit the other walls to test penetration." So they

---

bullets-how-do-they-penetrate-in-home-materials-4/

[28] R. W. Schiefke, Canadian Police Research Centre, TR-11-09 "Penetration of Exterior House Walls by Modern Police Ammunition," October 1997.

[29] Gary K. Roberts, "The Wounding Effects of 5.56MM/.223 Law Enforcement General Purpose Shoulder Fired Carbines Compared with 12 GA. Shotguns and Pistol Caliber Weapons Using 10% Gelatin as Tissue Simulant," *Would Ballistics Review,* Vol. 3 No. 4, 1998

built bigger wall panels and standard M193 bullets went through four drywall panels. Insulation made no difference, but for 5.56 rounds, the air gap of a room may make a difference.[30]

Their tests show that the bullets "keyholed" or turned sideways as they tumbled in flight end over end (after penetration), making the eponymous mark. The air gap of a room means more time to tumble and lose velocity. However, these walls were simulated interior walls spaced ten feet apart, not exterior walls. Velocity was not recorded, but death or injuries can't be excluded from probability of a bullet that made it through.[31]

A video from Paul Harrell, an ex-US Army marksman, demonstrated that .30 Carbine and 5.56mm bullets penetrated a simulated exterior walls of wood sheathing, plywood, and drywall, firing *first* through four panels of drywall before the exterior wall was contacted. He also noted the 5.56 rounds keyholing.[32]

A Canadian study found that .223 (5.56) and .308 bullets went through one simulated typical stucco wall. The .223 bullet was believed to have fragmented through the wall while the .308 bullet retained sufficient energy to wound or kill. 12 gauge buckshot was stopped while the slugs penetrated easily. Tests against vinyl siding walls showed the bullets going through both walls, when shot at a corner. 9mm and .40 pistol

---

[30] [30] The Box O' Truth, "#14 – Rifles, Shotguns, and Walls," undated, retrieved 6/15/21, https://www.theboxotruth.com/the-box-o-truth-12-insulated-walls/

[31] The Box O' Truth, "#14 – Rifles, Shotguns, and Walls," undated, retrieved 6/15/21, https://www.theboxotruth.com/the-box-o-truth-14-rifles-shotguns-and-walls/

[32] Paul Harrell, YouTube, March 1, 2020, retrieved 6/15/21, https://www.youtube.com/watch?v=Qw8IiRgSMFQ

bullets also penetrated the wall.

Clay and concrete bricks (solid) exhibited strong bullet resistance. Large-caliber high-velocity hunting rounds (7mm-.30 caliber) created holes and cracks but did not penetrate. This is consistent with US military testing that multiple rounds centered in one place were required to penetrate solid blocks.[33]

What does all this mean? The further away from where the shooter is, the better chance of survival you have. That is why I recommend that anyone taking cover inside the house do so furthest away from the street or wherever the shooter outside is. More material means more energy loss to the bullet and a greater chance for it to be deflected.

A typical home has all sorts of stuff in and on the walls, plus furniture and decorations, which might make a bullet go in a harmless direction. On the other hand, random chance could send it into you. For someone at the back of the house, down low, a stray bullet is not much of a danger. Intentional, aimed fire is, however.

The greatest danger is a bullet going through a window and continuing undeflected through multiple interior walls. Many people killed in drive-by shootings of homes were struck when bullets passed through windows.

- Homes with solid brick veneers or walls offer the highest bullet resistance.
- Stucco walled homes offer the second highest resistance, but bullets that penetrate can still kill.
- Siding covered walls offer very poor bullet resistance.

---

[33] Scott D. Kashuba, et al., *Resistance of Exterior Walls to High Velocity Projectiles*, Canadian Masonry Institute, Jan. 2001.

- Insulation offers no protective value but an airgap (a room) can cause 5.56 bullets to keyhole.
- Bullets fired inside the house can travel through the entire structure if not deflected.
- Things inside the home may cause bullets to be deflected instead of hitting someone.
- Stray bullets present a low level of danger but their danger is through their randomness.
- The velocity loss exhibited by stucco walls (most common in the Southwest) show that soft body armor has a benefit inside the home against some types of bullets.

Expedient cover

The Marine Corps found that the following common items will stop a 5.56 round fired at less than 50 meters[34]:

- One thickness of sandbags;
- 2-inch concrete wall;
- A 55-gallon drum filled with water or sand;
- An ammunition can filled with sand;
- A cinder block filled with sand (they note the block will likely shatter);
- A brick veneer; and,
- A car body (the bullet will penetrate but usually not exit).

Sandbags are the preferred method of creating cover where there is none. Laying in a supply of them may be a prudent investment. Otherwise, using earth in any sort of container will provide bullet resistance. You could use soil in garbage cans, plastic totes, or even in stacked plastic grocery bags. Cardboard boxes would work as long as the

---

[34] Ibid.

soil is dry. Other materials may be books, appliances, and furniture, but these will not provide the same level of bullet resistance as soil.

If steel sheeting is used, such as repurposed road trench plates, the metal should be at least ¼" to ½" thick and placed in combination with other materials. Bags of concrete can be stacked and used dry like sandbags or thoroughly wetted to set. Note that set bags of concrete will need demolition to be removed. Sections of sidewalks can also be broken and pried up by panel or in chunks.

Vehicles can be used as expedient cover preferably in combination with other cover. In front of a house, consider parking vehicles lengthwise in front to minimize through penetration. If possible, deflate the tires or remove the wheels entirely so the vehicles are flat against the ground. Dumpsters can be used as cover also, but preferably loaded with dense material. Thick trees can be cut down, sectioned, and stacked or layered to create a barrier.

It may be difficult to ensure total cover using expedient materials. Cover should be placed to offer shelter from the direction most likely to receive fire. Inadequate cover or concealment can be used in combination with expedient cover. Camouflage techniques can be employed to make inadequate cover appear more substantial to lure any shooters to fire in other places.

Inside a home with no basement, a designated safe area should be created with cover high enough for adults to comfortably lay or sit down. This area should be furthest away from the expected area of fire, such as the front of the house, and on the ground floor. During gunfire, residents can take shelter in this area.

Movement from behind cover

If you have to move, bound from cover to cover. Don't zig-zag, just run as fast as you can. Movement should only be done to seek better cover, to give yourself a better firing position, or to escape being in the direct line of fire unprotected. If you are safe and under cover, stay put. Pick where you are going to move to *before* you get up and move. Behind cover, you are better off in a semi-crouch, ready to jump up and move, then going prone. Always stay low to the ground when moving or in the open.

Take quick peeks by only exposing your eyes, rather than parts of your body. Peeks should be taken from low level, like under cars or from knee level or anything other than just standing up and popping your head out. If shooting from behind cover, expose as little of the body as possible.

For the 90% of us right handed people, if you have to shoot around cover to the left, shoot from your left side. When firing from behind cover, shoot so that the least amount of your body is exposed. As most people are right handed, when shooting around cover to the left, shoot left-handed so only half of your body and head is exposed.

Breaking contact

When breaking contact, fire a large volume of shots to

cover your retreat. Your goal should be to force the bad guy to stop shooting and put his head down so you can run away. If you can do this in sequence as a team covering each other, great. Fire a full magazine (aiming the best you can) before you peel off or while your buddy is doing so. Smoke can be used to conceal your movement as well (see discussion on smoke grenades in the "Riot and Crowd Control" chapter). Don't try to zig-zag; run as fast as you can straight for cover.

Snipers

A sniper in this context is any shooter that has concealed himself and is able to dominate an area, not necessarily a military-quality sniper. The shooter may be a good shot and adept at hiding or they may merely be hidden from view and taking potshots on easy targets. These may be trained shooters, hunters, ex-military, or just someone armed with a rifle.

Their goal may be to kill, prepare an area for an assault by other forces, or just to terrorize. The latter was the goal of the DC Beltway snipers in the early 2000s and a major motive for the notorious shooters of Sarajevo's sniper alley.

Your neighborhood security force may be confronted with shooters attempting to kill anyone manning a barricade. This is probably the most likely sniper scenario. Imagine walking out to confront a small group who are loudly demanding food or something, only to be shot at by an unseen gunman. As you are wounded, trying to take cover, or are looking for a target to return fire, the crowd draws guns and/or overwhelms you.

For this kind of problem, the best solution is that all members of your team disperse themselves. No one stands within a few yards of each other; make a sniper's task of re-aiming harder. A marksman or covering shooter stays concealed, behind cover, ready to return fire should you be shot at. An ideal situation is that your team members are behind cover themselves and there are extra men who can drag any injured persons to safety.

The more a sniper shoots, the greater the chance of locating them. Unsophisticated snipers will likely remain in place and continue to fire rather than take a single, well-aimed shot and leave the area. For the average urban troublemaker, they will likely shoot rapidly at all targets they can see and their positions are probably not going to be well-concealed.

Indications of a sniper's position may be a rifle muzzle pointing out of a window or gap, the muzzle flash, or dust kicked up from the shot. In an urban environment, gunshots will echo off of buildings and it will sound like the shooting is coming from everywhere. Locating where a shot was fired from is difficult to do by hearing alone. Even in training, the effect of a sniper shot can be terrifying because you do not know where it came from.

Your first reaction will probably be to duck or run for cover. There may be a moment of disbelief where you think "Is someone shooting at me?" or "Someone just shot at me!" You should get to cover next, not try to return fire, especially blindly.

To reduce collateral damage, return fire should only be

sent when the sniper is positively located. Do not shoot at a sniper without being able to positively identify his location and identity. You may harm innocent people in the line of fire. If you must use suppressive fire, take note of what collateral targets may be in the area of the suspected sniper's location. Suppressing fire could be used to keep the sniper down while anyone who is exposed removes themselves to cover.

To escape the line of fire and get behind cover, use concealment to your advantage. Hide in shadows or move behind objects that will protect you from view. Smoke grenades can hide your movement or at least when you initially start your run for cover. Don't try to zig-zag. Two persons running at once will give each person 50/50 odds.

For minimally trained personnel, counter-sniper assaults are not recommended. If you can see the sniper and shoot him from cover, that is one option, but you should take pains to make sure you are better hidden than he is. Otherwise, snipers should be assaulted from behind or the sides, known as a flank attack. Never attack within their line of fire.

Snipers on the perimeter

Another disturbing complication would be snipers shooting from outside your perimeter into houses. Houses that have a side facing your defensive perimeter would be most vulnerable to snipers targeting people in windows. Shots could be deliberate, random, or simply poorly aimed fire. In a civil war that sees a residential area become a battlefield, perimeter homes (especially the second floor) would be at the greatest risk of taking gunfire. Residents should be on the ground floor and, if necessary, evacuated to shelter in homes at the center of the defensive perimeter.

Dispersion

No two or more persons should stand so closely together that a single burst from a gunman could hit both. This goes for grenades, IEDs, and Molotov cocktails. Spread out, at least six feet apart. During darkness or inclement weather, there is a natural tendency to bunch up. Humans also like to be closer together and make eye contact when talking. Always have someone watch your back. If you are speaking, stand face to face and both of you watches behind each other.

WROL gunfights

In a WROL scenario, things are kill or be killed. You may need to proactively address potential threats in ways not permissible under justifiable homicide laws. Responses to violence that would be considered excessive in civil times may be necessary just to survive the encounter.

An example would be that in an attack on your neighborhood, you don't attack just those that are immediately shooting at you, but any "bad guy" with a weapon, even if they are running away. Someone who survives the fight today may return tomorrow with a badder attitude, more people, and more determination to finish you off.[35] A response to an attack not only has to fend off the attack but has to deal a decisive blow to your enemy that ideally prevents any further attacks through decimation of their manpower and morale as well as demonstrating your strength.

A well-conducted defense has an immeasurable psychological impact when dealing defeat to an enemy. You want them to be so demoralized and scared that they don't come back. Word can even get around that Maple Street is not a place to mess around.

If freed from the duty to let the other guy start the fight (as is required under law now), persons who you can actually say are going to attack you can be engaged first. If it's your life or theirs, seize the advantage and take them out. An example is that now, under the law, if a man approaches you aggressively and says "I'm gonna kill you," you can't just shoot him. He could be bluffing. WROL, taking the chance to see if he is serious is stupid, so you would be morally justified to shoot him.

Ambushes are defeated by soldiers who turn and run into the ambush putting down a massive amount of firepower. A surprise or in-force attack on your neighborhood should be handled the same way. Anyone who is willing to engage in combat comes out and fights hard. The more guns, the better. The tide has to be turned before the bad guys get into the street. House to house fights are hard and

---

[35] Shooting people in the back is poor form and if things are not totally WROL, could come back to haunt you. A judicious appraisal of the situation has to be made and the potential repercussions of allowing attackers to escape versus shooting them. Actions that could be seen as "unfair" by an opponent's group may be grounds for revenge upon you.

you may lose against an enemy who has been doing this week after week.

One technique would be to hold the attackers off at a barricade while the rest of your neighborhood's combatants respond. Once the planned response is in place, you could allow the enemy to come into a pre-designated kill zone and neutralize them there.

Machine guns

Some Americans legally own machine guns. For those who don't know, a $200 tax stamp and months-long FBI background check is done. Registered fully automatic weapons also cost thousands to tens of thousands of dollars because the supply was artificially limited by stopping legal civilian manufacture in 1986.[36] A machine gun is defined as any firearm that fires more than one bullet for each pull of the trigger. Fully automatic fire is when the gun fires as long as the trigger is continuously depressed.

There are some simulated rapid-fire devices out there that aren't machine guns but dramatically increase the rate of fire to be near analogous to full-auto. Bumpfire stocks were a popular workaround until the October 1, 2017, Mandalay Bay shooting prompted the ATF to ban them. Binary triggers or trigger cranks are legal as of this writing in many states.

Fully automatic fire generally isn't useful in civilian contexts and has limited military application. A real problem with full-auto is "spray and pray" where the shooter just holds

---

[36] This refers to registerable, transferable machine guns.

down the trigger and fires in the general direction of the enemy until the magazine runs empty. Especially in an urban area, every shot needs to be carefully placed. Rapid semi-auto fire will serve just as well in nearly all situations as full-auto fire will.

The problem is that unless the gun is heavy and mounted, the recoil of the constant firing will affect aim. Full-auto is useful when firing from a mounted machine gun to deny an area to the enemy or put down suppressive fire. Handheld full-auto can be used by a trained shooter to attack bunched up groups or in a small area, like a hallway.

There are more military uses, but in a civilian context, the only time you would typically use full-auto is when you are about to be overrun. This is known as "final protective fire" and military units use this when they need to use everything at their disposal to halt an attack or die, such as a human wave attack.

In very rare circumstances would a machine gun be beneficial over a semi-automatic rifle. Most attackers will be so undisciplined that any mass or accurate gunfire will stop them. A machine gun is likely to turn self-defense into a massacre rather than be needed in a one-in-a-million engagement. So, for reasons like cost, ammo consumption, limited utility, and the possibility of overkill, I don't think a machine gun is a necessary tool.

Fields of fire

When it comes to a potential gun battle, I don't

suggest you array yourself on a perimeter to gun down whoever is coming. This work is not intended to teach people how to do battle using small unit tactics against an armed and organized enemy.

The basics of a field of fire is that each person has an area, called a sector, that he is responsible for covering and shooting enemies in. These slightly overlap with the next guy. In practical terms, Bob and Tim are on the south end of the block. Bob watches the southeast corner and Tim handles the southwest corner. They both cover the central area where the street continues down towards the park. Or you cover the right hand side of the street and the guy who lives in the house on the left covers the left hand side of the street, both sharing responsibility for the area facing the street between the two houses.

Chances are you're not going to have a bunch of guys to put out, so the major consideration here is safety. I would boil this down to *shoot* and *no-shoot* zones. Your **no-shoot zone** would be in a direction you absolutely don't want to shoot; such as towards your barricade where your buddies are at. **Shoot zones** are the places where you are free to fire.

Everyone should have a defined field of fire that slightly overlaps with others, if possible. Individuals in their position can make discreet field of fire markers to limit where they shoot. Danger zones, such as occupied homes, need to be identified and clearly communicated.

In a typical suburb, your options are kinda limited here. So the basic firearm safety rules are the best guide to a bunch of bad options. Know your target and what lies beyond it. Your backdrop is the area where your bullet would fall if it wasn't stopped by what you are shooting at; on a range, this is the backstop.

If you fire a shot, you are taking a calculated risk. First, that the risk to *not* shooting the bad guy is worse than what your bullet *might* hit if it goes stray. That is, if you don't shoot him, a good guy will be seriously hurt or killed. Second, is the target standing in front of innocent people, or at least people you don't want to shoot? Maybe there is a garage, a yard, or the unoccupied part of a house behind them where if your shot misses, it is not as likely to kill someone in a house as if the bad guy was in front of a bedroom window.

"What about ambushes?" Again, we're not teaching infantry tactics here. If you want to learn about how to ambush people in a Mad Max scenario, find another book. A fatal funnel is basically an area where there is no cover and anyone in that area can easily be shot. An alley is a good example of this. You can turn the roadway portion of your street into an idea like this, but of course any attacker could take cover against the houses.

If you have the ability, you can create a "kill zone" just outside of your barricade. Any attacker or intruder who doesn't heed challenges or becomes violent could be shot in this area with relative safety to the surroundings. Pick this area carefully and consider placing obstacles to funnel anyone into the ideal spot in case you need to shoot. Clear any landscaping, brush, or other objects that make it harder for you to see bad guys and easier for them to hide behind.

When the shooting starts, think of where people will run and how they will hide, considering the paths of least resistance first. What areas might they hide behind and shoot from? Is there a brick house with a perfect little court yard someone could take pot shots at your checkpoint from?

If you have a tall house with a good view over the neighborhood, or even a hill that's nearby, consider putting an observer up there. Is there a good hunter or shooter in your neighborhood? Put him up there as a sniper. The high-ground advantage should be obvious.

Avoiding friendly fire

Neighbors should identify themselves through a particular piece of clothing, armband, or something else as discussed elsewhere. Everyone should understand where each other will be, at least generally. Non-combatants and uninvolved civilians should be told to shelter in place when gunfire is expected.

Kill zone (engagement zone)

Kill zones, or engagement zones, are anywhere you will encounter the enemy and use force on them. These zones are established to your advantage (versus fighting it out wherever). This is likely to be the entrance to your neighborhood or the end of the street, just beyond any barrier or perimeter you've established. You don't have to kill people here, but it may be your containment area for protesters, rioters, and looters. If you must use riot control weapons against them, it's best that they be in one concentrated area.

A kill zone:

- Is a trap but is designed so that it doesn't look like one.

- Can take advantage of existing geography, such as a large open area with no cover.
- Channels enemy movement to where the defender wants the enemy and restricts movement in that area.
- Does not provide cover or concealment to the enemy (nowhere to run or hide).
- Reduces (not eliminates) the need to defend in force an entire perimeter.
- Can be protected by you from covered positions.
- Has a free field of fire (no occupied homes or other collateral targets in the background).

Your engagement zone essentially puts the enemy where you want them so as to most easily observe and engage them. Like a good trap, it seems ideal to your opponent but isn't. An example of this would be setting up your barricade at the entrance to a neighborhood using the large intersection outside as the kill zone, strategically planting "disabled" vehicles and debris in the road to funnel attackers to the clear area where you want them to be.

Fighting from the yard

If you have to fall back to the house, you will have much greater mobility and fields of fire outside rather than in. By being outside, you can also direct any incoming gunfire away from where your family is. Don't stand right out front. Stay behind cover if you have it, preferably somewhere in the yard at an angle so you have maximum coverage of where your enemy is expected to come from. When using the house as concealment, try to stay on the sides of the house and fire from around the corners.

When coming or looking around corners, take a peek at ground level, only exposing your head as far as your eyes.

To go around a corner (to "clear it"); slice the pie. Bring your weapon up to eye level so you are looking through or over the sights (for faster target acquisition if you must shoot) and back away from the corner so you aren't right up on the edge to get a better view. Slowly come around the corner, checking out each area that becomes visible as you come around. Imagine taking the corner in angled sections like cutting one slice of a pie after another.

Stopping a vehicle with gunfire

You may face a situation where you need to stop a vehicle with gunfire. This is not likely to be effective with the weapons you will have access to and physical means to bar vehicle passage is preferred.

Never shoot at a vehicle when you can just as easily run out of the way. Stopping to shoot a vehicle or slowing down enough to shoot accurately on the move just makes you a target. It is *very* difficult to disable, or kill the driver, of a moving vehicle. Even if you do, the car has momentum (mass x acceleration) and will not stop instantly. Shooting at a vehicle should only be done to stop an imminent threat to life.

Do not attempt to shoot out the tires of a vehicle. It is easy to miss such a small target, especially if the vehicle is moving, and stray bullets can do unintended damage. Focus on shooting into the engine block with a large-caliber rifle, preferably a semi-automatic 7.62mm or .308 or larger. A large volume of fire may be necessary to compensate for misses, bullets striking non-vital components, and the energy of the bullets failing to deliver incapacitating damage. A .50 caliber bullet in the engine block will usually instantly disable a vehicle, but most people don't have a 50-cal. A giant M82 Barrett is not the kind of thing you can just shoulder, aim, and fire at a car in a hurry.

Chances are, you will need to expend multiple magazines to inflict enough damage to the vehicle that a vital component is damaged. You probably *won't* penetrate the engine block, but will certainly puncture the radiator, destroy the battery, and perhaps the alternator. The car may not be stopped before it does damage, but it will be non-functional without major repairs.

The main way to disable a vehicle by gunfire, particularly with *a lot* of fire, is that the driver is hit or is too intimidated to keep coming. Remember, if you're shooting, you're shooting to kill and you just might do that. So don't shoot at a car unless you're willing to kill the driver and any passengers, either intentionally or not.

Shooting outside

Experiences in urban combat demonstrate that most gunfights are relatively short-range, even between rifle equipped adversaries. Shooting will occur at distances below 300 yards and often well under 100 yards. Studies of infantry engagements show that the vast majority happen under 300 yards (90%) with 80% being under 200 yards. On an average suburban street, block length is typically not more than 200 yards (your neighborhood may vary).

The effective range for an AR-15 or AK-47 type rifle well exceeds this distance. A shotgun will be effective to 60-75 yards using slugs. Pistol caliber carbines will be effective within about 200 yards, if equipped with a 16" barrel. Most shooters will be effective with a handgun out to 50 yards.[37] Long-range scopes aren't necessary. A simple red dot scope without magnification is probably going to be sufficient.

Remember, there is a decent likelihood you will be shooting at very short ranges; perhaps 100 feet or so (2-3 houses away). Your enemies will probably be closing the distance to attack your home or will be such inept shots that they have to be close to make hits. Nonetheless, never underestimate your enemy. Assume he can shoot as well as you can or better.

Though it was said earlier, in a gunfight in urban areas, gunshots will echo making locating a shooter by sound very difficult and may create the illusion of multiple shooters. You are vulnerable to snipers or even being casually picked off, especially if there are a lot of places for an enemy to hide.

You will need to utilize cover and concealment effectively. There will be a lot of concealment in your neighborhood. Concealment is what can hide you but can't stop bullets (shrubbery and cars). Take into consideration the nature of vegetation where you live. Newer neighborhoods in Las Vegas or Phoenix aren't going to have a lot of trees or bushes, but 30+ year old neighborhoods in Sacramento or St. Louis are veritable forests.

---

[37] Note that for all weapons, the range at which a bullet is deadly will probably be far greater than any distance you will be aiming within. Generally, 1,000-2,000 yards are required for safe shooting.

Cover is going to be sparser than concealment, but depending on how your neighborhood was built, you may have things like retaining walls and terrain features to hide behind. However, one should take caution because many residential outdoor walls are often built out of hollow blocks that are not very bullet-resistant.

Being mindful of the direction you are shooting is as important as what is behind you. Remember, you might be shooting towards an empty boulevard but your enemy could be shooting at your house with your family inside.

Shooting and fighting at night

When shooting at night, the tendency is to aim high, sending shots harmlessly over the head of your target. Hold low. Low shots are much more likely to hit than missing high. Even a leg shot can be disabling. The "snap" sound of bullets hitting the ground add an additional psychological impact which is greater than the "whizz" of a miss.

Your shots will be seen as bright muzzle flashes by your enemy. This will cause your enemy to shoot at the flash, so move after taking a shot.[38] Invest in a quality flash suppressor for your weapon. Many variations exist and some do a better job than others, for instance the flash being the size of a cigarette cherry versus a flaming basketball. This will help preserve your night vision from flash blindness. Muzzle brakes *are not* flash suppressors. You can also use a suppressor

[38] Conversely you should fire at muzzle flashes for a higher probability of a hit or at least to provide suppressing fire.

(silencer) to get the same effect.

If one man has night vision, he can fire exclusively tracers from his rifle to designate targets. Everyone shoots at where the tracers are aiming. Some tracers do not illuminate at close range but need 50-100 yards to begin to burn. This is so that soldiers using them do not give away their firing point. Tracers can also have a psychological effect to bolster morale on your side and weaken your enemy.

Be aware that at night you will be silhouetted against any lighter backdrop. At ground level, this would be standing out as a dark shape in front of a light colored wall, fence, or building. Stick to the shadows and dark backgrounds when standing or moving. When an observer below you looks up and sees your dark figure against a lighter sky (the sky is always lighter than the ground), this is called sky-lining.

Often at night, you can see someone moving around because of the contrast of their shadowy figure on the lighter background, or if against the sky, stars or lights disappearing and reappearing. If you are elevated above a potential observer, be careful that you don't skyline yourself. Cross ridgetops or hills below the crest so your backdrop is the ground and not the sky. On rooftops one may have to crouch or crawl.

Be familiar with what your area looks like at night. Don't just drive the area, walk it. Walk the neighborhood streets and arterial roads. Walk those pedestrian or bike paths and in the woods, fields, or hills that surround your area. If you can do it during a power outage on a dark night, even better. Practice walking in the darkness, using only ambient light to navigate (more on this in the "Night Vision" chapter).

Shooting from inside the house

Obvious places to shoot from are windows and doors; this is apparent to someone who is targeting you. Do not stand or kneel directly in front of the openings, nor stick the muzzle of your gun out the opening. Stand back so that you are hidden in the shadows of the room. If you are going prone, put a table in the room and lie down on that. Get stools or other objects to stand on if you need extra height to stick a gun out the window to fire at people directly against the house.

Shooting from the roof is an option to gain height without actually shooting from indoors. This should be done shooting over the hip of the roof, with the body on the downslope that faces away from the line of fire. Parapets should be used if your home has one. Brick chimneys can be used for cover.

Probably the least desirable way to shoot from indoors is cutting a firing port, or loophole. This tears open your roof or wall. Not only does this expose the house to the elements, but typically provides a very narrow field of fire. Cutting a larger opening might as well be another window.

Be careful going outside. Take for instance a mob attack. The mob tosses a Molotov cocktail on your roof. You run out to grab the garden hose and suppress the fire. They shoot and kill you as soon as you expose yourself outside. Snipers may be lying in wait to do the same thing when you emerge for an ordinary chore. You are also vulnerable to being shot through a window if you are silhouetted by a light behind a shade/curtain.

- If your windows do not have a security film, tape X or # patterns on the glass or apply a transparent film to reduce shards if broken or shot out.
- Remove windowpanes from the openings if possible and place them somewhere they are not likely to be hit.
- Use blinds or thin curtains to help conceal you until you are ready to fire, or even shoot through them.
- Emplace sandbags, heavy objects, or appliances at your firing position for cover.
- Get any non-combatants to the ground floor or basement under any improvised cover or evacuate them entirely.
- Keep the inside of the house dark.
- Do not silhouette yourself in front of a door or window.

Marksman

If you have a particularly good shooter among you, consider placing him up high as a designated marksman. He can shoot particularly dangerous threats in the crowd or hold the crowd off if you need to retreat or fall back. The marksman would typically be used as a last resort or in a WROL scenario.

In warfare, snipers have an extreme psychological advantage because they often cannot be seen and seemingly randomly pick people off to die. Homicidal members of the mob that pose a threat can be picked off. Suddenly seeing the badass of the riot drop dead without seeing where the shot came from can take the piss and vinegar out of the crowd and maybe even force them into a panicked retreat.

Marksman rule of engagement:

- Do not fire unless death/serious injury would result to an innocent or team member.
- Do not fire if your shot would hit an innocent (non-rioter) or a friendly neighbor.
- Aim deliberately at specific persons that are a threat to life, i.e. the guy aiming a gun, or the guy who just drew a pistol at the foot of the barricade.
- Shoot those seriously physically assaulting a friendly neighbor.
- As a last resort, shoot at unarmed persons or indiscriminately into the crowd when failing to do so would mean innocents or friendly neighbors would be killed.

Hostages and standoffs

If a bad guy has taken a loved one hostage and tells you to drop your weapon (or anything else), don't comply. The bad guy will most certainly kill you the moment you have disarmed and have his way with the hostage, whatever that will be. Take the shot and fight. The worst that will happen is that you and the hostage both die. The same thing goes if a bad guy gets the drop on you; shoot, never drop your gun. Take the chance because in far too many cases, people that have "trusted" the bad guy not to hurt them died or suffered horribly.

Demands by an armed force

Scenario: You and your neighbors are met at your barricade by a group of armed persons who are asking for goods or services. Perhaps they want food, shelter, weapons, or women. If you give them what they want, they claim they will go away and leave you alone. They openly or implicitly threaten violence if you do not comply.

First note that at least someone within your group will want to comply for the sake of harmony. Do not do this. "We don't negotiate with terrorists," as the saying goes. Acquiescence will be taken as weakness and exploited against you. One demand will lead to another until you have been bled dry.[39] Politely refuse to give in and order the people to leave. Have long-guns out and be prepared to back-up your rejection by force. This is a time to look very tough and intimidating.

I would urge caution regarding shooting them then and there. If they will leave peacefully, why take the risk of a shootout or antagonizing them to come back? You should remain on the lookout and be wary in case they come back in force, try to sneak in, or start sniping at you. On the other hand failing to kill them then and there may just delay the inevitable. Use your judgement.

By the fact that the group is threatening you, rather than just barging in while shooting, you know that they are concerned about self-preservation. Their hope is that a weak group will give in to their threats and intimidation without a fight. Through a show of resolve, you may send these people packing without a battle, like standing up to a bully. Give in and they may milk you like a cow.

The same principal goes for persons claiming authority when authority means nothing, for instance a British soldier

---

[39] For an easily understandable version of this in action, see the children's book by Laura Numeroff, "If You Give a Mouse a Cookie" (Harper Collins).

after 1776 making demands of a new American. The redcoat had no legal authority and could only get and do what he wants through force. If the police and courts have dissolved and aren't coming back, why would you obey a police officer, especially if he is doing something illegal or for his own benefit? A badge and uniform when the government is non-functional is just symbolism for the gun on the man's hip. WROL, you don't need to comply with "authorities" simply because they had government power when the system was functional.

Overrun

What if your side breaks and runs?

Odds are the first time that your group "sees the elephant" they will be unprepared for what they are going to face. Your group will probably lack the experience and resolve to keep the enemy back and subdued enough to avoid a breach of your perimeter. By the time your group deploys crowd control devices (pepper spray, water hose, rubber bullets, etc.), it may be too late.

Let's say the crowd has guns or machetes and is forcing your barricade to burn you out. Shots get fired and/or blood gets spilled. Your neighbors retreat and run for their homes. In virtually every situation where a defensive perimeter is broken, the side that breaks creates a vacuum and open "hole" where the enemy floods in.

Any breakthrough encourages the enemy. It's what they were trying to achieve, after all. Expect to be violently attacked and even killed if this happens, especially if weapons have already been injected into the mix. Where are you going to go and what are you going to do?

Retreating

For a group of rank amateurs against a vicious enemy that is willing to do violence, I would expect that many average folks would wimp out when things got tough. They may be willing to posture and even engage in some light "action," but if things become life threatening, suburbanites might just run away. The most common defensive tactic in urban America is to leave the area, call the police, and lock the doors. Why would this be any different during suburban warfare?

You cannot fight alone. You will have to run and seek shelter. My advice in this case is to go home. In situations that *don't* call for lethal force being used on the crowd, use less-lethal means to cover your retreat, like smoke, pepper spray, and paintballs. Go home, put up the last-second barricades, and prepare to shoot from the house. If shooting has already started and you aren't under cover, fall back to cover behind a wall or in your foxhole. Don't stand out in the open. You may want to consider a secondary fighting point or barricade if your street/neighborhood has the room.

You are temporarily pulling back to get out of the "kill zone" or danger zone to place yourself in a more advantageous position. It is not a loss of face or weakness. It is a tactical movement to better protect yourself. You are not necessarily giving up ground. Don't let false bravery or pride keep you in a dangerous situation that could lead to avoidable violence.

You may need to conduct a limited amount of shooting to stop the people who are attacking you, or might be, and/or shoot your way out. Retreat to your home and button down the hatches tight. Prepare to shoot anyone who tries to breach your house or burn it down. A mob that got shot at may be ready to burn and lynch in revenge.

In a less dangerous situation, such as no one is using weapons, but the crowd is going to beat you up or vandalize your stuff, obviously hold your fire if they break through. Get away. Turn and run if you have to. Hunker down.

Stopping a breakthrough

To stop a breakthrough, you will need to show overwhelming violence of action and inflict as much fear, pain, and death (if warranted) necessary to break their resolve. Think of the mob as nervous cattle stampeding towards you; you want to be so dangerous and terrifying to them that they turn around and run away.

This would be a time to deploy your pepper spray, smoke grenades, flashbangs, and paintballs against the crowd. Fire hoses too. Anything that disorients or slows down the mob makes it harder for them to fight in an organized manner. Induce fear and panic in them.

The good thing is that against untrained, uncommitted individuals a determined use of force can be quite effective. Most attackers will be totally undisciplined, undedicated to any cause, and operating under false bravery fueled by drugs, alcohol, or peer pressure. Sudden, iron resistance can break up and even turn away a breakthrough.

Human instinct is to run away when shooting starts,[40] especially among amateurs. The mob will probably have far less cohesion than you think. Hungry, desperate, or stupid people will not be brave warriors who know that you can't shoot everyone. Only very dedicated and brave attackers will remain when things get kinetic.

Your goal in stopping a swarm attack before you are overrun is to do so early. Cool the heels of the individuals in the vanguard. Drive them back and don't retreat (if possible). Once the vanguard is dealt with, disperse the crowd. Early deterrence of the lead troublemakers disrupts the catalyst that create breakthroughs. Take cover if you must and hold the line. Whether this line is on the street or in your house depends on the exact situation and the legalities you may be facing.

Controlling panic

Your friends may shoot in a panicked retreat, whether this is legal or not. With a cooler head, rapidly assess if you can legally and safely shoot. Shooting indiscriminately into the crowd is not a good idea unless the rule of law has collapsed entirely and there is likely to be no legal repercussions at all (and you can morally stomach such a thing).

Over and over again, we see third world police or soldiers shooting into crowds during riots and protest. It's an ugly sight and it is condemned by governments, the UN, and

[40] This also includes use of less-lethal munitions, but gunfire is the superlative example.

the news anchor bringing us the story. Justified or not, shooting indiscriminately into crowds is *bad*. Even if you are a cold-blooded psychopath who doesn't care, remember that your actions could sway people against you or serve as a cause for revenge. Doing this when this is *necessary* to protect life is discussed elsewhere.

There is a well-known history of panic leading to massacres:

Boston, MA, 1770: Rowdy colonists pelted troops with snowballs and harassed them. A soldier was knocked to the ground, then without orders fired his musket. A scuffle with the officer ensued, after which, the troops fired on the crowd without being ordered to.

Orangeburg, SC, 1968: State troopers who were attacked and thought they were under small arms fire shot into a crowd. 31 casualties resulted.

Kent State University, OH, 1970: National Guard troops dispersing a crowd of war protesters opened fire for reasons undetermined, resulting in 13 casualties and bolstering the anti-war movement.

Torrance, CA, 2013: In the midst of the manhunt for murderer and ex-police officer Christopher Dorner, LAPD on a protection detail shot up a truck of a mother and daughter delivering newspapers. Shortly thereafter, Torrance Police rammed and shot another pickup belonging to a surfer. Neither truck matched the description of Dorner's vehicle.

These are just a sample of high profile incidents where poor discipline and fear resulted in innocent people being shot. In each case, highly agitated soldiers or officers in a tense situation mistook stimuli for actual danger, leading to sympathetic fire from others.

What is sympathetic fire? That's when one person, who is under threat or feels that they are, begins shooting. Other armed persons also begin shooting at whatever the first person lit up. The others do this, not necessarily because they feel that they are in danger, but an unconscious reaction takes over that they too need to suppress the threat. There is also the tendency to assume or imagine an order was given to fire.

Another danger is that if the finger is on the trigger, a sudden start, like a gunshot, can cause the person to jerk and unintentionally pull the trigger. In one instance with a police department in my county, an officer tripped while chasing a suspect and fired a shot. Keep your finger off the trigger until you actually are going to shoot!

In a standoff type of situation with a hostile crowd or group of bandits/looters, an accidental massacre is a real danger. Trigger discipline is absolutely vital. Keep your distance from your opponents and have anyone on your side who is too terrified or emotional to stay calm step back from the line. Lethal force should be used against specific point targets and not indiscriminately if at all possible.

If your side breaks and your barricade is overrun:

- Immediately retreat and run for safety.
- Use overwhelming force (lethal or less-lethal as warranted) to cover your retreat and slow the mob.
- Consider using distraction devices (flashbangs) or pepper spray grenades.
- Shoot only when you absolutely must to survive.

- Don't fire indiscriminately on the crowd unless the overall situation is so far gone you will not be prosecuted and you know you will die otherwise.
- Secure your home and defend the doors and perimeter.

Arson and IEDs

Arson attacks can take many forms. One form might be a brush fire lit surreptitiously behind your home or neighborhood. Buildings may be burned in the middle of the night to deny their use or kill someone inside. One domestic terrorist used a lighter and a can of WD-40 as an improvised blowtorch. Most commonly, we see Molotov cocktails used during unrest and insurrections.

A Molotov cocktail is a glass container filled with a flammable liquid and burning wick inserted. These can be extremely devastating weapons. As an anti-personnel weapon, it would be like dousing someone in gasoline and lighting them on fire. They can easily be thrown against buildings or into other flammable material to start fires rapidly from a distance. Their low cost means that they can be thrown in overwhelming numbers.

Please note, this section goes for other types of firebombs in general. Fireworks launched horizontally into open windows or otherwise into flammable areas could be considered as dangerous as Molotov cocktails.

Self-defense

Generically speaking, states allow the use of deadly force (justifiable homicide) "against one who manifestly intends or endeavors to commit a crime of violence" or "in defense of an occupied habitation." The exact wording and conditions vary (some states require retreat, when possible), but usually the protections are similar. You are allowed to defend yourself or another against someone who is:

- Trying to kill or cause great bodily harm; or while
- Protecting an occupied home against someone trying to do the above.

Arizona is one such state that allows the use of deadly force to prevent arson of an occupied structure (ARS 13-411). Other states have less explicit protections in the case of arson, like Washington (RCW 9A.16.110). Check your state laws.

The reasoning behind shooting an arsonist is what the potential of the fire is. Fire to destroy an unoccupied business may devastate someone's livelihood, but the law frowns upon taking lives merely to protect property.

When it comes to an occupied building, especially a home, in combination with the circumstances, an arson attack has the potential to be deadly. A defense attorney may argue that the arsonist just wanted to destroy the property without hurting anyone, but this is like arguing that "I shot him but I didn't mean to kill him."

An arson terrorist may set your house on fire to:

- Destroy where you live to demoralize you or drive you out of the area;
- To kill you;
- To force you outside for apprehension; or,
- To draw you outside to be ambushed, perhaps by a sniper.

Let's say your house is surrounded by an angry mob for whatever reason. Some in the crowd are armed. Many of them are threatening to beat or kill you. There is no safe escape route. You see a Molotov cocktail being lit and the thrower's arm cocked. You take the shot and hit the thrower, who drops the cocktail, burning him (if the shot didn't kill him) and several others nearby.

I would articulate my defense something like this:

"My home was surrounded by a hostile, aggressive mob. We received repeated threats from multiple people threatening to storm our home, to beat us if we came out, and to kill us. They were banging on the front door with such intensity I thought it might give in at times. It was clear that the crowd had the intention to seriously assault or kill us if we were not inside.

"Because the street was besieged, it was impossible for us to exit out the front or drive away without risking injury or death. We couldn't go out the side gate because they were in the alley, too. Nor could we go over the back fence because the hillside is too steep. If we tried to get out through the neighbor's yard, the mob could see us hopping the fence and we knew they had watchers down the street just in case we tried that. We were trapped.

"We called 911, but they wouldn't come and the fire department has said they would not respond to fires in rioting areas because it was too dangerous for them. Without leaving my house, which would put me at great risk of being attacked by the mob, I couldn't put out any fire and the garden hose is not a proper substitute for a fire hose.

"If our house burned, we would have no choice but to flee the house, putting us in the hands of the mob. I was afraid that if we stayed inside a burning house, we would burn to death or suffocate. If we ran outside to escape the flames, we would be severely beaten or killed by the mob. With no safe avenue of retreat, I had no choice but to keep our house from being set on fire. In fear of my life and that of my family, I had no choice but to shoot that arsonist before he could throw that fire bomb."

The above is merely a generic example for illustrative purposes. No one should ever make a statement to police or prosecutors after any instance of self-defense without attorney representation.

Allowing arson terrorists to set fire to occupied homes greatly increases the risk to someone who flees and complicates self-defense in the midst of a mob. Rather, shooting an arsonist who is committing a crime that could quite easily lead to death is a targeted response against an immediate and most-urgent threat. Waiting to fire until all reasonable options are exhausted shows great restraint and deliberation.

In a more strategic sense, should courts allow the prosecution of citizens who shoot arson terrorists it would set the evil precedent that harassed persons need to decide between death by fire or the "mercy" of the mob. Citizens would be forced to comply with their antagonists' demands and even allow themselves to be victims at the risk of prosecution. Permitting arson of homes would be nothing more than governmental endorsement of lynching.

A time may come when calling the police to break up a riot or stop the mob from burning people out may not be possible. Your choice might be survival or death. A tyrannical system that allows mobs to burn out their political, social, or economic opponents with impunity is a system that is no longer legitimate. Shooting an arsonist might seem like a sure ticket to a trial today, but if the system continues to be prejudiced against those who use self-defense against politically favored mobs, what obligation do you have to obey? I would rather take my chances with a kangaroo court than being burned alive.

Dealing with arson attacks

Use distance to your advantage; Molotov cocktails cannot be thrown more than 25 yards by most people and 50 yards would be extremely unusual. Keep potential throwers away from you or your vehicle away from them. Anyone within that distance or approaching that distance to throw should be considered an imminent threat. In lieu of lethal force, use less-than-lethal force like rubber bullets, shotgun baton rounds, or paintballs. Anything that stuns and interrupts the attack is a good thing.

In a vehicle, get away from the scene. Your best defense is to accelerate away and steer the vehicle to dodge the glass as it lands. If it hits your car, roll up all windows (if not done already) and accelerate as fast as you can to try and blow out the flames. Once you have driven to a safe area, abandon the vehicle if it is not operational.

How to put out a Molotov cocktail

When the glass container of a cocktail breaks against a hard surface, the liquid spreads out in a puddle and may spray, rapidly igniting from the burning wick. This creates a Class B (burning liquid) fire. Class A, or water fire extinguishers, or water itself should be avoided to douse the initial conflagration as there is a non-zero chance the water may spread the pool of burning liquid at first. If you do need to use water for this purpose, be prepared for the fire to initially spread.

Class B fire extinguishers, or a common household dry powder fire extinguisher (known as ABC for the three common classes of fires) should be used. When using a fire extinguisher, always aim at the base of the flames from about eight feet or so away. Move the extinguisher in an even manner to equally spray the base of the flames. Do not spray at the top of the flames themselves. Buy multiple extinguishers, not just for multiple rooms or large fires, but so that you have spares in case the first round is exhausted.

If you do not have a dry chemical fire extinguisher available, use dry sand or earth to smother the fire and absorb the liquid. A lot of material may be needed and the saturated material will need to be removed after the emergency is over. Another common tactic is to use a wetted *wool* blanket[41] to smother the fire.

Should *you* catch on fire, STOP—DROP—AND ROLL. Your first instinct will be to run. Fight this because running just

---

[41] Wet wool is somewhat flame retardant and most importantly won't melt like synthetic blankets.

fans the flames. Immediately drop and roll, vigorously and violently until the fire goes out. Bystanders should smother the flames with jackets or blankets. Your defense team should have a fire blanket and fire extinguishers on hand at the barricade. Some fire extinguisher models are small enough to put into a vest pouch or a cargo pocket; even a wet extinguisher is better than none.

IEDs, or Improvised Explosive Devices

An IED is an Improvised Explosive Device, or a homemade bomb. These weapons often take the form of pipe bombs made out of gunpowder, fireworks, or home brewed explosives. A notable recent attack of these weapons domestically was during the 2013 Boston Marathon. They usually cause death or injuries by blasting metallic shrapnel, like nails or other pieces of hardware, into people. They can be quite devastating.

I put bombings in two risk categories; incidental and widespread urban warfare. The former category would be similar to how Molotov cocktails are used. These would be bombs thrown at your house or your defensive team's position. A bomb might also be dropped inside the crowd or near your barricade/checkpoint either to harm you or create a "false flag" incident to blame you for a bombing. The risk of this will be low for most people.

A more frightening prospect is if the security situation devolves enough that Iraq or Northern Ireland type urban warfare starts happening. This will be sectarian in nature (racial, religious, or political) and terror bombings will be a feature. Car bombs and blowing up public places will be common. This will be harder to defend against.

A terror bombing's purpose is, beyond fear, to inflict as many deaths or injuries as possible. I foresee smaller weapons being used mainly in an anti-personnel role. Some areas in your suburb to expect a car bomb would be:

- Neighborhood entrances/exits.
- A security post or barricade.
- An area with a lot of pedestrians (market, park, meeting).
- Along a roadway where the bomb can be remotely detonated to target a passing vehicle or group.
- Outside a particular building (like a church).

Bombs in these areas would tend to do the most damage. In other conflicts, we've seen bombings done in busy commercial areas or near an opposing group's building. Car bombs while out and about are getting beyond the scope of this work, so I'm looking mostly at the hazards in a neighborhood.

There is good news. America has tight controls over explosives and this would continue somewhat into a dystopian future. Our Army isn't going to desert leaving stores of artillery shells unguarded like the Iraqis did. We also don't have a tradition of bombing. I would even speculate that a lot of veterans who might fight in a civil war would eschew use of IEDs in a terrorist role because of their negative experience with them.

Americans do have firearms. From psychos shooting up schools to gangland mass shootings, our killing tends to be with guns. Firearms are our tradition of violence and resistance, so I personally see bombs in the USA as much less likely than sniper attacks, drive-by shootings, or small gun raids.

It is cold comfort to think shootings are less frightening than bombings. Gunfights are less frightening than bombings because we typically can prepare for a fight, whether we have the advantage or not. We can fight back against guns. With bombs, they explode in surprise. An invisible menace we can't do anything about lurks out there, literally ticking away. Vigilance is the defense against bombings.

Injuries and employment

Unsophisticated bombs anarchists may use will likely be weak in nature. They will cause injuries primarily through shrapnel injuries as projectiles or debris hit flesh like bullets. Most wounds produced from this fragmentation effect are to limbs. However, this data is based on military experiences where the torso and head are protected by body armor and the limb injuries still present a risk of death due to blood loss (exsanguination).

Eyes also need to be protected from fragments, so ballistic goggles or glasses are a good precaution. Larger weapons will cause injuries primarily from blast trauma (overpressure squishing organs) and burn injuries from the explosion's heat up close. Shrapnel will be the secondary means of major injury causation.

I would expect to see most weapons made from gunpowder (black or smokeless) taken from reloading components or fireworks. Homemade chemical explosives are a little more difficult to make. Keep in mind that binary explosives for target shooting (popularly known as Tannerite, a brand), could be used as part of an IED. A device could be emplaced and then shot at by a sniper.

Not only can these bombs be set down for detonation after the bomber has left the area, but they can also be thrown like grenades. The first grenades were little more than metal spheres loaded with blackpowder and detonated with burning fuses. Video from Portland shows a suspected thrown IED of an unknown type being used at the federal courthouse in July of 2020. Firecrackers can be easily modified into ersatz grenades.

IEDs can be remotely detonated (versus timers or movement). Remote detonation requires someone to be physically observing the device or remotely via camera or drone. Be aware of secondary devices. Secondaries are designed to detonate after you've been drawn in to examine the damage or treat the wounded. Hoax weapons (fake bombs) may be used to distract you or slow you down. A fake bomb might be planted so you investigate further, drawing you into a trap for snipers.

Personally, my concern is for hand thrown bombs being used against neighborhood security team members or a checkpoint. A bomb placed at a barricade to kill any sentries is another troubling concern. Last would be static car bombs parked to target a checkpoint or vehicles coming in and out of a neighborhood at a chokepoint.

Prevention and mitigation

Vigilance and patrols (inspections) are necessary. Check the area around your checkpoint, barricade, or other chokepoints for suspicious packages or vehicles. Watch crowds or intruders carefully if you suspect bombs are a threat. Be aware of anyone filming from a long distance away as videos of bombings have been used by jihadis as propaganda (and may be used so here).

Look for suspicious packages, such as a backpack or parcel left in close proximity to people or where they might pass. An abandoned backpack suddenly appearing in a neighborhood near a pedestrian gate could be suspicious. Likewise, a protestor who sets down a bag or package and then leaves they area could have just set down a bomb. Opening the flap of a bag and seeing a pressure cooker inside would be considered a clue.

Keep the area near your sensitive points clear of any hiding places. For New Year's Eve, New York and Las Vegas authorities clear the streets of any garbage cans or things that could hide explosives. Do the same (and keep parked vehicles away). Prevention to ensure a bomb isn't planted is absolutely necessary if such a threat exists.

For thrown weapons, treat anyone lighting/throwing a bomb (or suspected device) like an arson terrorist; shoot them. In the beginning, fireworks and smoke bombs might be thrown, so discretion and judgment will be necessary. However, once use of explosives becomes common, you may need to institute a stricter protocol to deal with anyone about to lob a suspected bomb at you.

Confirm: make sure it is a bomb

- Is the item out of place?
- Does it have wires coming from it or smells oddly (like gasoline or chemicals)?
- Does it make sense someone would place a bomb there?

Cordon: close the area to pedestrian and vehicle traffic.

Clear: get everyone out of the danger zone.

- Nearby homes and businesses within the blast radius should be evacuated.
- Anyone outside should be under cover and well away from the bomb, preferably around a corner (no line of sight).

Call: call for the Bomb Squad

- Military EOD may be necessary if in a martial law type situation.
- Veterans who have experience with explosives may need to be found if the police/military are not functioning.

Control: get the situation safely resolved.

- Disarm or safely detonate the device if authorities no longer exist.

First of all, make sure the suspicious package probably is a bomb. Is there a bomb threat (specific or general) and does it make sense a bomb would be in that place? Eliminate other probabilities for the suspicious package, like a pepper sprayed protestor dropping their bag and running. Inspect the item remotely if possible. Use binoculars or drones if you can.

Ideally suspicious packages shouldn't be closely inspected by civilians. Call professionals if you can. If you must approach it, be sure to remove any electronics from your person, like a phone or radio, so a stray signal won't set off a wonky detonator.

Be gentle with the device and slowly peek inside. Sophisticated weapons dropped in place may have anti-tamper mechanisms to detonate the explosives if the device is moved, inspected, or is disarmed. Carefully lift flaps, unzip zippers, or lift covers.

The area around the device needs to be cordoned off. If you can close it off with tape or cones, great. It is more likely you will need to verbally warn people. Outdoors, get as far away as possible. Solid cover should be several feet of earth, a solid wall, or on the far side of a building. Being out of the line of sight from the device makes it hard for shrapnel traveling in a straight line to hit you, so be around a corner. Remember debris may rain down from above.

Indoors, get to the part of the building that is furthest from the device. Stay away from windows or anything that could fall on you. Get under a table or sturdy piece of furniture and cover your head.

The below chart[42] shows distances in feet for typical threats (explosive weight in TNT):

Threat	Evacuate buildings	Shelter in place	Outdoors
Pipe bomb	70	71-1199	1200
20lb bomb	110	111-1699	1700
50lb bomb	150	151-1849	1850

[42] Taken from "Bomb Threat Stand-Off Card," Dept. of Homeland Security.

Car	320	321-1899	1900
SUV	400	401-2399	2400

For comparison, a US standard M67 fragmentation grenade uses 6.5 ounces of plastic explosive, has a fatal injury radius of 15 feet, an injury radius of 50 feet, and some fragments can go over 800 feet. Hand grenades can be thrown by a competent thrower up to over 100 feet.

If the package must be disturbed or detonated, the nearest houses should be evacuated. All other residents should shelter in place inside, on the floor, in a room furthest from the device. A brave soul, from behind solid cover, should attempt to use a fire hose, paintball gun, or other projectiles to disturb or detonate the package.

Car bombs (VBIEDs)

Car bombs, or VBIEDs (Vehicle Borne IED) are more of a threat if America is hit by a protracted sectarian crisis. I see this as more of a threat in mixed business areas where a lot of people will be. Downtown and densely populated areas (shopping centers) are at risk. Suburbs probably not so much. In a suburb, these would likely be detonated remotely to ambush vehicles, large pedestrian groups, or detonated statically to destroy strong points.

Note that car bombs have a large blast radius and many houses would need to be evacuated. The preferred evacuation zone, indoors and outdoors, is a quarter to half a mile (depending on the size of the bomb). There is no disarming or safely detonating one of these except by an expert. Evacuation and waiting the blast out is the only defense.

A car bomb would likely be parked overnight near a position where it would do the most damage (like your checkpoint). No vehicles should be allowed to park near where people will be. Unfamiliar vehicles that are parked overnight, or where the driver parks and leaves the neighborhood, need to be carefully examined.

The biggest red flags will be vehicles parked where they shouldn't be or obvious wires or detonators visible. Others are:

- The vehicle sags under the heavy weight of the explosives (often overloaded for maximum blast effect).
- Dark or covered windows.
- A load that is suspiciously covered (like rear seats folded flat and blankets covering odd shapes).
- Visible wiring or antennas inside the vehicle.
- The smell of diesel fuel in gas powered vehicle or unusual chemical smells.

A lone male driver fits the historical pattern for car bombs. This person would typically park the car and rapidly flee the area, perhaps getting into another vehicle. Virtually all Western bombers will park the vehicle and detonate the weapon remotely or via a timer versus a suicide bombing. As said before, Westerners are highly unlikely to engage in suicide bombings.

Bombs planted in roadways around town are unlikely. In Iraq, roadside bombs were designed to target coalition military convoys that were impossible to mistake for anything else. Average groups probably will not be using bombs the same way against civilian traffic here. In Northern Ireland, bombs were placed in neighborhoods to be used against the other religious group (when civilians were targeted). If there is an insurgency going on, there may be a collateral risk to civilians from roadside bomb ambushes against military forces on patrol.

Night Vision

Most Americans have no idea how dark night really is. New York and Las Vegas are bright enough to blot out virtually all stars. Out in the vast farm fields of the Oxnard Plain of Southern California, it's dark and we used night vision to catch agricultural thieves. Still, the city lights on a clear night glow orange on the horizon. One has to go to the western deserts, far from cities or roads, to find dark skies.

Total darkness is hard to get but can come in the right circumstances. In my novel *Hard Favored Rage*, after an Electromagnetic Pulse (EMP) destroys the power grid, night vision becomes essential for the survivors to defeat an enemy drug cartel. Being able to see clearly in the dark becomes a necessary tool for survival. Your situation may never be as dire as my fiction, but it could.

City dwellers probably have never seen total dark outside, which is possible on a moonless, overcast night with no ambient light. We practically never are plunged into total darkness. If the power goes out, its usually only a neighborhood or portion of the city because of the way the electrical grids are divided up for redundancy. One city-wide blackout I remember wasn't totally dark because we still had starlight and the rest of the cities in the county had electricity. Their light pollution made skyglow on the horizon.

Yet that night was so dark I had trouble distinguishing the outlines of trees and houses 50 feet away. Cars and landscaping were dark blobs. The details of the ground were lost. After my eyes adjusted to the darkness, I was able to make out some parts of the houses, but only because the light paint contrasted with the dark. It would have been impossible to see a person approaching, especially if they were careful not to be outlined against anything.

So what does this mean for you? Take an ordinary suburban block, maybe 200 yards long at the most. In moonlight, it's not hard to see someone at that distance. By starlight alone, in a dark neighborhood that distance drops to perhaps 100 feet if you're observant.

Depending on the situation, you may face a deficit of light. I would not count on illumination from houses or streetlights in any case. Cities may go dark because of:

- Sabotage or deliberate interference with electrical supply.
- Brownouts/rolling blackouts.
- Economic conditions making streetlight illumination too expensive.
- Disaster.

Neighborhoods are more likely to go dark due to:

- Streetlights being shot out.
- Copper wire theft.
- Preparation for attack.

Not only is your own source of electricity for your daily life necessary but being able to see and fight effectively in the dark is imperative.

Night vision is a force multiplier

If you cannot see in the darkness, you don't know what's out there. Seems so simple it's cliché, right? Think about the average person's feelings in the dark. Ever whistle to keep yourself company while taking the trash out at night? Do you stay within the light of the campfire? How many times have you jumped at the odd noise in the night that you would have ignored during the daytime? Now imagine that in the darkness a determined adversary is coming to kill you. Will you be alert, eyes adjusted to the dark, and catch the bad guy in time to stop him?

Without night vision devices, you will be limited to what you can see with the naked eye. That means the area you can cover and the distance at which you can fight will be limited. By revealing what the darkness cloaks you can engage more persons, at a greater distance, over a wider field of fire. You can detect and identify threats earlier than they can observe you.

Night vision allows you to do several things white lights will do but without detection. That initialism is SIN:

S – Search

I – Identify (friend or foe)

N – Navigate

These three are all passive uses of your night vision gear. Identification and navigation (marking waypoints) can be boosted by use of infrared markers such as reflectors, glow sticks, strobes, or IR flashlights. The latter will also enable you to control and communicate just as you could with a white light.

Night vision Optical Devices (NODs)

Types and employment

There are three kinds of Night vision Optical Devices (NODs). The first are *image intensification* tubes that amplify ambient light. This is usually done in the infrared spectrum using a light sensitive tube. This technology was invented during World War II and used by German and American troops. The first such unit was a huge infrared spotlight and scope larger than a Pringles can mounted on top of the M3 carbine. This technology was refined through Vietnam to today.

Image intensification night-vision devices come in three generations. Gen I is the WWII stuff; the intensifier scope is really crummy at amplifying light and is basically useless without an infrared spotlight. Some Russian stuff that is battery free is sold, but this is basically a novelty; don't bother. Gen II is Vietnam/Gulf War One era. It is useable, but heavy, might not work anymore, and is far from optimal. Gen III is the current military issue stuff. The picture is basically what you're familiar with from recent movies showing night vision (*13 Hours* is a great example).

The next category is *thermal vision*, or FLIR (a brand). This is a device that is like an optical thermometer. It picks up the difference in temperature of the surfaces around you and displays it. This will give you basically a black and white picture. Some models have color for different temperature gradients, but in darkness, you just want stuff to stand out from the background. Thermal scopes are sold and frequently used by hunters. They are expensive and suffer the same problems regarding navigation as a weapon mounted traditional night vision scope (see below).

The final category is *digital night vision*. This is not so great. It basically is an image sensor from a digital camera that amplifies light. It cannot amplify light that well. Some models do a great job for the technology, but don't hold a candle to true night vision. If this is all you can afford, then get a top of the line model, $600-$1000. I don't recommend it, but it's better than nothing.

Light amplification technology will allow you to identify stuff, distance, focus, and light permitting. This means you can ideally recognize faces, read license plates, etc. Thermal vision is not good at this, unless you are close up or spending a lot of money on military quality gear. Thermal optics basically show you that someone is hiding in the brush. With a night vision scope, although that guy will be green, you could put an infrared light on him and see just who he is, in theory.

If I had the money to buy multiple devices, I would use thermal vision for area surveillance, especially in forested or brushy areas. You could see a white blob moving through the brush, then check it out as it gets closer with your light amplifying goggles or monocular.

Check out some videos on YouTube, see the differences between the types of gear, and how they are employed. You'll see what I mean and understand more about what will and won't work for you.

Note: Some of this stuff may be regulated or illegal in

your state. For instance, California prohibits devices that mount to a weapon and project infrared light as a "sniperscope."[43] Clearly some retard legislator saw something in a movie or magazine and thought it should be banned. So caveat emptor.

Devices and accessories

This isn't a what-to-buy guide, but I will recommend the PVS-14 monocular. It's affordable at around $3,000.00 and it is military grade, in current use by the US military. There are dual tube goggles and newer monoculars, but this is the best bet for your money. It will cover one eye and leave the other free for navigation. It comes with a "skull crusher" head mount that is a bit like 1970s orthodontic headgear. You will probably want to look into upgrading that with a helmet, but then it gets pricey.

So why the PVS-14? Because for the money it can't be beat. If you go cheap and buy $300 Russian night vision gear, you are getting utter rubbish. A Sony camcorder with the green Nightshot mode will do better. Cheap night vision gear sucks. Some of the mid-grade digital night vision scopes are better than nothing, but you won't be using it except as a pair of nighttime binoculars. Forget about using it to shoot bad guys with. Seriously; don't bother with it. Embrace the suck and buy a PVS-14.

NODs don't work like a magic eye that you put on and suddenly everything is visible, but green. First off, you have

---

[43] 468 PC

something hanging off your head. You cannot physically get your eyes down on a rifle to look down the sights with a NOD on your face. Even if you could, the focus doesn't work like that. NODs focus is on one point in space.

What a "night vision compatible" red dot means is that if you mount your PVS-14 on the rail with the scope, the dot won't wash out the amplified picture. That is, the dot has a dimmer switch. To aim with a NOD, you must have the device mounted on the weapon in line with the scope and focused for your optic and the range you're shooting at. Again, you aren't putting your head down and looking through the scope like it's daytime, just with the goggles or monocular on.

So okay, you put the NOD on the rifle. Now you can't navigate or scan the area without looking down the barrel of your rifle. You really don't want to be holding a rifle up to your face and walking around or even just scanning an area. That NOD has to go on your head. So how do you shoot? Unless you're a millionaire or Delta Force, no one is getting two night vision devices. Also be aware that a PVS-14 mounted on a weapon can cause the internal tubes to be battered under recoil over time, rendering the unit worthless.

This is where infrared lasers come in. Yes, another expense. Buy once, cry once. I recommend the civilian version of the PEQ-15 laser illuminator/pointer, known as the AITPAL-C. The difference from the military version is that there is no high-output setting for the laser; you aren't going to be guiding in smart bombs and the FDA or whoever doesn't want you blinding yourself. This will come with an infrared illuminator that can light up your target at a distance just like a flashlight, but in infrared.

When you want to shoot, you activate the aiming laser

and put the dot on your target. The dot will be visible in the NOD you are wearing. This is where it gets sort of like a video game and the only time I recommend using lasers on weapons. But you are still shouldering the weapon and aiming it, not shooting from the hip like Rambo. Remember, without a laser on your weapon, your head-mounted NOD can't be used to accurately fire a gun.

"But I can't afford all that!" You might say, freaking out when you realize all of this is going to cost you like $6,000 to do what an 11B line infantryman in Iraq was shooting with. "I still want to be able to see what's out there in the dark, though." Okay, then get a *quality* digital night vision device. Or a thermal device. You can scan the area and at least see that someone is out there, then use white or ambient light to shoot them, should it come to it. This is where you will want glow-in-the-dark night sights on your weapons.

The goal is to be one step ahead of the bad guys. If a gomer doesn't know you can see him, he's going to sneak up right through the bushes as you watch. Then when he's at the final line of bushes before the open ground, you can light him up and kill him. The alternative is that you don't know he's there until he starts shooting at you or is rushing your position.

You need: A night vision monocular or goggles and an infrared laser and illuminator.
You should have: A quality night vision helmet with counter-weight and NOD mounting arm.
It's good to have: A thermal spotting scope.
If you want a gunsight: Get a purpose made thermal gunsight.

Small infrared beacon strobe lights can mark friendly positions and individuals. Very small beacons are designed to attach to 9V batteries and can be attached easily to clothing. This can also be accomplished with infrared glowsticks. A laser or illuminator beam can be circled in the air like a lasso (known as "lassoing") to indicate to others a position like shining a flashlight in the air. Alternatively, a glowstick can be twirled in a circle from a string or length of paracord ("buzzsaw"). Phosphorescent tape or reflective tape can be used to mark positions and people as well.

Don't have night vision?

Don't have/can't afford NODs? Use your eye's natural night vision. First, allow about 30 minutes in darkness for your eyes to adapt to the dark. If you have to turn on a light, close one eye tightly to preserve night vision in that eye. Make sure you are well rested as vision tends to deteriorate with fatigue.

Have you ever noticed that if you try to look directly at something in the dark it "disappears"? Your eyes are only able to focus on an area of about 2-3 degrees with your sharp central vision (fovea); the rest of what you see is peripheral vision. Try looking indirectly, that is just away from the object, and you will be able to see it again. This phenomenon is known as averted vision.

Averted vision is possible because your eyeball's rod cells, which don't distinguish color, are far more sensitive than your eye's cone cells. Cone cells are responsible for color vision and are used primarily in bright light. Rods are roughly 100 times more sensitive to light than cone cells but produce blurrier vision (or else everyone would have great peripheral vision).

To visually scan areas you are watching at night, use averted vision by moving your eyes in a pattern. Scan in a grid: up and down, left to right. This will allow you to see things off to the side of your fovea and avoid the problem of looking directly at an unidentified something only to have it disappear.

If you are going to be exposed to bright light, such as muzzle flash, headlights, etc. close one eye to preserve night vision in that eye until the light is gone. Use red lights or filters to preserve your night vision.

Your depth perception and ability to distinguish outlines will be affected after dark. Distance tends to be underestimated by up to a quarter; dark objects appear further away while light objects seem closer. Hats, hoods, and helmets reduce your field of view, especially at night.

I'm the only one in my group with NODs. If it's totally dark and a "weapons free" situation, you should be firing exclusively tracer rounds (which look like laser beams). What you can do is identify a target, pop off a couple of tracers in the direction everyone should fire, then the group directs its fire that way until you can see the target is neutralized. Note that tracers don't always illuminate as soon as they are fired (to help conceal the point of firing) and are better at longer distances. Tracers can also indicate to the enemy where you are shooting from.

Tips

Remember that traditional night vision (intensification) only amplifies light that is already present. Total darkness (totally overcast, moonless night), underground, and the interior of structures at night (absent any ambient illumination), will require an infrared light source.

Streetlights and other neighborhood illumination can wash out the intensified image due to too much light. Anything reflective will reflect infrared light just like visible light. While bright flashes (muzzle flash, lightning) will not "blind" the operator, they may brighten the optic enough to cause the user to lose his night vision or have a problem with after-images.

Both image intensification and thermal will be degraded by flames, smoke, dust, and fog. Thermal does better in fog or smoky conditions at short-range, but through dust, image intensification is better.

To help alleviate flash blindness when shooting, ensure that your rifle has a flash suppressor on it. A muzzle brake does not suppress the flash. Some models of flash suppressors are better than others. A suppressor (silencer) can also be used if you have one.

"What if the bad guys have NODs?" and light discipline

If stuff is so bad that your adversaries have night vision,

start praying. It is overwhelmingly likely that whoever you're facing is some fool with more bravado than training or technology. A NOD equipped adversary is unlikely. Imagine you are the average member of a mob, or even a hardcore gang member. Suddenly you are shot at in the dark by someone you can't see. How are you going to react? Most people that you shoot in the dark before they see you will likely be terrified, run away, and seek an easier target.

Remember at night your team should always maintain strict light discipline. This applies to infrared emitters as much as it does visible light. The Taliban has detected American troops operating in their area by using cheap point-and-shoot cameras with IR filters to scan for infrared light emissions.

If the opposition is using night vision as well, remember they can see any infrared light you produce, such as flashlights, supplemental infrared illumination, or targeting lasers. Through a NOD, it will appear just as visible as it were visible light to the naked eye. Use passive NODs to amplify ambient light or consider using thermal scopes, including thermal gunsights.

When using an infrared laser or illuminator, avoid using it to scan your field of fire like waving a flashlight around. This is distracting to other NOD users and if your enemy has an infrared device, he can see you. Illuminators and lasers should only be switched on for momentary illumination or for firing. Be careful to keep track of your laser if multiple people are using laser targeting devices so that another's laser isn't mistaken for your own and vise versa.

If you are concerned about visible light giving away your position, it should not be used except under total cover. An example is draping a poncho over someone who must use a visible light to use a map. Red lights or infrared filters should always be used to preserve night vision. Blue light is the hardest for another observer to see but does not protect night vision like red light.

When darkness is being used for concealment, visible light should only be used to disorient or identify. Lights should be remotely mounted when possible or flashlights held out to the side of the body at arm's length. A weapon mounted light or a flashlight held in front of the body is a tempting target to shoot at. Although if there is enough ambient light already it doesn't matter much where the light is held.

Firearms and Tactical Accessories

Firearms[44]

The most important rule of having firearms is "have one." Not what kind of gun to have or multiple ones for different roles, but simply owning a gun. Weapons for self-defense are so important that Jesus admonished his disciples to sell their cloaks to buy a sword.[45] A weapon is any object capable of inflicting death or injuries that increases your natural ability beyond that which you can do barehanded. That could be a heavy stick acting as a club, a sharp blade, to a projectile throwing device like a bow and arrow or a gun.

Today the most effective weapons are firearms. There

[44] **Note:** This section is intended for persons who do not have firearms or are new to owning them. This is not a firearm instruction manual. This is a general introduction for persons who don't know what to buy or what to do with a gun once they've bought one. Please see other works or an instructor for how to shoot.

[45] Luke 22:36

is a valid argument about the primal fear that a bladed weapon like a large knife can cause an opponent. For soldiers, being on either end of a bayonet charge is one of the most difficult things they can experience in combat. Yet no one in this day and age would be in their right mind to trade a gun for a blade if they have the option.

Firearms distill killing and disabling capacity into a package that weighs from two to ten pounds. While the ability for a rifle to shoot hundreds of yards is great, even a small caliber pistol allows one to shoot an attacker from outside the range of the attacker's grasping (or cutting) distance. Guns give even the weakest person the ability to kill a bad guy; something that was formerly reserved to only those strong enough to throttle, beat, bludgeon, or slash their enemy to death.

A pistol in the hands of a frail, elderly person or a petite woman allows them to defeat a large, angry and possibly drugged up killer. A repeating firearm (semi-automatic, pump action shotgun, etc.) allows for multiple shots in case the attacker keeps coming or if there is more than one person trying to kill you. The noise of a firearm discharging can have an incalculable effect on bad guys who may have expected little to no resistance. Even being seen with a gun in hand or on hip has turned the tables in many would-be attacks.

It has to be stated that a gun is not a magic talisman that keeps evil away (and to that point "no guns" signs don't stop crime). A firearm is a tool, that if used properly, can save lives. Just owning one and putting it in the closet won't protect you. The same goes for carrying it outside or pointing it at someone. Not every criminal will be scared by the sight of a gun, especially if you are not prepared to use it. If you choose to own a gun, know how to use it and, should it be legally and morally necessary to shoot someone, have the willpower to use it.

What gun do I buy?

Maybe you have your grandfather's old shotgun in the attic; that's a good start. Any gun (with ammo) gives you the ability to kill a bad guy. Many people have been killed by the "puny" .22 LR round lots of us have shot starting as children. A gun is your last line of defense. Even if it is a single shot weapon, that's one bad guy who doesn't get you. If there is more than one, it could deter the others.

As of this writing, the gun supply nationally is a mess. The time for choices and low prices in firearms was 2019. This is about what you can get. Don't necessarily think *brand* but think *role*. If you need a good defensive handgun, don't worry about getting a tricked out Glock. An economy model semi-auto pistol in 9mm will work just fine. The same for shotguns; it doesn't have to be a "police" model or even a black, self-defense shotgun. A wood hunting shotgun will fit the bill.

Firearm basics

This is not intended to be a comprehensive explanation of all things firearms, but a brief introduction. Research online (particularly YouTube) for introductory information about firearms. Reputable gun store employees will also help educate you on the basic differences. The time and money spent with a firearms trainer is well worth it.

Handguns

If you can only have one firearm (due to affordability, supply, or other reasons), get a handgun. Handguns are excellent starting places for shooters who may be intimidated by long guns. Pistols can also be easily carried and concealed, whereas a rifle or shotgun cannot. A refugee from an Eastern European conflict said that a handgun was better than a rifle. Long guns made one look like a combatant while handguns could still be used for protection while maintaining a civilian profile.

To dispel any ideas about "stopping power," a handgun in a major caliber is sufficiently lethal if aimed properly. This means semi-autos in .380 or larger and revolvers in .38 Special or larger. Handguns, unlike rifles and shotguns, are easily transported and concealed. They can be kept in a pocket, on the hip, or easily placed at hand in/on a desk or nightstand.

Handguns come in two main types; semi-automatic pistols and revolvers (though technically both can be called pistols). Semi-autos load through a magazine (sometimes erroneously called a "clip") in the grip of the gun. Once the slide has been cycled back and forward to chamber a round, the gun will fire for each pull of the trigger until empty.

Revolvers require each of the chambers in the cylinder to be individually loaded with a cartridge, although most modern revolvers will eject all the empty cases out at once.

Which to buy is a personal question. Some shooters, generally the elderly and women who have poor hand strength, find it difficult to work the slide on a semi-auto, so they prefer a revolver. Double-action revolvers are somewhat "foolproof" in that once it's loaded, all the shooter has to do is aim and pull the trigger. Some shooters find the revolver trigger to be stiff and heavy or cocking the hammer difficult; try one out is the only advice I have. Revolvers are also slower to reload and you only have (typically) six shots.

If cycling (racking) the slide of a semi-auto is not a problem for you, they are a much better alternative. There are even models and accessories that make racking the slide easier; consult your local gun store. The major advantage is ammunition capacity. Magazine (AKA "clip") feeding gives you in nearly every case more shots than a revolver and vastly easier reloading. Most large and medium revolvers will have a capacity of at least ten, if not 15-17 rounds.

My advice to women is not to buy a small handgun because of the trope that women are smaller and thus need a smaller gun. Well-meaning husbands and gun salesmen often try to steer women to subcompact pistols. Smaller guns transmit more recoil to your hands whereas many women find larger guns to be more comfortable to shoot because there is less felt recoil. Even so, a smaller gun may be the one that you can carry, so I don't wish to discourage you from that. A gun that you don't carry is useless.

Don't worry about what caliber to buy. So many people have engaged in the "caliber wars" that if it was a real war, half the gun owning population would be dead. .45 is not a magic bullet because it is big. People who bought .44 Magnums because Clint Eastwood used one in *Dirty Harry* found that the most powerful handgun in the world is very unpleasant to shoot. Modern 9mm defensive/hollow-point/JHP bullets are just as effective as larger calibers are. It is shot placement that counts, not the size of your bullet.

Rifles

The next stop is a rifle. This book is about defense, so I'm not recommending rifles for hunting. Most rifles suitable for self-defense can be used for hunting as well (local legalities aside). Ideally, what you want is a semi-automatic rifle in a centerfire cartridge that uses a detachable box magazine. Your .22 or bolt-action hunting rifle is far from ideal. Specifically, I am referring to AR-15s, Ruger Mini-14s, and AK-series weapons. There are other types of weapons, but if I had to boil it down to one concept, get a civilian variant of a military rifle.

Modern semi-automatic rifles are known as "modern sporting rifles" or the misnomer "assault weapon." There is no such thing as an "assault weapon;" any object can be used to assault. The term is a play on "assault rifle" which is specifically a military weapon that has the capability to fire on fully automatic (legally a "machine gun"). You aren't buying that in California, or anywhere else unless you have tens of thousands of dollars.[46] "Assault weapon" is intended to

---

[46] Machine guns are technically not illegal in most states. They are

scare people into letting politicians ban them.

Your average semi-automatic rifle uses the recoil or gas from firing to cycle the weapon without any intervention from the shooter. All the shooter does is load the magazine, chamber the first round, and pull the trigger until the gun is empty.[47] A semi-auto may look like a wood hunting rifle or it might look like an "evil black rifle" like the M16. Whether they appear like something Elmer Fudd would take into the forest with him or dressed up in a tactical guise, functionally, most of these guns are identical. It's just about the accessories.

Without waxing too political, the idea behind "assault weapon" bans are to restrict firearms that are optimized for tactical use in the incorrect notion this limits criminal use. It also places limitations on citizens who one day might fight back against a tyrannical government or the angry mobs out to harm average citizens. Trying to fight back with a slow-loading double-barrel shotgun against soldiers or radicals supplied with military weapons is not an easy way to resist whatever evil they might want to visit upon you.

The Second Amendment was not about hunting or even ordinary self-defense (although records clearly indicate the Founding Fathers thought carrying and owning guns for self-defense against criminals was so obvious they didn't think they needed to clutter up the bill of rights with it). The Second Amendment is about resisting a tyrannical government and

---

regulated under a 1934 law known as the National Firearms Act (NFA) that requires a $200 tax, registration, and an extensive FBI background check that can take up to a year. New machine guns could not be publicly sold after 1986, causing an artificial constriction in supply that drove prices up from slightly more than a semi-automatic gun to the price of a car.

[47] A "machine gun" (the legal term) is fully automatic and fires as long as the trigger is held down; semi-autos require the trigger to be released and pulled for each shot.

the police or soldiers that would enforce their edicts. In this day and age, it goes for angry mobs that the police and partisan politicians won't control.

As of this writing, it is not beyond reality to imagine that future totalitarian politicians will send mobs to target their political opponents. In 2020 and 2021, we see almost exclusively leftist groups and mobs like Antifa rioting with little opposition from police or government. History shows us that communist or fascist, left or right, civilian groups that organize into partisan paramilitary forces are often the vanguard of genocide. Research the history of the Nazi's SS, the Khmer Rouge, and the atrocities in Rwanda.

Why am I harping on mobs and going down the "fight the government" rabbit hole? Because that is a very real potential threat in the near future. Yes, you can fight against a government with rifles.

For an idea of what one man can do to disrupt policing, look at the Christopher Dorner manhunt of 2013. Southern California police were totally consumed and scared over one man who was killing cops. We doubled up on patrol, motorcycle cops were put in Crown Victorias, and the civilians/volunteers taken off the street. Extra patrols and special details were laid on to find this one guy. Imagine if hundreds or thousands of people were attacking police that were committing Nazi-like atrocities?

Now I'm not advocating rebellion, just that it is possible to defeat tyranny with civilian arms. The Founding Fathers intended the Second Amendment to put civilians on the same footing as armies with the ability to self-organize into militias against tyranny, but that has been forgotten. If you're reading this, I'm not expecting you to take on a future leftist or rightist insurrection. But that AR-15 rifle *does* give you the ability to stand relatively on par with the stormtroopers any tyrant might send.

More importantly, a semi-auto rifle is a great tool for dealing with a mob or multiple attackers. With a standard 30 round magazine, you can fire 30 shots as fast as you can aim and pull the trigger. That's a lot of firepower. Look up the stories of AR-15 self-defense incidents. If your house is surrounded by a mob of hundreds of angry people, ready to burn you out and kill you, you can potentially take out 30 bad guys without reloading. Do you really want a two-shot, or even a nine-shot, shotgun, or a bolt-action rifle that holds five rounds?

An AR-15 is simply the most common semi-auto rifle out there. It has been proven in combat and civilian service for over 50 years.[48] It is the most supported and developed rifle in the country. Countless variants and manufacturers exist. It has more accessories and configurations than Barbie. The ergonomics can't be beat. With the "Why do I want an AR-15?" question out of the way, let's move on to practical matters.

Sure, some states have regulated the AR-15 to death, but there are several workarounds and so-called "featureless" builds. If you want an AR in California, New York, or Massachusetts, it is possible. Be sure to do extensive research

---

[48] Ignore the stories about how the M16 was unreliable in Vietnam. Problems in Vietnam were because the rifle was issued with little training and often without cleaning gear. Troops were mistakenly told the rifle was "self-cleaning." Worse, the Army changed the gunpowder formula in the cartridge without considering how it would affect the rifle's operation. In the hot, moist jungles with poor maintenance, the guns did have problems. This was fixed by correcting the powder issue, issuing cleaning gear, and teaching the troops to fire the rifle. The AR-15 is as reliable as the AK-47 is said to be.

on your options. Once/if things have collapsed to the point that there is no way in heck "assault weapon" laws will be enforced, you can simply configure the rifle to its intended configuration sans the goofy compliance stuff.

But an AR-15 might not be for you. There are plenty of semi-auto rifles suitable for self-defense you can buy. Research online and check them out at your local gun store. As I said earlier, you want a rifle that takes a 20-30 round magazine standard, detaches with the push of a button for easy reloading, and has the ability to take a scope. Tell the gun store clerk you want a rifle suitable for self-defense and listen to their advice.

These rifles should be in either 5.56mm (also known as .223), 7.62 NATO, or 7.62x39 (the Russian AK-47 cartridge). Other cartridges exist, but these are the most common and easiest to find. They are all adequate. 5.56/.223 is the standard US military caliber in M16 rifles, used in AR-15 type rifles. Both rounds are essentially interchangeable. 9mm rifles and carbines are also available. If you choose an uncommon caliber, expect to have difficulty finding it (especially during the ammo crunch) and expect to pay more.

For ban-states, an M1 Garand is a good compromise rifle. It is semi-automatic, holds eight rounds in an en bloc clip, doesn't have any of the evil banned features on it, and is a reliable weapon. The .30-06 cartridge is powerful on both your target and your shoulder. This is my compromise choice of weapon in California. If you don't want the gun that won WWII, there are other similar options.

Perhaps you don't want, can't have, or can't find a semi-auto rifle. The old standby are lever action guns; for older folks, think of Lucas McCain (Chuck Connors) in *The Rifleman* or any rifle in westerns. These rifles can be fired and cycled quickly without the same eyes-off-the-target motion a standard bolt action rifle requires. They do take longer to load, with one cartridge going in the tubular magazine at a time. However, many of these guns can be bought in calibers that will also work in a revolver.

If you can't do better, get a "tactical" .22 LR that is an AR-15 clone. Its close resemblance to an AR-15 might scare criminals and you will have 20-30 shots that can be quickly reloaded vs. an older style .22 rifle you may have shot as a child. A "scary" gun with lots of shots is better than none at all. Plus, many of these clones serve as good practice for AR-15s which have virtually identical controls.

Finally, there is always what you have. Dad's old hunting rifle with a scope is good for long distance, but are you really going to be a sniper? Most combat kills with small arms take place at 100-300 yards; that's the length of your street. Beware that any rifle (or pistol round) will penetrate through walls and hunting calibers are even more likely to penetrate deeply, so consider that if you are using one.

Shotguns

Shotguns are great compromise weapons. Why a compromise? Because they can do many things adequately but none well. For self-defense, shotguns are not obsolescent, but getting there. They are limited in capacity (maximum of nine shells in the largest commercial models), limited in range, and suffer from heavy recoil. All of this can be mitigated, of course, but a pistol and an AR-15 is a better choice.

But don't despair! Shotguns are still viable self-defense weapons, especially inside the home. As a compromise long-gun, shotguns can be used for self-defense and hunting. They can fire slugs for medium range shooting (<75 yards) or even shoot less-than-lethal rounds. A basic defense load of buckshot, from a single shell, sends usually nine 9mm sized lead pellets out at 1000-1200 feet per second.

First, let's dispel some myths. You are not going to rack the slide of a shotgun and scare a burglar away with the "*shuck-shuck*" noise. Life isn't a movie. If a burglar is going to be that intimidated, he will probably run from your presence alone.

Two, shotguns aren't "point and shoot." They have to be deliberately aimed. If you shoot down a hallway, the shot isn't going to spread out like a cone of death and just hit the bad guy. The old saying "Shot spreads out one inch for every yard it travels," is a sort-of myth. I say sort-of because it depends on the shot type as well as the gun. For modern guns and shotgun shells shooting buckshot (the kind you want to shoot a person with), they spread out about a half-inch for every yard they travel. Inside a house or your yard, assume a target impact area the size of a fist to a large open hand.

With that out of the way, let's talk about what kind of shotgun to get. Again, any shotgun is better than no shotgun. A double barrel model is better than a single barrel model and a repeating (slide action or pump) shotgun is better than a double barrel one. With a double, you get two shots; great if all you have is a single shot because that gives you another round to fire without the bad guy getting the jump on you if you miss or there is two of them. A repeating shotgun can get you from five to nine rounds.

When it comes to shotguns, I recommend a simple pump shotgun, like a Mossberg or Remington. Semi-automatics are a possibility but are usually for shooting clay pigeons or bird hunting. They can be finicky with some types of shells. Inform the gun salesman you want a shotgun for self-defense and they'll help guide you.

You may also have access to an old hunting shotgun; don't discount these. There is very little difference functionally between hunting pump shotguns and self-defense models. Often hunting shotguns have better sights, oddly enough. There are lots of aftermarket accessories to turn a hunting gun into a defensive one. Do keep note that some hunting guns may have wooden plugs in the magazine tube to limit capacity to three rounds. This is a bird hunting regulation, so be sure to check the magazine.

Now we return to the compromise aspect for disadvantages. Shotguns are heavy, their ammo is bulky, and they are slow to reload. Their maximum lethal range is somewhere about 50 yards, depending on many factors such as the type of projectile, the wind, and luck. Slugs might get you out to 75 yards, but that's it. All of this is within typical neighborhood distances that an average person could expect to shoot at.

For ammunition, there are three main types: birdshot, buckshot, and slugs. Birdshot is very small lead pellets (non-toxic metals are required for hunting in many places). Birdshot is lethal at close range and can cause serious injuries further out. I would highly recommend against using it for self-defense unless there is absolutely nothing else available to use.

Buckshot is intended to kill deer (hence "buck") and is

used for self-defense. A typical 00 ("double ought") buckshot pellet is roughly the size of a handgun bullet; nine to 15 are carried in a typical shell. Slugs are basically a giant lead bullet. They are powerful manstoppers (one-shot stop kills are possible if the slug hits the right area) and can reach out to extreme ranges, for a shotgun. The recoil is harsh, but they are great at what they do.

12 gauge is the most common caliber of shotgun with the smaller 20 gauge being the next most popular. Shotgun shells are measured by gauge, an antiquated form of measurement, and the caliber gets larger as the number gets smaller. A .410 shotgun is roughly 10mm and is inadvisable for self-defense (though slugs can be used). As a strong man, I would recommend nothing smaller than 20 gauge and suggest 12 gauge most of all. You will also find 12 gauge ammunition almost anywhere that has ammo in stock.

What about less-lethal rounds? I do not recommend these for the average person or any non-civilian.[49] These shotgun shells are packed with a bean bag, small rubber shot, or a rubber slug. Some sold at sporting goods stores are intended to shoot predatory animals without killing them; not for use on people. Even highly engineered police-grade bean bags, etc. can kill or seriously wound. I've seen a man die after being shot with a bean bag shotgun.

I know what you may be thinking: "I don't want to kill them, just make them go away." It's nice you are hesitant to kill, but don't let your sensitivity get you killed or prosecuted. A gun, no matter what it is firing, is a lethal device. Bean bag, rubber bullet, or not, you are using lethal force and using lethal force (justifiable homicide) needs to be permissible by

[49] For self-defense use. Riot control is a different story.

law. You are not a cop who gets the benefit of the doubt or an excusable homicide by misadventure defense by statute.

If you want to use bean bags, make rock salt shells, or ricochet birdshot off the pavement, save it for the true end of the world or prepare for the consequences of your actions.

Less-lethal

Note: this section discusses less-lethal means of self-defense from a perspective of everyday carry, not riot control. Contingency riot control use for these items in that context is discussed separately in the "Riot and Crowd Control" chapter.

Some of you may not be able to own or use firearms. Some of you are downright unwilling to kill someone. What are your options that aren't bludgeons or blades?

For those who are willing to kill, a less-lethal[50] option would be used in a situation that hasn't yet escalated to deadly force but would justify an ordinary use of force. In layman's terms, if you could legally punch someone in self-defense, but not shoot them, it would be okay to use a less-lethal weapon.

The first is a Taser. I'm talking actual Taser brand Tasers; perfectly legal in most states. You can carry one concealed even in California. These are the electrical conduction devices that shoot out two probes on metal wires that stun

---

50 "Less-lethal" and "less-than-lethal" mean two different things and even things like Tasers and pepper spray can result in death, but we're keeping the things not meant to kill under a simple term here.

the attacker, overriding his nervous system for a short period of time. In civilian models, there is a "run away" feature that gives you 30 seconds to drop the Taser and run.

Tasers are great because they don't require you to be within arm's reach of the bad guy. The usual distance is 15 feet. Stun guns, the kind with probes you touch to a person, require you to be at bad-breath distance. That's close enough to be beaten, stabbed, or disarmed. Tasers aren't magic. Often both probes fail to penetrate deeply enough into the person (usually heavy clothing) and they are not incapacitated. This is why cops don't carry Tasers alone.

I personally don't own a private Taser. I see no need. If I can't hold them off by physical strength or with pepper spray, I'll shoot them. For civilians, I see Tasers as a tool for those unwilling or unable to carry a gun. You will not need to temporarily incapacitate someone to handcuff them.

Next is pepper spray or oleoresin capsicum, known as OC (covered in greater detail in the "Riot and Crowd Control Chapter"). Some people call it Mace, although that is a brand name and refers originally to a product that is based on CN tear gas. Pepper spray is pretty much what you've seen on TV. It works by creating intense pain and quasi-blindness through pain that forces the eyes to water and close. Attackers are too busy screaming in pain (in theory) to continue the attack.

Lots of different sprays exist from gels to foggers to streams. Do a little research on what you're getting. You might have to go out of state to buy it (some states restrict the potency or volume of the spray), but police-strength stuff in big canisters is a good tool to have. The riot or bear sized ones are perfect for dousing a mob.

There is a good chance if you use pepper spray that you will feel the effects. Some cops don't even bother using it because of the risk of self-exposure. I don't recommend testing it on yourself. Never shoot it upwind. If you do spray yourself, the only advice I have to give is *don't* take a hot shower. Hot water just opens up your pores and makes things start burning.

Be prepared for your less-lethal option not to work. A Taser with good contact will drop a bad guy, but he can always get up and fight or yank out the probes. The probes might not make contact either. Pepper spray is purely pain compliance; some people seem miraculously immune to it and fight on, smearing *you* in that burning stuff. Have a back-up plan if your less-lethal doesn't work.

Some have brought up non-firearm projectile devices, like airguns and BB guns. These are a bad choice; they can get enough velocity for those small metal projectiles to cause wounds, someone to lose an eye, or in freak incidents, kill someone. High-power airguns are used to kill game frequently. Do you really want to shoot someone who might just go "Ow, stop!" and get even more upset with you? Or worse, you cause them to lose an eye, find out your use of force was unjustified, and now you're looking at decades in prison over a mayhem charge?

Ammunition

Cartridge is the proper term to refer to any packaged firearm ammunition round. *Shell* has the same practical meaning, but usually refers to shotgun shells. *Round* is parlance for "cartridge" and is used interchangeably. The *case* is the big part (usually brass, or plastic for shotgun shells) that holds the powder. *Caliber* in the context of ammunition refers to the size and exact type of the cartridge; this doesn't necessarily mean the diameter of the bullet.

The *bullet* is held in the front of the case. If you call the whole cartridge a bullet, you'll sound stupid but people will know what you're talking about. Remember, the bullet (which can be lead or lead covered in a copper jacket) is what flies down the barrel whereas the empty case or shell flies out of the gun.

FMJ or *Full Metal Jacket* is a bullet that is coated in copper. Most sporting, target, and military rounds are of this type. You should assume this is what you have if you aren't sure. *JHP* or *Jacketed Hollow Point* are the most common types of self-defense ammunition. There are many brands; some work better than others but almost any **handgun** JHP round will work better than a **handgun** FMJ round. JHP rounds are designed to expand once they've hit a target, destroying more tissue and causing faster incapacitation. They also are less likely to expand once they've left the target. I do not recommend hollow-point or soft-point rounds for defensive rifle rounds; use FMJ or do extensive research before using specialty rifle rounds for defense.

+P rounds are higher pressure rounds usually used in defensive handguns. They are safe to shoot in most modern

handguns, except where the manufacturer says not to. +P+ ammunition is overpressure ammunition and should not be used except by experienced shooters. A lot of handguns cannot safely handle these rounds, which were intended to be used in submachine guns.

Supply

Since COVID-19, ammunition has been hard to get. Coupled with the George Floyd riots and the election, America has entered an unprecedented ammo drought. Ammo prices were up to 200-300% over their lowest low, January of 2020. Expect to pay 50¢ to one dollar per cartridge for anything useful in self-defense if the shortage continues or another one happens. Hopefully, none of this will be true by the time you read this and the gun market will have normalized.

For Californians, you're hosed. Sorry. Your only choices are in store. You might pay full-freight and have your ammo shipped to a dealer to do the background check thing, but if you want to stay off the radar, you're driving to another state and playing the waiting game. Of course, it would be illegal to self-import ammo into California and no one would ever do that.

For people new to the gun world, your local gun store is your best bet. Buy what they will sell you when you buy a gun. Return every week or two and buy your quota. Stock up. Sure, you can bet prices will decline in the future, but if they don't, you'd wish you could pay a dollar per round now. What if things get worse and there is no more ammo?

How much ammo should you have on hand?

My personal rule is a minimum of 3,000 rounds per caliber; one grand to shoot, another for the end of the world, and another as a cushion. Space is my major limiting factor on why I don't have a jillion rounds stored up. Other sources will tell you to have 1,000 rounds on hand. Buy as much as you can afford, store, and feel comfortable having.

A lot of shooters simply bought what they shot. If they planned on shooting 100 rounds, that's what they bought at the range or at the gun store the day before. Some might not even have that much at home, buying only when they went shooting. That's stupid, like only having enough gas in your tank to get you to the gas station, where you buy just enough gas to get to work. If you have the money, buy the ammo.

Now most civilian gunfights involve a handful of rounds. Soldiers will tell you that a firefight that takes even more than one magazine—30 rounds—is a really bad place to be in. Even in law enforcement, the only incident that comes to mind where a ton of rounds were fired from handguns, exhausting the usual three magazines an officer has, was the North Hollywood Bank Shootout. Realistically, you will be fine with a 50 round box of ammo, but we're talking-worst case, right? Buy as much as you can.

For those who *must* be told what quantity to buy as a minimum, here goes. A pistol will typically be sold with two magazines; I recommend you buy a third mag. If each magazine holds 15 rounds, that is 45 rounds, plus one in the chamber, for a total of 46. Cartridges are sold in 50 round boxes (except for some defensive ammunition that is sold in boxes of 20). You will have 50-60 rounds for carrying purposes. Buy double what you think you might need to carry. Most casual gun owners shoot 100 rounds at a range session, so buy for two range sessions. Total: 300 pistol rounds.

For rifles, buy enough ammo to fill every magazine you have, whether you fill it or not. You're less likely to shoot a rifle than a pistol unless the world ends, so I'd say two to three complete magazine loadouts. A combat loadout (traditionally) for the M16 is seven magazines or 210 rounds, so 420 to 630 rifle rounds. If it's a .22, buy as much as you can afford. .22 is a great training caliber.

For shotguns, I would recommend buying at least 20 rounds of buckshot (your defensive rounds). That's two to three reloads depending on capacity. Buy at least ten slugs. Defensive rounds usually come in five round boxes. For birdshot, which is a good hunting, emergency defense, or a training round, buy 100 shells, which is five twenty-round boxes. Pricing for birdshot used to be less than $10 a box for lead shot, so if you can get those kinds of prices, stock up on it.

And for whatever gun you have and whatever ammo you plan to defend your life on, buy a small box to test. You will need to fire the ammo to make sure it feeds and cycles correctly in your weapon. The range is the right place to find out you bought 3.5" shotgun shells that won't work in your 2 ¾" chamber, not the dark of night.

When buying ammo, know what your weapon takes. If you don't know, ask questions. You don't want to buy 9mm Browning only to find out this is a specialty caliber for odd imported European firearms when you want 9mm Parabellum (AKA Luger). A smaller caliber bullet will not fire in a larger caliber gun or vise versa. And the lord help you if you try and fire a .300 Blackout from a 5.56mm chamber.

Don't get hung up on brand. Buy what you can find. I would highly advise you to stay away from Russian steel cased ammo ("Wolf" and "Tula" brands). Yes, it is cheap, but like anything cheap, you are making sacrifices. This ammo is often underpowered, causing guns to malfunction. I've had several steel cases jam inside my rifle that I had to hammer free with a steel rod. Pay the money for defensive ammunition, especially in a handgun. Your life is worth it.

Your ammo will store indefinitely. If you have a relative who has ammunition older than you are, chances are it's probably still good. The enemy of ammunition is moisture. Stored in your home, in good packaging, you can expect ammunition to last for years unless you have terrible humidity problems inside. Keep your ammo dry, in sealed containers (preferably with desiccant packs), and away from high temperatures, and it'll be just fine.

I do recommend changing out your defensive carry ammunition at least once a year. Shoot it in practice to remember what your premium defensive ammo feels like when fired.

Unless you are an experienced shooter, I don't recommend you attempt to reload cartridges on your own. Mistakes can cause death or injury and destroy a gun. On top of that, at the moment it is nearly impossible to get common reloading components, so one might as well just buy packaged ammo instead of "rolling their own."

Magazines

Magazines are the things that go into a gun that hold the cartridges. You'll see them slid in and out of pistol grips and into the magazine wells of rifles. The term also applies to the tube under the barrel that holds .22 cartridges or shotgun shells in those weapons.

You may have called them "clips;" this is the wrong term but most shooters will understand and only laugh at you behind your back. Clips are pieces of metal that hold cartridges for easy loading into magazines, usually in certain older firearms like surplus military rifles. You'll sound a lot more sophisticated if you use the term magazine, often shortened to "mag."

How many magazines should you buy? Like ammo, as many as you can afford. Magazines are intended to be somewhat disposable. In a gunfight you won't be carefully pocketing the empties or stopping to reload them cartridge by cartridge. They also do break and wear out over time with extensive use. Consider that if guns are banned you can't buy anymore.

You need a minimum of two for a pistol, ideally three. Most cops carry two spare magazines on their belt. When you are target shooting, you'll quickly find out that two magazines go really fast and stopping to reload them sucks. You'll buy more magazines just to keep shooting. A realistic minimum for convenience and spares is 6-10 per pistol.

For a rifle, we previously discussed a combat loadout was seven magazines (six in pouches). Your gun will come with one, so buy six more, giving you seven. I'd buy at least six more as spares, preferably a dozen extra. In a gunfight, you will be fumbling with magazines. If you are in a bad gunfight, like end of the world type, you'll shoot more ammo than you would think possible and drop the empty magazines on the ground without hope of recovery.

If you are in a capacity restricted state, like California, or if you are reading this at a time when Congress has banned 10+ round "high capacity" magazines, do what you can to acquire the standard capacity magazines. For Glocks and modern pistols, that number is 12-17 rounds. Rifles are 20-30 rounds. Many quality aftermarket magazines hold more than that. So what if it is illegal? Go out of state and buy them at a gun show or something. The law is arbitrary and your life is more important than political points.

Magazine capacity arguments are stupid. Studies have shown that limiting how many rounds in a magazine doesn't significantly reduce the body count. The whole idea of limiting capacity is to limit your ability to shoot back against people who deserve it. Whatever idiot originally came up with the idea might have been sincere, but there is evil in this world and that evil wants you to stand as little chance as possible. Remember, the Founding Fathers intended the Second Amendment to enable each American to have their own military quality equipment.

If you can't or won't buy "high capacity" magazines, buy a lot of 10 round ones. There are various ways to attach 10 round rifle magazines to make reloading quicker. Just don't "jungle tape" magazines together where one is upside down. That could cause damage to the magazine or fill it with dirt and crud so it doesn't work when you need it to.

In California or other such states that prohibit drop free magazines, be sure to have a spare magazine release catch.

If SHTF or WROL, you don't want to be stuck using your bullet button or Patriot Pin work around if no one is enforcing those stupid laws. There is nothing illegal about owning a standard magazine catch as a spare part.

Suppressors (silencers)

Firearm suppressors, also known as silencers, are basically car mufflers for guns. Literally the guy who invented the first silencer (the Maxim Silencer) also invented exhaust mufflers. Contrary to what movies show, suppressors don't lower the sound level of a firearm shot to something that can't be heard. Most weapons with a suppressor just aren't as loud as they normally are. Using the right ammo, this can be lowered to a sound level that is comfortable to shoot outside without ear protection.

If you have a suppressor, it can be a great tool to use especially when shooting inside or in an emergency when you don't have time to don ear protection. It may not make the gunshot not painful, but at least you will not go deaf. On the contrary, using a suppressor all the time may deny you the benefit of the noise of firing. Most people who are not combat hardened are frightened by the sound of gunfire. This fear could be to your advantage. I personally would choose a suppressor.

If you would like to buy a suppressor, they are legal in most states. However, they require a $200 tax and an extensive FBI background check under the National Firearms Act of 1934 (NFA). The waiting period can take months to a year, due to overwhelming volume. Be sure to see a dealer licensed to sell suppressors and don't make your own unless you are prepared to go through the procedures to do so legally.

Accessories

For your firearm, you will need cleaning supplies. Most guns will come with a simple brush and jig to fit down the barrel. I would recommend buying a simple universal cleaning kit from a sporting goods store. As far as oil and solvents, Hoppe's No. 9 is the standard that will help you clean and lubricate any gun. Don't get hung up on which magical spray cleaner or oil to buy; gun "CLP" products (Clean, Lubricate, Protect) are functionally identical, no matter what the manufacturer says. If you want to buy a can of three-in-one CLP spray and call it a day, you should have no trouble.

Scopes and red dot sights

The next thing you should buy is a red dot scope (for a rifle). These provide 1x magnification, which is actually no magnification. These scopes project a red dot that you use to aim. As for magnification, the 1x scope will work at neighborhood shooting distances. These are much better to use than the iron sights already on the gun.

If you bought a so-called "optics ready" gun with no

old-fashioned iron sights, buy iron sights or a scope. Weapons without sights are useless. I recommend having either both Backup Iron Sights (BUIS) and a red dot, or a scope that has an engraved reticle that does not need power. If you only have a red dot scope and your battery fails, without an engraved reticle or BUIS you cannot aim.

Don't buy cheap stuff. Cheap scopes will fail when you need them. I've had a $20 scope eat through a battery like a motorhome guzzling gas. A lot of sub-$100 scopes are barely qualified for your .22 rifle, let alone an AR-15 or something more powerful. Some scopes and electronics are made for airsoft guns and simply cannot handle the recoil of real shots being fired. Do your research; buy once, cry once. Law enforcement quality scopes/sights can be had for $400 and some good consumer grade sights less than $200.

Again, for the novice I don't recommend a pistol scope, often called "RMRs" or pistol red dots. Learn to shoot using the sights. Slide mounted red dots take practice to learn correctly and aren't like a video game. Do put glow-in-the-dark night sights (tritium dots) on your pistol though so you can see your sights in the dark. Your night sights will only help you see your sights and they must be used in combination with a light to illuminate your target or for a search.

Flashlights and weapon mounted lights (WML)

Do get a Weapon Mounted Light (WML) for your pistol or your long-gun; target illumination in the dark is critical. Night sights do not help you illuminate or identify a target.

Light models exist for both pistols and long-guns. For shotguns, several different types of replacement slides exist that integrate a white light or allow you to easily add a flashlight of your choice.

Never wave your weapon light around like an actual flashlight. Your gun should always stay holstered or pointed in a safe direction except when you intend to shoot someone. A general search (or heaven forbid just looking for innocent stuff in the dark) requires a separate flashlight. You've never seen hate like when a sergeant catches a deputy with his pistol drawn using the WML on it searching his trunk for something.

Flashlights are critical for multiple functions, which can be remembered as SINCC or "sink."

S – Search
I – Identify (friend or foe)
N – Navigate
C – Control
C – Communicate

Searching is an obvious use of a flashlight. Anytime we aren't using a flashlight to illuminate something we're working on in a dark space or to navigate, we're searching for something. In this context, a handheld flashlight will allow you to look around for someone who is hiding or to inspect defenses, etc.

A WML is used when you are searching for a threat you might have to shoot. Never conduct a general search or inspection with a WML in lieu of a handheld light. WML illumination during a search is when you are looking through the sights of your weapon ready to shoot. In other words, use a WML to search in situations when you would be searching in daylight with your gun up.

Identification also seems obvious and this is where in a potential shooting scenario, WMLs shine, pardon the pun. If you have your weapon up on a dark figure, activating your white light to see who it is might mean the difference between hesitating and being assaulted yourself or killing an innocent person.

Navigation is so obvious I'm skipping that. *Controlling* (as in commanding) others can be done by briefly shining a flashlight on a target that needs to be engaged. Lasers can also be used in this role (especially in infrared). Defensive control is done via intimidation or using the light to blind or disorient the subject. *Communication* is also simple; colored lenses can mean different things or the light can just blink a certain code.

One tip I learned is that when searching a large room (maybe you just want some general lighting in the house) is to aim the flashlight at the ceiling. This will reflect the light downward and create general area illumination. Flashlights can also be shone into water bottles or a reflective box to create a lantern effect.

Don't buy cheap flashlights either. Harbor Freight or dollar store flashlights won't cut it. Law enforcement quality flashlights retail for around $40 and up. I recommend against CR123 or other special batteries whenever possible because they are harder to find and aren't rechargeable. Plenty of great lights exist that take AA and AAA batteries. Remember that non-standard rechargeable batteries can't just be swapped out quickly as a pocket full of AAs can be. I always carried my super special rechargeable Pelican light and a D-cell Maglite in my warbag just in case.[51]

Lasers

I recommend against lasers for the new gun owner. A laser is a crutch that will hurt your shooting. You need to learn to shoot using the sights (on a pistol) or through a scope of a rifle. Real gunfights aren't like video games where you put the "red dot" on what you want to shoot. So if you buy a laser or a light/laser combination, learn to shoot *without* the goodies before you try shooting with the laser. Infrared lasers are necessary for most night vision shooting but see the "Night Vision" chapter.

Lasers can also be used as a less-lethal tool for warning people off. The little red dot of a weapon laser is a great persuasive tool when you can shoot but don't want to. To someone who sees the laser and doesn't have a death wish, it is a picture in a thousand words moment warning them "back off or die." Never rely on this, however. Not everyone will be intimidated or see the red dot. Also, legally speaking, pointing a firearm mounted laser at someone is still pointing (brandishing) a gun at them.

Retention

Buy a sling for your rifle or shotgun. You may need both

---

[51] Large flashlights were usually kept in the vehicle and put in the sap pocket of our pants when exiting our units at night. I always carried a small flashlight on my belt, 24/7. You never know when you will need to look into a vehicle or find yourself in a dark building (or locked in the supply closet).

hands and the last thing you'll want to do is put down your rifle in some circumstances. I recommend a tactical one-point sling that will allow you to hang the rifle in front of you. The traditional hunting style goes over the shoulder and usually doesn't have enough slack for you to move the rifle around easily.

Get a holster for your pistol. You may start with some cheap piece of trash Nylon holster that fits every pistol known to man, but you will want to get a holster made for your gun. If you live in an open carry state and plan or think you might openly carry, get a retention holster. A retention holster has some mechanism, like a strap or a button, which must be overcome before the gun comes out of the holster. This will prevent guns from being snatched. If you are carrying concealed, make sure the holster snugly fits your gun.

Load bearing equipment

Magazine pouches are important if things seriously go nuts. You will need reloads. For pistols, these are usually dual magazine pouches that go on your belt. For shotguns, I don't recommend the bandoleer of shells around the chest. Get a belt pouch like trap and skeet shooters use, although any shells carried in the tube, on the side-saddle, or in a butt pouch will be enough most times.

For rifles, the options are a lot more complex. The War on Terror and militarized policing has made us all familiar with vests carrying spare magazines and other goodies. If the vest holds body armor, it's called a plate carrier. If not, it's Load Bearing Equipment or LBE. You may also hear the phrase "chest rig." Basically, it's putting stuff in pouches on your torso.

Do some research for what works for you; you don't need to be Rambo.

Body armor and PPE

Should you buy body armor? That's up to you, but I'd first ask if you can engage in heavy physical activity with an extra 20-30lbs of gear on. Like most Americans, you probably can't. Armor that will stop rifle bullets is known as Level IV. These are heavy, hard plates made of steel or ceramic. Imagine running a mile in your gear to get to the fight, then doing a ten minute exercise routine, while shooting and being shot at, only to have to run back home. If you can do that, consider armor.

Soft armor, like what cops wear, at the highest Level III, will only stop most pistol bullets. Remember, effectively they won't even "slow down" a rifle bullet. Soft armor is basically invisible to rifle bullets, so don't think you'll get *some* protection from rifles. I have soft plates in my plate carrier. I can't comfortably afford the 3.5lb super space age lightweight Level IV plates. Soft armor, like under-the-shirt vests, are much lighter weight, but they hold in heat and can make you feel like your chest is being constricted.

One option, if you do buy armor, is to use it in a static position, like the front of your house. Most American residential construction is very weak when it comes to gunfire, so if you aren't moving more than a few feet, you could benefit from hard plates inside. However, you will want a plate carrier where you can quickly drop those if you need to move around.

Outside, I would recommend that you forgo armor and rely on stealth and rapid movement to avoid being shot. If you are shot, and the armor stops the bullet, you will hurt. The bullet might break a rib. You will have a very nasty bruise unless the bullet is deflected off something hard first.

The same thing goes for helmets. Forget a ballistic helmet; military helmets are designed to stop artillery shell fragments, not bullets. You don't need a ballistic helmet. If you want something to protect your dome from a rock or bottle, then get a good plastic helmet. This can be a bike helmet, a police model, or even a construction worker's hard hat. Surplus military helmets work too and will give you cheap protection from artillery fire in case Antifa ever gets howitzers.

Goggles? A must. You can always use your shooting safety goggles (get clear or yellow ones for night use). Face shields can also be used to protect from whatever stuff the mob might throw at you, but if you're shooting a gun, true ballistic eyewear is important. The range safety officer might not care to check if your sunglasses are ballistically rated, but if there is a catastrophic malfunction of your gun, you can bet the shrapnel will.

Ear protection? You probably won't have time to put it in if SHTF. A lot of people have reported that when in life-and-death gunfights, the adrenaline rush and the body's own defense mechanisms block out the gun fire. I wouldn't trust this. You won't care about the tinnitus if you survive. If you want ear protection, get electronic mufflers that amplify soft sounds and mute loud ones. You can hear the bad guys, perhaps better, without going deaf from gunshots.

Be sure to always wear ear protection when shooting

on the range. My grandfather, a Korean War vet, was always told "Don't worry, you won't hear the shots after the first one." That was because his ears overloaded and he was temporarily deafened. He wore hearing aids from his sixties to his death.

Safety

If you don't know how to use a gun, get training. Take a hunter's education course, a CCW course, or a basic gun owner's safety course. Heck, even watching YouTube videos is better than nothing. Learn how your gun works. Treat it like an obsession; this thing can kill you, strangers, or loved ones if you screw up. You can't take back a bullet once it has been fired.

Know the four basic firearm safety rules:

1. Treat every firearm as if it is loaded.
2. Keep your finger off the trigger until you are on target and ready to fire.
3. Do not point the firearm at anything you are not willing to shoot.
4. Know your target and what lies beyond it.

These four rules ensure that to cause death or injury, you have to make multiple mistakes. Follow them and you should be fine.

1. Every time you pick up a gun, check to ensure it is unloaded (if that is the state you want it in). Pull back that slide or charging handle and look inside the chamber. Do you see a cartridge? Be sure you see a black hole. You might even want to check with your finger.

Never, ever assume a gun is unloaded. For all you know, some idiot relative might have found the gun and loaded it without telling you. Plenty of people forgot they loaded a gun and then were surprised it fired.

If you act like a gun is loaded all the time, you will instill discipline in yourself. You won't get careless because you "know" the gun is empty and start pulling the trigger. You won't point the muzzle at people.

2. Don't put your finger inside the trigger guard until you're ready to pull the trigger. Lay your index finger along the side of the slide or receiver above the trigger. Up until recent decades, it was common for people to rest their finger on the trigger. Don't do this! Safety mechanisms aren't foolproof. Plenty of cops have been chasing people with their finger on the trigger, tripped, and fired a shot. You also don't want to be the idiot who accidentally pulls the trigger on a loaded gun.

3. Don't go waving or pointing the gun around. Don't point or aim it at a person unless they are a threat to life and you can legally shoot them. Imagine you break Rules 1 and 2; the gun is loaded, but you were too stupid to check, and you are too careless to keep your finger off the trigger. The gun is casually pointed at your child across the room. Something startles you, your finger jerks, the gun goes off, and your child is killed. You broke three rules to make that happen.

4. Know what you're aiming at. Every hunting season, some hunter is shot because a retard with buck fever sees movement, aims, and shoots. Elmer Fudd just shot his friend. Know what you're shooting at. Make sure your target is a bad guy and there aren't people behind him that are innocent who might be shot. This is where a weapon light comes in handy.

Mind your backstops. On the range, the backstop is a berm or a solid wall. In an emergency, you might be shooting at a bad guy who is up against the wall of your child's bedroom. Virtually all bullets will penetrate through residential walls. The same goes for in the street; sure, there might be no one behind an arsonist, but will your misses go through the front wall of the neighbor's house and kill someone hiding inside?

Securing weapons

Keeping your gun safe from relatives is vitally important. Children die regularly because some mouth-breathing moron leaves a gun out for them to find. No matter how well hidden a gun is, kids can find it. Remember your childhood days; if you were like me you got into *everything*. No hiding place is safe. Don't trust that your kids won't get to the guns on the top of the shelf or in the attic. Guns and children are no place for hubris.

Unless you live alone, a gun needs to be secured in a safe, etc. when it is not physically on your body. And especially if you have kids, don't put the gun down, ever. They might come into the room or you could get up and forget about it. Don't believe me? Start Googling stories about how kids accidentally shot themselves.

Get a safe or gun cabinet. Anything that locks away guns from curious kids will dramatically improve their safety. You don't need a one-ton monster safe.   Quick action safes can also be had. This allows you to keep a loaded gun at the ready, but not on your body, in a reasonably childproof manner. Smart teens and burglars can defeat them but they are a good compromise for safety and anti-theft while still leaving the gun readily accessible. It beats an unloaded gun up in the closet for both safety and accessibility.

At a minimum, guns are sold in cases with locks. Use the cable lock to go through the action to disable the weapon. If a kid gets their hands on an exposed gun, they can't shoot themselves with an unloaded firearm with a plastic coated chain through the breech.

Lacking a safe, most guns are sold in a lockable plastic case. Store it with the gun unloaded and the magazines and ammo locked away separately. Keep this all very high and out of reach. No case? Unload the gun, hide the ammo far away, and utilize a trigger lock, cable action lock, or both. Virtually every police station and gun store will give you a lock for free.

If your child is mature enough, talk about gun safety with them. This is about the age that they can learn "Stop, drop, and roll!" The NRA Eddie Eagle program recommends: "Stop, don't touch, run away, tell a grown up." Like the basic firearm safety rules, this provides multiple fail-safes. Children stop and assess the situation, remember that they aren't to play with guns, don't touch it so it can't fire, run away—which is important if another child gets the gun—and tells an adult so the situation can be made safe.

Even if you live alone, I highly recommend locking up your guns when you are away. A huge number of "black market" guns are stolen by burglars from cars and homes. Burglars *love* unsecured guns. Don't be *that guy* who loses his guns to a burglar and puts them on the street. At least make the scumbag work for whatever he is going to steal. This goes for cars too; get a purpose made locking car safe that is chained or bolted to the vehicle itself. Never trust a glove box.

Training

For a novice, a basic firearm course is an absolute must. Concealed weapon courses are also a good introduction but do little to teach someone how to shoot or defend themselves. CCW classes are basically the classroom portion of driver's ed. You still need ample instruction from someone who knows what they're doing to learn to fight effectively. The minimum required course is just to confirm you can pull the trigger safely.

Training comes in three forms: basic courses (i.e. NRA Basic Pistol and CCW courses) that teach essentially safety; shooting instruction (like a coach on how to shoot better); and specialized courses for advanced techniques. The first two can usually be found locally, but one needs to research specialized instructors in tactical techniques or attend a school like Front Sight in Nevada or Gunsite in Arizona.

Just because someone was a cop or in the military doesn't mean that they are instantly qualified to be an instructor. Your dad might have done fine to introduce you to guns, but if you need training, see a certified trainer who is well-reviewed. "Trained with/by special forces" is not the same as someone who was in the special forces. It's a marketing gimmick. And often private instructors are better shots than a lot of veterans or cops.

Family, friends, and standardization

If you expect that family and friends will be using your weapons, familiarize them with not only the operation of the weapons, but safety as well. Take them shooting. Men, if your wives don't care about shooting, at least make sure they can use a gun well enough to defend themselves in an emergency. Teenagers who can be trusted should be taught to shoot as well.

If you have the ability to, purchase handguns for those who are currently unwilling to use them. You may want to extend this to long-guns as well. Once things get bad, your loved ones may change their mind or they may have no choice. This could include buying multiple firearms to give to neighbors. Cheap shotguns would make a good expedient choice.

Standardization is a good idea. The easiest is picking the same caliber and magazine types. Using standard weapon platforms allows for personalization, but the controls and main characteristics stay the same. For example, there are only two major variations of pump-action shotguns, any rifle will probably be an AR-15, and pistols are all very similar.

Do standardize on caliber and magazines where possible. That probably means 9mm or .45 for handguns, 5.56mm or 7.62mm for rifles, and 12ga for shotguns. AR-15s will take standard NATO magazines. Handguns do not have to be any certain type or caliber (magazines are generally *not* interchangeable between brands) but should be in a common caliber.

Other than having common calibers, standardization is great but not vital in a casual group. Pooling guns, magazines, or ammo in the heat of battle is rare in the civilian world. I've never heard of patrol officers doing that. If things are so bad that you need an ammo resupply mid-battle, you probably need to retreat or evacuate.

So you're gonna carry a gun

Don't buy a gun and keep it unloaded, expecting that waving it around will deter people. If you do that enough, eventually someone will call your bluff. Having them steal the gun and beat you up will be getting off lightly.

The same goes for carrying air guns and BB guns instead of the real thing; they might sting and scare someone, but a determined attacker will not be stopped. A gun that is not capable of killing someone is worthless as a weapon. It is a lie that only the weakest and stupidest criminals might believe, and worst of all, it is a lie that you believe. The last thing you want when your life is on the line is a false sense of confidence that will get you injured or killed.

So you're gonna carry illegally

Please note by "carrying illegally" I mean carrying without a concealed weapon permit in a place that requires a permit. If you cannot legally carry a gun because you are a prohibited person, this is not advice for you. This is not a debate of the ethics of violating arbitrary carry restrictions.

Don't get caught

You are breaking the law. Once upon a time, carrying a concealed weapon was not a big deal, but now it is. In some states, it could cost you your right to bear arms if you are caught. This is for a situation where it is better to be armed and fight back, not because you want to engage in some nefarious deed. You should *only* be carrying because your local area is unconstitutionally denying your right to bear arms.

Henceforth, carrying in violation of a law that prevents you from bearing arms without a permit or license from the government will be known as "unauthorized" carrying. All you are doing is innocently exercising your right to self-defense and bearing arms without obtaining prior government permission.

You may not encounter an officer who is "cool" and lets you off with a warning. The threat must outweigh the risk of being caught. For instance, I wouldn't recommend carrying unauthorized just because of the day-to-day threat of robbery, etc. that exists generally in normal life. The risk of being killed, etc. must be greater than the consequences of getting caught toting a gun.

Don't be stupid and break the law. Cops who want to jam somebody up will look for any excuse from jaywalking to expired registration. Mind the law and don't do something stupid like litter or speed in a car with expired registration. Any interaction with a cop may result in you being detained and searched. You don't even have to be arrested for an officer to frisk you down for weapons. Even a "friendly" conversation could tip the cop off that you are nervous or he could see a suspicious bulge on your waist.

Don't carry into places with security screening. This includes:

- Places with wanding or metal detectors;
- Bag checks;
- Hidden advanced detection devices (like Las Vegas casinos or federal buildings);
- Random searches or inspections;
- Government buildings; and,
- Places with particularly alert security or cops looking for armed people.

Also be smart and don't leave your gun in the glove box or someplace like that. If you are going to keep a gun in a car, keep it in a combination locked box. They can take your keys but not a combination, and without probable cause something illegal is in the box, they can't force it open.

"Printing" is a term in the concealed carry community for when the imprint of your gun is visible beneath your clothing, often because a shirt is too tight. A concealed gun can also become visible due to a shirt that is too short or isn't tucked in. If you are carrying unauthorized, this is an absolute *must* avoid. Buy clothes a size larger and wear baggy clothes or outer wear.

The vast majority of the public is *not* looking to see if you are carrying a gun. Even tactically oriented people who know what signs to look for aren't scanning all the time if it were even their business. Heck, even a lot of police officers don't have the recognition skills or are observant enough to spot someone carrying a properly holstered and concealed gun.

Even though most people and cops don't have x-ray vision, don't take a chance that someone sees a dead giveaway. Many inexperienced carriers often pat their gun for reassurance like it might have left or something. Another tell is adjusting the belt from the weight of the gun, snugging the gun back into a belt, or the weight of the gun moving like a pendulum as the body moves. There are guides to spotting a hidden gun online that are worth studying. Don't be stupid; get a quality holster.

Creating reasonable doubt

Always consider what to do if you need to ditch your gun. You might have to drop your gun at the scene or discard it further away, so in case you are stopped and frisked, the gun isn't found on you. Sure, you may have been in the area, but the gun doesn't come back to you and it wasn't on you, so there is reasonable doubt for a jury.

Don't remove the serial number; most people fail at this and getting popped for an obliterated serial number is much more serious than just a concealed weapon violation.

Unauthorized carrying is best done with a firearm that is not registered to you (if your state has registration) or was purchased face-to-face with no dealer involvement. The ATF can trace a gun down to the dealer you purchased it from. Remember, even a bill of sale could tie you to a gun if the police trace the gun to the person you bought it from. An 80%

pistol you completed yourself is also a good idea (presuming you never registered it).

Be aware of your cartridge cases ("brass") as those may be evidence against you. A revolver is better than a semi-automatic in certain situations where you don't want to leave brass behind. Revolver cylinders do not automatically eject the empty cases when fired.

Load your firearm with ammunition that you have not handled with bare hands to avoid leaving fingerprints on the cartridge case. Not wiped down, but never touched by hand. Wear gloves when loading the rounds into the magazine. Also be sure to wipe down the magazine thoroughly with a clean cloth and preferably alcohol. This way if you use the weapon and drop a magazine (you aren't going to be picking up your brass) they can't get your fingerprints.

Since you aren't committing a moral crime, ditching the gun isn't strictly necessary. Yes, if you do shoot someone and you are politically prosecuted, there is the chance that having the gun could be a bad thing. But on the other hand you might need the gun unless you have several. I'm not going into detail how to dispose of a gun. You were just protecting yourself and trying to avoid a concealed weapon charge, right?

Be a sympathetic defendant. Carry a gun that is legally yours; not stolen or with an obliterated serial number. Apply for a permit even if you will get denied in a restrictive area ("I tried, but I couldn't do it the legal way."). Carry only for true self-defense in *really* dangerous circumstances when the police are not effective.

Be an upstanding, law-abiding citizen. You will stand a

better chance in court if you're doing almost everything else right. A family man who legally owned the gun and can articulate why he was afraid of being robbed is going to be cut a lot more slack than a gang member. Be someone that is so sympathetic that the prosecutor won't want to bother with a trial (or even to file charges) or that a jury might see themselves in your shoes and will acquit.

Never attempt to hide or destroy evidence of a shooting incident. Even if you acted legally, this could make things worse by incurring charges for destruction of evidence or obstruction or even make you appear guilty.

California: In California, if you are unable to get a CCW permit or the delay is too long, use retired peace officers to your advantage. Off-duty officers are an obvious benefit, but they may still have to work and can't stick around guarding the neighborhood for you. Retired peace officers can already openly carry *without* a special permit.[52] Of course, these officers can carry concealed in most cases, but it may be handy to have someone with a rifle in plain sight the cops won't be able to *legally* hassle.[53]

Summary

- Decide if you will need to suddenly discard the gun or not:

---

[52] 25900-25925 PC

[53] There were instances of this during the 2020 George Floyd riots in Southern California.

- If yes, try and use one built from an 80% receiver or one that you bought privately and never registered;
- If no, carry a gun that is registered to you, if registration is a thing in your state (in California, this is the difference between a misdemeanor or a potential felony).
- Decide if you will need firepower (a semi-automatic) or no empty cases left behind (a revolver).
- Carry the gun in a proper holster paying attention to good concealment under loose outer clothing.
- Load only ammunition you have never touched with a barehand (use gloves).
- Never obliterate a serial number.
- Don't carry anywhere there is security screening.
- Do not do anything to draw police attention to yourself.
- Be familiar with any local laws that may provide a defense or loophole.
- Practice carrying concealed at home to get used to the feeling and *not* touching your gun or adjusting your holster.
- Do whatever you can to create reasonable doubt. If you are a law-abiding citizen just trying to protect yourself in rough times, never underestimate the ability of the jury to sympathize with you.

Vehicles

Generally

Much of this advice *may* only apply in life-threatening circumstances, such as near-WROL and WROL. **Your state may have new protections for motorists in riot/protest type situations. Not all states have adopted enhanced protections for motorists. Look up your local laws and obtain an attorney's advice.**

If things go pear shaped in the world, get used to driving with your windows up and the doors locked. This is a standard practice in third-world countries or bad neighborhoods. The glass is just one more obstacle an attacker has to overcome. It also prevents them from just reaching in to open the door or assault you, plus it keeps thrown objects out. If you must lower your window, drop it no more than two inches, just enough to talk.

There will always be cameras and video of any incident where you have to use force with/from your vehicle. Thugs will obtain your license plate and turn that over to authorities. Whether or not you will be prosecuted will depend on your conduct and the politics in your area. You should also expect that you will be personally exposed and your home and your employment targeted by a vindictive Internet mob even if you escape any legal charges.

Should police become involved, any defensive driving was a use of force, the same as shooting someone. This was not a traffic collision. Never make a statement to police. Shut up and ask for an attorney. Do not talk to the police.

Avoidance

One of the major concerns currently is how to respond if a driver finds their vehicle in the midst of a hostile crowd. Mollycoddling of rioters and mobs have made being a motorist caught in a crowd a legal risk instead of just a safety one.

Remember that if you drive into a crowd (for any reason) and have to use force of any kind, you may be branded as the aggressor for driving in to the wrong place at the wrong time. Prosecutors who are looking for a conviction or plea bargain would suggest that the "right" thing for you to do was allow your car to be vandalized and burned while the crowd beats you to death rather than use force against them. Unfortunately, some of us live in areas like that in this day and age.

Self-defense applies when driving a vehicle even with the crowd. However, it is the motorist who will be on the defensive in any morally correct use of force. Few weapons are more effective against humans than several tons of metal moving at high speed. When a vehicle is used deliberately to kill or injure someone, the crime is "assault with a deadly weapon." You can put yourself ahead of the game by not being near an angry mob in the first place.

Situational awareness and monitoring the media, including the dreaded social media, is important here. If you can learn that there is a protest downtown starting at 5 PM, wouldn't you leave the area or stay away? Who cares what rights you have to self-defense if you can avoid the legal problems from exercising them if you use common sense instead and stay away?

A little bit of awareness can mean the difference between life and death (or an expensive trial). I understand that sometimes the crowd might come upon you suddenly, but can you say that you were realistically informed on what was going on? Reginald Denny was taking a shortcut through the ghetto on the day the jury in the second biggest trial of the '90s returned a verdict. Surely he *must* have known that there might be trouble. Despite this "storm warning" he was taking his shortcut listening to music. Had he been smarter, he would have been listening to news radio and learned of the riot unfolding in his path. Your first defense is to be informed.

Your next defense is to look ahead of you and see what's going on. Most drivers have no idea what's going on a few car lengths ahead of them. They don't look down the road and suddenly they are surrounded by angry people with signs. Look down the road as far as you can see. Are cars making strange turns or stopping for no reason? Are there protesters on the sidewalk next to you? If so, get out of there.

Another mistake people make is assuming the only way to go is forward. You are never forced to continue through the crowd. Take alternate routes or turn around through the beginnings of the crowd where people are thinner and less likely to box you in.

Don't be afraid to make a U-turn, legal or not. Although none of us enjoy backtracking, it is preferable to being attacked in a riot or being forced to choose self-defense. Your car has reverse; use it. Any surface your vehicle can traverse to get you away from the area should be used, even if you have to drive the wrong way, on the sidewalk, or across lawns. High clearance vehicles can hop curbs and low medians.

Be observant or face the consequences

In 1992, America watched as Reginald Denny was beaten nearly to death because he drove into a riot. Unfortunately, a majority of drivers are not truly paying attention to the road and actually perceiving what's going on. Not that they didn't *see* what's going on but that their brain didn't associate that visual stimulus with either danger or the need to take action. This is how people end up driving into a riot and being surprised by it, even though it should have been obvious.

Something else I noticed was that many drivers don't really see what's going on. Despite a police car parked in the road, lights flashing, other cars would often stop just behind our unit and have to slowly merge into traffic. It became clear to me that these drivers weren't looking ahead down the road, but just one car length ahead. These drivers could have seen the lane blocked off hundreds of feet away and gotten over but didn't until they found the police car blocking their path.

Flash floods are another example. Some people drive right into flooded roadways without knowing they are there.

Others underestimate the depth and power of the water and are washed away. Driving into a riot is a lot like a flash flood. By the time you realize you can't navigate the hazard, it's too late.

You need to have a realistic discussion with yourself and figure out if you might be one of those people. You have to be aware of your surroundings, actively observe the terrain, and not be afraid to turn off your intended path or turn around entirely.

- Don't drive into a protest or riot area if you can at all avoid it. If you live in the area, don't go back until the protest is over.
- Reversing instead of going forward may be the safest and fastest way out of danger. Make a U-turn and drive the wrong way if you have to.
- If you see a group of protesters in the road, even if they are "peaceful," get out of there. Turn in any safe direction and leave the area. Do not try and parallel the protest on the next street over; go *well* out of your way to avoid the unrest altogether.
- Plan your route to avoid places popular with protesters, like the scene of a critical incident, law enforcement stations or government offices, and the city hall or state capitol building.
- Never assume the crowd has a survival instinct *not* to be hit by a car. Some want to be hit by a car or force a confrontation.
- Never assume you have solidarity with the crowd because of your race or bumper stickers.
- Do not try to negotiate with the crowd or expect they will give you permission to pass through because you live there, etc.
- Utilize places you wouldn't normally drive, from different routes to parking lots, open space, the opposing lanes of traffic, etc.

Navigation

Have paper maps, know your route, alternate routes, and diversions, as well as the surrounding area. Be prepared to navigate without GPS or directions. The US military has the ability to jam GPS signals, reduce accuracy enough to make turn-by-turn worthless, or turn them off entirely. Also, does anyone recall how Apple phones wouldn't give people directions to DC in advance of January 6, 2021?

When directing traffic, at least once per collision someone asked verbatim "How do I get home?" Not, "How do I get to my home at X and X?" I would have to know where this person lives to give them directions. Their question, phrased as it was, told me that they could not find their way home except by their usual route down the main thoroughfares. Simply diverting a block and paralleling the blocked road for half mile was beyond their abilities.

A small detour destroyed their mental map and induced fear in some people. GPS made this better, but what if you had no GPS? What if you were unfamiliar with a neighborhood or city? Familiarize yourself not with just where you live or where you will be, but anywhere you plan to travel. Is the city on a grid pattern where you can just go up a couple of blocks and make it back to a major roadway going in the same direction you want?

Does your family know the layout of your neighborhood? As a kid, I could draw a map of my neighborhood from memory. Can your kids do this? If you are forced to run, either on foot or by car, you must know the immediate area well enough to navigate without getting lost or turning down a street where you can be trapped. Drive and walk the neighborhood as well as study the maps.

The ability to navigate is more than just knowing what exit to take and what alternative routes there are. You have to think critically about where danger points might be. What are the risks and benefits to using certain routes? A direct freeway route may be fast, but any sort of traffic jam will disrupt the whole plan.

Freeways can be deathtraps because their entry and exit points are controlled. The way they are often constructed in urban areas make them ripe from attack from above (bridges) and create long stretches of free-fire zones perfect for snipers. Protesters flood through on- and off-ramps to stop traffic. What if these "protesters" started pulling people out of cars or shooting them? The controlled access is also a boon to military/law enforcement who want to control the movements of others.

If you have alternate routs, like rural highways, those should be considered or at least kept in mind. Out west, we don't have really great options for alternate routes. We often have to go through massive sprawling urban areas that even at their edges are potentially dangerous. The roads that skirt LA, for instance, are well-known to locals and can be busy when freeways are closed or stop-and-go around holidays.

In the desert, there often is only the Interstate to make several hundred mile journeys. My novel *Blood Dimmed Tide* features a very circuitous and dangerous route through rural, desert areas because a chokepoint was created. As any LA resident knows when driving to Vegas or Phoenix, if the Interstate is closed, in most places there is no alternate route to get around without going at least a hundred miles out of your way.

Best practices

- Know local protest routes/areas and avoid them (don't drive into a riot);
- Avoid police stations, courthouses, and other government buildings;
- Avoid sites of looting, like major malls and shopping centers;
- Know multiple ways home and memorize the layout of your neighborhood;
- Be observant and monitor the news/social media; and
- Pay attention to the behavior and "mood" of the traffic and pedestrians around you.

Defensive driving

Roadblocks and protests

Even if you practice avoidance, you may still come upon a roadblock of one kind or another. This may be a checkpoint to screen people out or it could be nothing more than a bunch of petulant protesters annoying drivers. Should things totally destabilize in America, this may be where one faction may rob, rape, kidnap, or kill their enemies.

While it may be infuriating to have the road closed by armed insurrectionists or criminals (as well as dangerous), playing possum may be the best tactic here. Police are often present but not willing to interfere with the protesters or rioters for fear of agitating them, but they will arrest *you* should you attempt to force your way through. You may very well be shot at by the antagonists. In most states, the armed protesters will have the benefit of the doubt when it comes to a self-defense claim.

As of this writing, such roadblocks have not been especially dangerous or violent. The protesters are blocking traffic mainly as a stunt to advertise their presence and get mainstream and social media to notice their grievances. Most protests of one kind of another can be reduced to public temper tantrums that gives the participants a way to express how they feel to the public. Part of it may be to antagonize their opponents (both the left and right does this). This is an oversimplification but know that a lot of protests and blocking traffic is symbolic at its heart *for now*.

From a devil's advocate point of view, the crowd doesn't want to hurt anyone. They are there to use the delay in traffic to spread their message to a captive audience. A misdemeanor or infraction of playing in traffic doesn't justify assault or use of deadly force, no matter how angry or inconvenienced anyone is. Thus, in an unsympathetic (to the motorist) prosecutor's perspective, the crowd was not presenting an imminent threat to the motorist.

If a motorist then gets out of the vehicle and initiates a fight, the motorist is the aggressor. Should a motorist try to force his way through the protesters (or if he gets out and yells, etc.) and protesters draw weapons, the protesters would only be responding proportionately with deadly force (guns) against deadly force (the vehicle). After all, the protesters are not doing anything worthy of being run over or shot, so they would be justified in using force to avoid being run over.

No one should be stopped by civilians for political reasons in the road, especially under the threat of violence. Legally, the protesters should be arrested for illegal detention of the motorists. In a sane world, using reasonable force to overcome the illegal detention should not be controversial or risk prosecution.

In a semi-rule of law situation or when protesters are just being jerks, I recommend playing possum. Don't escalate the situation. Remain calm and get through the moment without being shot or arrested. Getting out of the vehicle only exposes you to risks. Yelling at the protesters won't get you through and may provoke them to violence. You are playing into their hands by getting angry so they can escalate their behavior.

Remember an armed roadblock is their strong point and you will be fighting presumably at a disadvantage. Never fight on someone else's terms. Getting through the situation peacefully looking like another sheep is the best option many times. For violent and life-threatening situations, see below.

Fake and planned accidents

A popular scam in third world countries is the fake pedestrian collision, where a pedestrian jumps on a slowly moving or stopped vehicle to later claim (perhaps with witnesses) he was hit. A dashcam proves your innocence. In a world where police and insurance still care, drive to safety and immediately call the police to make a report. Save a copy of the video for yourself before turning it over to police.

Ad hoc checkpoints and roadblocks could include a staged traffic accident or some debris to force you to stop. Look for vehicles without damage or parked unnaturally in the road. After most accidents, cars are not stopped in a way that the road is totally blocked. The biggest giveaway that an accident has been staged is that there is no glass or debris in the road. If the crash is hard enough to disable both vehicles and block the road, there will be stuff on the ground.

I recommend that people should not stop because it could be a way to get your vehicle stopped so you can be robbed, carjacked, or worse. Don't stop. Keep moving, don't stop, even if you do have a collision. Stopping makes you easy prey for any confederates waiting in ambush. If there are no police to call, just leave. They wanted to hurt you and they got what they deserved.

In either case, if you can drive off the roadway, do it. There doesn't have to be a hard or dirt shoulder, just something that won't stop your vehicle. If you have to slowly hop the curb and drive on the sidewalk or a lawn, do it. I wrote a very dramatized version of this situation in my book *Late For Doomsday* complete with gunfire.

Being shot at

If you are shot at in a vehicle, duck. Get down as low as possible and behind the B-pillar (the center pillar where the doors latch). Ride low and slouched like a gangster. The reason cops and gang members both tend to drive like this is the extra material of the pillar affords slightly greater protection than just the door and window.

If the shooter is in another moving vehicle, don't just hit the gas. This is what the other driver is prepared for and expecting. The other driver's plan is to accelerate away after killing you. You'll experience a lot more change in velocity (Delta-V) by braking hard than by trying to gas it, even if you have a powerful vehicle. Braking hard and fast will cause the other vehicle to overshoot and rapidly get you out of the line of fire.

By reacting quickly and moving your head and torso, it can throw off the point of impact the shooter was aiming for. Any additional material the bullets hit might be deflected or eat up precious terminal energy.

Do not stop or exit your vehicle until you are clear of danger or unless your vehicle is disabled. Continue to drive a damaged vehicle to safety as long as you are able to, even if this means destroying your vehicle by driving it on the rims, etc.

Don't do anything predictable. Places of safety may be a police station if they are operational. Do not take aa predictable route and go to an expected place, like home, immediately.

Do not try and shoot back. Get out of the kill zone. I don't care how pissed off you are or how good you think you can shoot; your job is to maneuver the vehicle to safety. Get out of danger and don't worry about returning fire. You can't shoot car-to-car well and you can't drive well if you're shooting.

Freeway: consider slamming on the brake pedal, hard. The other vehicle will expect you to evade by swerving or accelerating. Use caution if other vehicles are close behind you and that an astute driver in the shooter's vehicle doesn't also slow down. Turn around and drive the wrong way if you have to, otherwise exit the freeway and immediately take a circuitous, alternate route.

Streets: Hard braking as above may be a possibility. Make an immediate right-angle turn into any roadway that is not a dead end. Ideally you can put other cars, buildings, or walls as a barrier between you and the shooter. Also consider left turns if the other vehicle is out of sight. Right turns are easier and thus can be anticipated by someone following you. Be sure not to circle back to where the shooting began.

Sniper/ground shooter ambush: If gunfire is coming from your side of the vehicle, or in front of you, make a fast U-turn if you are able. This will put at least half of your vehicle between you and the shooter if you have no passengers. Put obstacles between you and the shooter. If you are unsure where the shooter is, try swerving and being unpredictable. Turn as soon as you are able and drive at high speed from the area of the attack. Be aware of barricades, crowds, vehicles, or even staged accidents designed to keep you in the kill zone or divert you into one.

Vehicular self-defense legal principles

Barring any new (as of 2021 laws), standard self-defense laws apply even in vehicles. You cannot hit someone with a vehicle on purpose in self-defense unless they are an imminent threat to your life. A vehicle is deadly force versus pedestrians or even occupants of other vehicles. People die in car accidents all the time so I hope I don't have to explain further. You must have an actual, reasonable fear that if you stop or don't hit that rioter, you will be seriously injured or killed.

Remember that crowds will likely take *your* vehicle to be a lethal threat and act in their self-defense, regardless of the purity of their motives. Your behaviors may take a riotous mob that wanted to harm you and turn them into the victims. Expect that even in a WROL situation, the mob will try to shoot you in their defense.

You cannot drive through the crowd merely because you were afraid. A "bare fear" is not enough to justify lethal force. You need to have an actual threat with imminent danger (and be able to articulate it), such as someone pointed a gun at you, they broke the window and were trying to pull you out, a Molotov cocktail hit your vehicle, etc. Seeing someone pulled out and being beaten to death in front of you like Reginald Denny could be a good justification if you had a real fear of the same happening to you.

An armed attacker in another (moving) vehicle would probably be a legitimate use of ramming against a vehicle. Smashing your car into their car could shake the aim of the gunman or screw up their firing position. The other vehicle could crash. An armed motorcyclist is easier; just slam the car into the bike and knock it down. Be aware that any collision may cause your vehicle to become disabled or crash.

If you have to drive through a crowd

- Honk judiciously to warn people (not constantly) and turn on your hazard lights.
- Keep moving, but slowly enough for people to get out of the way. Don't panic and don't accelerate in fear.
- Keep your gun handy, but secure, and out of sight until necessary to use.

Keep your doors locked and windows rolled up. You would be shocked at how many people haven't done this, drove into a riot, and were pulled out of their cars. There is no reason for you to roll down your windows. You don't need to warn these people or say anything to them.

Keep your firearm secure but handy in your holster. Consider where your gun is and what happens if you have to stop suddenly. Will it slide out of wherever and disappear under the seat?

This is why I highly recommend always having your firearm on your body. During the 1986 Miami FBI shootout, one of the FBI agents set his revolver on the seat. After the collision with the suspect vehicle, the gun was not there. If you have to exit the vehicle in a hurry, there won't be time to grab your gun, holster it, and run.

If you must draw your gun, keep it out of sight of the rioters. Don't let them see it as it may escalate the situation. In plenty of videos from the past several years, we've seen rioters/protesters draw guns on vehicles. Assume that the crowd is armed and they will shoot you if they see your gun.

If the mob is non-violent and you are stopped, don't try and force your way through. Try and stop your vehicle in a place and with enough room that you could take alternative exits, like driving on a sidewalk or lawn, if things get ugly. Always stop your vehicle so you can see the rear tires of the vehicle in front of you. This will give you enough room to turn out.

Forcing your way through a non-violent crowd, as much as they may be behaving like jerks, will aggravate the crowd and will turn you into the aggressor. It is frightening and you will be infuriated, but in most cases it will be over soon. Don't give into people trying to incite a reaction by becoming hostile.

If the mob is violent, don't stop. Moving slowly at a predictable pace allows people (who are willing) to get out of the way. It could also be considered reasonable, or proportionate force, to move just enough to get your vehicle out of danger while giving the protestors a chance to flee. 5-10 MPH is faster than most people can walk/run in a riot. If you must hit someone, slow down to below 5 MPH to inflict less injury.

Whatever you do, keep moving slowly through the crowd. Driving through will look bad on video and will enrage the crowd. If you drive slowly, you are being careful, minimizing risk, giving people a chance to get clear, and doing minimal damage. Your lawyer gets to make a powerful case for restraint in front of the jury. Always look like the reasonable, controlled, and cautious one.

Don't get out of your vehicle unless it is disabled. Take off your seatbelt in case you need to make a quick escape or draw your gun. Even if the protesters are forcing their way in, it is easier to defend yourself from inside the vehicle. Think of it as a cage that keeps them (mostly) out. Anyone fighting a shark or a lion would prefer half a cage instead of no cage at all. Only exit your vehicle if:

- The vehicle is on fire or surrounded by fire.

- Your vehicle is non-operational (or stuck), you are not surrounded, and you have a place of safety you can run to.

Don't run people over if you can avoid it. So you ignored the first piece of advice to not drive into the crowd *or* they came out of nowhere and surrounded you. Remember that using your vehicle as a weapon is a crime; deliberately running someone over is murder. A vehicle vs. pedestrian self-defense claim may be difficult to argue. All of your actions must be deliberate at this point to minimize injuries and get you out of the crowd.

As said above, keep moving slowly. Honk if people in your path aren't paying attention; a horn is to be used as an emergency signal that you can't or, aren't going to stop. If you honk excessively or constantly, the horn loses all meaning, you might attract more members of the crowd, or agitate them. Use a horn as a final warning to someone who won't get out of the way or someone who was oblivious and had their back turned.

At 5 MPH or less, which is a walking pace, anyone in the way of the car should be able to get out of the way. Judicious use of the horn can help. Anyone still in the way of the car should be pushed at this speed rather than be seriously struck and injured. You would rather have them knocked to the side rather than run over, which looks bad, is more injurious/deadly, and could stop your car. Be prepared if they land on your hood or shatter your windshield as it will probably startle you.

If you must hit someone, try to do it as slow as possible and with the corner of the vehicle (so they aren't knocked under) or with something like a mirror. Even if you do run someone down, don't stop moving. The damage is already done and you don't want to be drug out of the car and beaten. Your vehicle may have an impact shutoff sensor and you may find yourself in a disabled vehicle surrounded by a hostile crowd.

While driving through a crowd, they will beat on your car body, the windows, and try to vandalize the car. They may even succeed at breaking windows. Jumpers will try to get in front of the vehicle, on the hood, roof, or in the bed of a truck. If the car stops or the windows are breached, the crowd then gets more violent and starts trying to assault the driver or break windows with the intent to hurt the driver.

The crowd will already be mad at you for driving through and will take it as a mass personal affront if you start hitting people. Most drivers stop when they hit someone. The mob then surrounds the car and tries to force entry. As the driver panics and tries to get away, they hit the gas and strike more people at high speed. **Stay calm and don't panic.** Aggression will increase once you accelerate and people in the mob may draw guns and even fire. Keep your foot off the gas unless you're being shot at.

Control yourself and think your way out. Use only the minimum accelerator necessary to keep moving. Use minimum force if you must hit someone and maneuver your vehicle to minimize the impact. Utilize openings in the crowd or drive though non-roadway areas like lawns to get away. By being judicious and thinking outside the box you can argue your intent was to escape, not to hurt or kill.

Drive until you are not just away from the rioters/protesters, but also out of sight. You might *feel* safe a hundred yards away in a clear street, but they might be pursuing you. In Los Angeles, protesters employed a chase vehicle that literally chased down someone that drove through a pursuit. In a violent riot, especially in a WROL or a near-WROL situation, this chase car may be coming to kill you.

Breaches of your vehicle

You may be forced to stop due to circumstances beyond your control and surrounded by the mob. It will be loud as the crowd yells at you and bangs on the car. Don't panic. Do not try and bail out of the car. Stay in the vehicle. Even with windows broken it will be hard to extract you and you may get a chance to just floor it and get out of there.

If your car is breached, you may have a right to self-defense in your state, a "castle doctrine" in your vehicle. Your legal standing and physical safety are better with the car around you. As I said before, stay in the car.

A breach would be a very bad environment to use pepper spray in as you may be affected by it if your target is up close or the breeze is against you. One could toss out an airsoft smoke grenade or flashbang to startle and disorient the crowd. Using a gun should be a last resort even if legally applicable.

Should you shoot anyone, only shoot those who actually are a danger to you, such as someone with a crowbar breaking the window or someone trying to drag you out. In some states, you may have additional protections if you need to outright run someone over, though as of this writing, the legislation is pending and I believe it is geared towards more incidental collisions vs. using a vehicle in self-defense.

If you draw a gun or start shooting, chances are good someone in the crowd has a gun. Expect to be fired upon. In Texas, an off-duty Army sergeant was driving for rideshare when he was confronted by a protester with an AK-47 who pointed the rifle at the car. The sergeant drew his pistol and fatally shot the man with the AK. He was charged with murder over a year later. In another protest in Utah, shots were actually fired into a vehicle that was blocked by a protest.

Ramming

If you are being pursued or shot at, avoid ramming the other vehicle if at all possible. If you must hit the other vehicle, do so gently—a push, not a shove—to the rear side of the vehicle. Specifically, match speeds with the other vehicle. If the bad guy's vehicle is on the left, put your vehicle's left (front) fender against the other vehicle's right rear quarter panel, about where the bumper and quarter panel meet.[54] Once the vehicles are in contact, steer the vehicle gently to the left and keep steady pressure on the accelerator.

The other vehicle will pivot 90 plus degrees in front of you, so be prepared for this. Maintain the gentle turn as the other vehicle (hopefully) goes around you. Brake gently. Expect a collision once the vehicle goes broadside. Odds are you will not be able to steer around the vehicle and will end up having it make significant contact with your front end as you go around.

This technique, known as the PIT maneuver, is best

---

[54] Reverse directions if the bad guy's vehicle is on the right side.

accomplished at lower speeds and in areas where there is low risk to other parties. Beware of other drivers, pedestrians, crowds, and bystanders. If you are being shot at by the other vehicle, other evasive maneuvers are probably best.

For parked or stopped vehicles that are blocking the road (as part of a roadblock or a fake traffic accident), aim for the trunk or rear of the vehicle. The heavy part of a vehicle is always going to be the engine compartment up front. Aim for the rear of the vehicle with about a quarter of the front edge of your vehicle, whichever side is easier in that situation, and hit the other car. A steady, but low speed of 5-15 MPH is best.

Whenever colliding with another vehicle, expect airbag deployment and even engine shutoff. Many modern vehicles kill the engine or at least the fuel pump if a significant impact is detected. Evasion and a defensive collision may cause your vehicle to lose control as well and strike another vehicle or fixed object, disabling it. If this happens, you must expect to evacuate the vehicle as soon as it comes to a stop.

When ramming is expected, or if you plan to crash through barricades, use a large, heavy vehicle, like a full-size pickup or SUV. Make sure the gas pump impact shutoff is disabled or bypassed. It may be desirable to do the same to the airbags, if possible. Install bumper guards or push bars (that attach to the frame) to protect the vehicle during collisions. In a convoy, this should be the lead vehicle.

Remember that using a vehicle deliberately to hit another car could be construed as a crime. Most insurance companies would consider this a deliberate act and deny your claim, meaning your vehicle isn't getting fixed through your full coverage. An insurance liability claim denial may potentially result in a lawsuit against you which you would need to defend against from your own pocket.

Best Practices

- Avoid the area by all means. If stuck, try and stop in a place or leave enough room from the car ahead of you to escape over a median, sidewalk, gap, etc. if an opening presents itself.
- Stay in your car with the doors and windows locked. Remove your seatbelt.
- Remain calm and try to ignore them. Do not make eye contact, honk, flip them off, etc.
- Keep your firearm secure and concealed.
- Have your family members duck down on the floor.
- Avoid a shootout at all costs. Handgun bullets will easily penetrate a vehicle and rifle bullets even more so.
- If an opening presents itself, slowly drive through the opening without hitting anyone. If you do hit someone, continue moving until you are safely out of the area and call the police.

Convoys

You will most likely form a convoy as part of an evacuation. Families and groups of friends often do this in the Southeast when hurricanes threaten. A convoy is simply a group of vehicles traveling together to a shared destination.

Stay close together; maintain a safe following distance but discourage the entry of other vehicles between members of your convoy. To close the distance, 1-2 car lengths of clearance may be necessary, so put your best and quickest reacting drivers behind the wheel. If a random vehicle sneaks in, more vehicles may also come in and quickly separate the group. Variations in speed and closing distance may be necessary, including cutting off or forcing other vehicles from entering gaps. Separated vehicles may need to pass and work their way back into the convoy.

If the convoy gets broken up, the vehicles should coordinate by radio to rejoin each other on the move. The farthest back vehicles should catch-up. The lead vehicle(s) should avoid stopping and waiting for the others to catch up if the slow vehicles are in radio contact and can just speed up. Habitually slow drivers should be placed in the middle of the convoy and "pushed" to the desired speed by the rear vehicles.

If radio contact is or is about to be lost, only the leading vehicles should pull over and wait. Waiting on the side of the road without radio contact is risky because the stragglers might pass by the waiting vehicles if the drivers are unobservant. Should a rendezvous not be possible to coordinate by radio, all vehicles should continue to a pre-designated rally point and rejoin the convoy there. This rally point should be known to all, safe, and easily accessible from the travel route. Only after a pre-designated waiting time beyond what is safe or reasonable to wait for stragglers should the lead vehicles continue to the next rally point.

Agree on a pre-set speed to travel. I suggest the speed limit because it avoids any traffic stops and it is easy for everyone to remember and maintain. It will also give the best balance between speed and fuel consumption.

On multiple lane roads (in each direction), stay in the middle lane of three or more lanes or the far right lane of two lanes. When changing lanes or passing, the lead vehicle should call to the rear vehicle to "take the lane," at which point the rear vehicle will make the lane change and slow down to prevent any other vehicles from going around until the whole convoy completes the lane change. Large convoys should be broken up into sub groups of half a dozen vehicles traveling about one-quarter to half a mile apart.

Do not pass other members of the convoy. A convoy should only pass much slower vehicles and only when there is sufficient room for the entire convoy to pass at once. When passing, the rear vehicle will initiate "blocking" of the passing lane and slowing as necessary to prevent any vehicles to the rear from going around. Starting from the rear and working forward, each vehicle should pull into the left lane. The lead vehicle then begins passing, continuing in the left lane until the rear vehicle has safely passed the slow vehicle. Then the rear vehicle will move back to the right lane and each vehicle will also move to the right working back to front.

Crowding/tailgaters

One way of getting tailgaters off you is to slightly accelerate and touch the brake pedal to light up the taillights. A driver who is paying attention and *doesn't* want to hit you should back off. If someone is tailgating aggressively, try and change lanes, slow down, and let them go by. Divert to a new route.

If someone is crowding you or trying to get alongside your vehicle to run you off the road, try swerving your vehicle slightly. Be unpredictable in your movements. If you feel confident enough, use the PIT maneuver against another vehicle trying to force you off the road. However, the best defense is to slow down, turn away or around, and leave the area.

Evacuation

Being able to safely navigate through areas of unrest while evacuating is of vital importance. While very few of us are going to be able to "bug out" when SHTF, knowing what to do if you have to flee is important. Running out of your house in your underwear into the hands of the mob is a bad idea. Remember that evacuating includes leaving an unsafe situation at work and going home, so some of these principles apply to commuters.

Where are you going?

Have a destination in mind, specifically one that has the capabilities to support you *and* is willing to accept you.

Evacuation isn't driving to some place that isn't wherever you are leaving. Unlike a hurricane or earthquake, you simply can't outdrive a total catastrophe like nuclear or civil war. Even if California turned into a raging hellhole overnight (more than it already is), most people wouldn't have the gas to make it to Nevada or Arizona. You can't just drive aimlessly and hope there is a motel or Red Cross shelter to take you in.

You don't want to end up as a refugee yourself. You don't necessarily need a "bug out" location, but plan to go somewhere you will be welcomed. Living circumstances in such a case won't be ideal yet having a roof over your head and not being dependent on an impersonal organization beats the alternative.

The same goes for relatives. If your plan is to show up and hope that familial ties will be all you need, think again. Is whoever you're trying to stay with able and willing to accept you? Your elderly parents might let you stay with them in their retirement condo in Florida, but the only sleeping may be on the floor. A wise move would be to show up being able to say, "I brought food" and not just enough for you, but your hosts as well.

When some godawful catastrophe strikes LA (for example), people are going to flood out of the city and into the local mountains. These people will be *fleeing* into the wilderness, ill-equipped and unprepared. Only a fraction of the population can camp without logistics that resemble a military deployment, let a lone bushcraft. The overwhelming majority of people who go out into the woods will either die there or return home. I wrote about this in my novel *Hard Favored Rage*.

Long-term wilderness survival, even as an expert bush crafter, is far from ideal and non-sustainable in the long term. If you are a suburbanite, forget any idea you have about "roughing it" in the wild. There is not enough food or water to sustain everyone who goes "innawoods." Estimates show that if everyone began hunting deer to survive, the American deer population would last six weeks.

Getting out of your house

You may find yourself in a situation where you need to flee your home in an instant, such as during an arson attack or if intruders are forcing their way in. Just running out the front door or hopping in the car isn't always going to work.

Alternative exits and escape routes will be necessary.

Avenues of retreat/escape from homes will be limited. Escape from homes in most suburbs will be through adjacent yards, over fences and walls, or through alleys. Your escape route might be nothing more than over the fence and through the neighbor's yard, but have it planned. Stage ladders or other climbing aids nearby so even children can easily get over. Consider planting shrubs to make a concealed pathway. Escape routes might be through exposed alleys, drainage channels, or across open ground to the woods.

I don't recommend creating escape holes in neighborhood fencing, etc. A weak point for you could be exploited by a bad guy who finds it. Cutting padlocks off emergency or back gates that are never used and replacing with your own could be problematic. The landscaper can deal with the inconvenience, but it may be a different matter if it is the fire department's lock. This is a bad idea for a gate that is frequently accessed. I recommend that everyone have a set of bolt cutters capable of cutting chainlink fencing up to common size padlock shanks.

Going yard-to-yard may not be viable, even if one is physically fit, for several reasons. First, going over walls and fences is dangerous due to objects, thorny shrubbery, or animals. Many cops and suspects have been hurt jumping over walls without looking and landing on stuff, dropping into cactus, or being bitten by dogs.

In a neighborhood attack, your next door neighbor may attack you for hopping the fence, not knowing who you are. You may be a total stranger to someone several houses away or even your next-door neighbor may overreact in chaos or panic. Enemies could easily see you jumping the fences or walls or running through unfenced yards. Observation and tracking by drone are not an impossibility. When planning, imagine you're trying to avoid police after taking foot bail at the end of a car chase.

If you are very lucky, there is an alley, storm drain, creek, or other natural feature that the enemy hasn't placed security in that you can follow out. Since most cities are in some sort of a grid fashion or organized into blocks, these alternate routes can easily be bottled up on either side. They are also avenues of attack to flank your house or defensive position. Even without alleys, all an enemy has to do to prevent you from "fleeing out the back" from the neighbor's house is walk around the block and then you're trapped within a few bordering lots.

Realize that you may need to escape through force. You may have no choice but to ram through a crowd in your largest vehicle. Be prepared for this eventuality and having to ditch said vehicle. I would highly recommend parking a second car several blocks away if it won't be stolen. This way, once you get clear of the house you can use the second vehicle.

Have escape routes planned. Sure, you might have the wash you can follow for a half-mile until you reach the park, or you can go through the Thompson's yard, but where do you go from there? Set rally points in locations well known to each member of the family and determine how long everyone will wait and where they will go if it is necessary to move on.

Commuters

The key to not finding yourself caught needing to evacuate from work (or away from home) is preparation. Keep up with the news and your intelligence gathering so on the day of the apocalypse you aren't downtown when the riots begin. This section shouldn't even be necessary because a wise person wouldn't be out if things are so bad that they will have to run the zombie apocalypse gauntlet on the way home.

Take common sense measures like never letting your gas tank fall below half, keeping a well-stocked "get home bag" in your vehicle, and wearing or keeping a pair of comfortable shoes. Tell friends/family your intended route in case you do not arrive when expected and they need to search for you. If your family is evacuating as well, have several rally points planned to meet up along the way.

If you find yourself in an evacuation situation at work, you will probably be able to leave by vehicle. Leave early. Avoid freeways and main routes that could be clogged with other people. Take secondary routes and avoid dangerous areas. Travel by vehicle as far as possible. Much advice applicable to vehicles and incidents along the way a commuter might encounter can be found elsewhere.

Best practices

- Memorize the layout of your neighborhood and know multiple ways in and out.

- Walk your area both day and night, exploring natural areas, storm drains, and other places off the beaten path; this may be your avenue of escape in an emergency.
- Be observant and monitor the news/social media.
- Have a destination in mind instead of fleeing blindly.
- Have bug out bags for each family member ready to go.
- Bring your own food and supplies so as not to be dependent on others.
- Plan on how you will get out of your house if you can't leave through the front door.
- Screen or secure your escape route from the yard so you can leave unobserved.
- Carry cash or other barterable valuables to secure rides, pay bribes, or meet vehicle needs.
- Have pre-planned escape routes and rally points.

Refugees and Tent Camps

Internal refugees who have been displaced by disaster, war, or civil unrest will appear. From the Syrian Civil war on back through history, civilians who have lost their homes or are seeking to avoid becoming a casualty of conflict have sought refuge in areas less affected or unaffected by tragedy. This means that if dense urban areas become battlegrounds or unsurvivable, the residents will move out to the suburbs and countryside.

The overwhelming majority of people will be unprepared for even short term disruptions in the financial and logistical systems. Even those who did prepare may find themselves dispossessed of home and supplies. You may even become one of the destitute. Having nothing and limited prospects of survival makes people desperate.

America experienced a vast domestic refugee crisis in the 1930s as the Great Depression and Dust Bowl devastated the Midwest. As best told in John Steinbeck's *The Grapes of Wrath*, California was inundated with more mouths than could be fed and men looking for work than could be employed. A future economic crisis and famine will likely be *far* worse than this and at some point it will be combined with a kinetic aspect. War, starvation, and civil strife will be ugly.

Scarcity and competition drive migration. This is exacerbated by safety concerns; if someone is going to kill you, you will leave a moderately survivable position to accept the uncertainty of being a refugee to avoid the certainty of being killed. Whether through famine or war, internal migration for survival will occur. The severity of the crisis will dictate the behavior of the refugees.

Hungry and scared people who see others that have it better than they will often become resentful. This can be anything from a socialist attitude of "everyone should go a little hungry so all can be less hungry" to full-on deprivation of what the better prepared have. A desperate band of refugees who has been camping in a field next to your neighborhood and starving may one day decide to try and overrun your defenses in order to kill you, eat your food, and live in your houses. While this sounds extreme, it is not outside the realm of possibility and violent attempts to rob or loot are of very high probability.

The point is, as awful as a refugee crisis is, and that it could affect you, if you are not a refugee you have a duty first to you and your family. Strangers come second. You must be prepared in mind, heart, and defense to deal with refugees who want to take what you have. I suggest a certain hardness of heart during this time; this will not be the society that came together to survive the Great Depression.

Remember that morality adjusts itself to present reality. People will easily discard the norms of their behavior in order to survive. Desperate refugees may resent you and consider you a valid target to kill and steal from. Likewise, you have to consider them a threat and be willing to protect yourself, your family, and your neighbors. Survival of the fittest and kill or be killed will be the rule for both desperate and defender.

- The destitute seek better/safer conditions and move to areas that can provide.
- Resources in the new area are taxed until they are depleted;
- The refugees then either move on like locusts or are ejected by the locals; or,

- If refugees remain, the more desperate they become, the dangerous they will become as they will do anything to survive; and,
- Refugees may challenge locals for hegemony or to steal their resources.

- The prepared will be targeted for begging or theft by those who are unprepared and desperate.
- The unprepared will beg you for aid and threaten you when they don't get it.
- When you refuse, you may be accused of inhumanity; that is you will be called a "murderer," a "racist," selfish, etc.
- Desperation and coveting will drive these accusations, retaliation, and attempts at theft. That they "have not" will be used as justification for whatever evil is done to you.
- If you look like you have something to protect, you may be a target.
- You can survive the aftermath of a disaster but still have to deal with the human element.

Dealing with refugees

An *alien refugee* is any refugee who is unknown to your group; this would be most refugees. A person seeking refuge from a friend or relative, who is expecting them or will welcome them, will be an *evacuee* for our purposes.

Alien refugees are a potential danger. Rural and distant suburb residents should plan for and expect large numbers of individuals leaving large cities. Not insignificant numbers of these urbanites will have low impulse control and proclivity to violence. Significant resentment may exist and will quickly develop between the refugees and the suburbanites.

Evacuees

Residents of your neighborhood will have **friends and family** that live in affected areas that may come to stay. Some of these guests will be wanted and others unwanted. The evacuees become the responsibility of the sponsor resident who is their family or friend. Unless the person or persons trying to join your neighborhood would be a clear threat to your community, you need to let them in.

That is, the risk of alienating the neighbor who is related to/friends with this person is *less* than the danger of letting the refugee(s) in. A flock of sheep doesn't let a wolf in, so the community may need to vote to reject someone's felon, gang member, or sex offender relative no matter how much the neighbor wants "their" evacuee in.

Absentee property owners or temporary residents should always be let in. They own property in your neighborhood and may consider their home a "bug out" location. Verify ownership before letting them in. For landlords seeking to evict a resident of the area, it must be carefully considered by the community if the neighborhood will be strengthened or placed at risk either by allowing or rejecting the eviction.

Anyone coming in after a situation has become dire may be rejected if they present a security threat or if the existing resources can't support more people. Someone bringing in their own food and occupying their empty second home may not be a threat, but one family's 30 cousins arriving when the water system can't support them may need to be rejected by the community.

Refugees

Refugees should *never* be admitted to your neighborhood unless the refugee has a specific, specialized skill that your group needs and that person will add significant value to your group. This could be young veterans for security in a senior community or a physician when hospitals are closed. Bringing in unskilled persons for manual labor so residents don't have to toil is a bad idea. **Skilled persons** who are candidates should be vetted carefully and the community should vote to include them or not. It is preferable that any refugee who is admitted has their own supplies.

Moving them along

Requests will be made for food, water, shelter, and supplies. With the exception of maybe water—if in ample supply and easy to provide—requests should be refused. Beggars should be directed to a charitable distributor (see below). Those requesting shelter should also be refused. If you house them, expect to be feeding them and there is a *major* possibility they will refuse to leave and will require forcible eviction with all its attendant problems.

Letting someone pass through your defensive perimeter (safe passage) is also problematic. They could be on reconnaissance for a raiding force or plan on fighting/escaping once inside. Large groups are far riskier than individuals or small groups. If your defensive perimeter is large and/or has closed a main throughfare, you may need to have an armed escort team to escort the refugees through your perimeter or town.

Resistance is to be expected. This may be passive-aggressive hostility. The people could just sit down and see if they can wait you out. Others may attack you or try to sneak in. Your guards should always have weapons in evidence to signal that entry attempts will be met with force. Denials should be made politely, but firmly. No attempt should be made to reason, bargain, or argue with refugees once the denial is made.

- Persons who hang around your barricade/checkpoint need to be moved along. They may persuade or wear down a guard to get what they want or attract others to remain. Order them away, physically escort them away, or use other means to dissuade them from remaining. Do not let them set up a camp.
- The perimeter and any possible infiltration points should always be guarded, patrolled, and inspected for anyone trying to sneak in. If a negative encounter with refugees occurs, these efforts should be stepped up.
- Non-violent infiltrations should be resisted through capturing intruders or by utilizing crowd control measures. Surreptitious infiltrators should be dissuaded, blindfolded, and removed far from the area to discourage them from coming right back. Repeat offenders may need to be neutralized or subjected to corporal punishment to dissuade them from reentry.

- Violent attacks should be repelled with equally violent if not overwhelming force until the threat is totally eliminated.

Charity and beggars

You will face beggars at your gate asking for food, water, and other items. I would highly recommend denying these requests politely (and appearing you are equally desperate). Not only does this kind of charity deplete your resources, but as mentioned elsewhere, your neighborhood could get a reputation as a place for handouts. Hobos in the Great Depression marked homes where meals could be had and shared the information by word of mouth. You may face a situation where word spreads and you eventually run out of giveaways causing beggars to become hostile (or signaling to raiders that you have ample supplies).

Charity should be entirely anonymous and directed through a church, emergency management agency, or a Non-Governmental Organization (NGO). This allows you to give away any charitable supplies you stockpiled for this purpose without giving away the appearance of having the "luxury" of extra food, etc. It also allows more equal and equitable distribution. If no such organization exists, your community could create one.

I would also recommend a charity shelter that can provide limited shelter to the sick, injured, disabled, or elderly. Perhaps this is just a simple Red Cross gym-and-cots type setup, but it's better than having them sleep out in the cold. Being able to direct the lame to a church or someplace where they can sleep indoors will be easier for you than simply rejecting them to sleep in the cold.

Camps

Refugee camps

There is no long-term management of refugees within your abilities. If you allow them in, permit them to setup a camp or set one up for them, they may never leave. They may begin to agitate for homes in your community or for you to supply their needs. You will need to be ruthless. Unless they have something to offer that makes you stronger, move them along.

A camp in the immediate vicinity of your home is a danger. Homeless camps that abut residential areas are already problematic, bringing theft, drugs, and violence into the area. Now imagine that instead of vehicular burglaries, these people are jumping your fence, stealing your vegetables, and some of them are even robbing homes. If you have open land or a park near your home, ensure it does not become a place for refugees.

You may need to burn out camps or terrorize these people to avoid them being a threat to you. Polite efforts to establish them elsewhere can be used, but ultimately having a horde of desperate "have nots" next door to the "haves" is a bad combination. The potential for trouble is just too great to risk. Harden your heart.

Any refugee camp that is a necessary evil in your area needs to be established *far* from your neighborhood or any other locals who are surviving. This could be in an idle industrial warehouse area or in a field in rural areas. I suggest that a refugee camp be setup three miles from town, which is an hour's walk for average people. Such camps need to be sited so there is a water supply and any sewage will not contaminate water sources. They should also be located away from main highways.

Existing homeless camps

A SHTF situation is probably a good time to remove encamped homeless people from near your home. Many homeless people are drug addicted and mentally ill. As illegal and legal drug supplies dry up, expect symptoms of mental illness to increase and addicts to become more desperate to get a fix. Some of the unmedicated mentally ill will become violently delusional. As soon as you can feasibly do so, you may want to force any homeless out of your area.

A disturbing trend my partners[55] have noticed lately is that some of the homeless are using slingshots to discourage people from getting too close to their camps. Now these are of the mostly harmless variety, but it shows that these bums are getting bold enough to use force against "intruders." You may need to use less-lethal force to remove these people. Ideally, you would enter the camp when the squatter is not

[55] In Southern California.

there and dismantling it.

When tearing down a homeless encampment, you need to remove everything they brought; that includes all personal effects, any food, and anything that can be made into a shelter. In short, if it is manmade, take it and throw it away. Dispose of the stuff *far* away or burn it *in situ*. You have to ensure that nothing remains that can be used to rebuild the camp. Be ruthless.

Cut down vegetation used to conceal the camp and make the area undesirable for reoccupation. Brush removal may be something you want to do preemptively to avoid "urban outdoorsmen" from colonizing that natural space near your home. Causing the area to stink with disposal of pet waste, fertilizer, manure, or stink bombs is a short-term area denial solution. Remember that hidden paths frequented by the homeless could be rigged with alarms or trip lines, but nothing lethal or injurious.

Autonomous zone comes to you

If you live in an area where it is likely an autonomous zone could be established, I highly suggest you move. This would be the downtown areas of very liberal cities in blue states that have high occupancy rates of far-leftists and probably has seen protests in the last few years. Even areas that have had their autonomous zones removed, like the Capitol Hill (CHAZ) area in Seattle, remain at risk for reestablishment.

Evacuate as soon as the zone is announced and

begins to setup. Do not wait to see what politicians and police are going to do. Empty your home of any valuables or items that you would not want to lose, as it is highly likely your home will be burglarized and occupied by squatters. Return only after the zone has collapsed and dissolved or police have broken it up. Sell the house and move.

If you have no place to go, and you have the skills and manpower, offensive action may be required to eliminate the threat. This is a WROL response only. However, this will be resisted and retaliations are highly probable. Cutting losses and evacuating is the best option.

About the Author

Don Shift is a veteran of the Ventura County Sheriff's Office and avid fan of post-apocalyptic literature and film. He is a student of disasters, history, current events, and holds several FEMA emergency management certifications. You can email him at donshift@protonmail.com.

Fiction works include the Ventura Sheriff EMP series, *Hard Favored Rage* and *Blood Dimmed Tide*, where deputies must survive after a devastating electromagnetic pulse destroys the electric grid. *Late For Doomsday* and *Limited Exchange* are novels of surviving and evacuating after a nuclear attack.

All works explore the realities of emergency planning and personal survival in the face of low probability, high impact events that highlight the shortcomings of a technology and infrastructure dependent nation.

While this work is free from profanity and crude or offensive humor, some of my other works do feature such elements and may not be appropriate for sensitive readers. — Don

Printed in Great Britain
by Amazon